J. M. Coetzee

J. M. Coetzee

Truth, Meaning, Fiction

Anthony Uhlmann

BLOOMSBURY ACADEMIC
NEW YORK • LONDON • OXFORD • NEW DELHI • SYDNEY

BLOOMSBURY ACADEMIC
Bloomsbury Publishing Inc
1385 Broadway, New York, NY 10018, USA
50 Bedford Square, London, WC1B 3DP, UK

BLOOMSBURY, BLOOMSBURY ACADEMIC and the Diana logo
are trademarks of Bloomsbury Publishing Plc

First published in the United States of America 2020

Cover design by Eleanor Rose
Cover image © Sharon Zwi

Selections from the J. M. Coetzee Archives are reprinted
courtesy of J. M. Coetzee and

Harry Ransom Center
The University of Texas at Austin

Library of Congress Cataloging-in-Publication Data
Names: Uhlmann, Anthony, author.
Title: J.M. Coetzee : truth, meaning, fiction / Anthony Uhlmann.
Description: New York : Bloomsbury Academic, 2020. | Includes
bibliographical references and index.
Identifiers: LCCN 2019025902 (print) | LCCN 2019025903 (ebook) |
ISBN 9781501357473 (hardback) | ISBN 9781501357466 (paperback) |
ISBN 9781501357480 (epub) | ISBN 9781501357497 (pdf)
Subjects: LCSH: Coetzee, J. M., 1940–Criticism and interpretation.
Classification: LCC PR9369.3.C58 Z923 2020 (print) |
LCC PR9369.3.C58 (ebook) | DDC 823/.914–dc23
LC record available at https://lccn.loc.gov/2019025902
LC ebook record available at https://lccn.loc.gov/2019025903

ISBN: HB: 978-1-5013-5747-3
       PB: 978-1-5013-5746-6
       ePDF: 978-1-5013-5749-7
       eBook: 978-1-5013-5748-0

Typeset by Integra Software Services Pvt. Ltd.,
Printed and bound in the United States of America

To find out more about our authors and books visit www.bloomsbury.com
and sign up for our newsletters.

For Andrea, Liam, Xavier, Nicola, and Alistair

CONTENTS

ACKNOWLEDGEMENTS

I am grateful for funding support from the Australian Research Council. This project began as part of an ARC project, 'J. M. Coetzee: Making Sense in Literature' (DP140104427), as part of my contribution to a collaboration with Nicholas Jose and Bruno Clément. Yet the book continued to develop after this project and overlapped with and has been informed by two other collaborative ARC-funded projects, 'Spinoza and Literature for Life: A Practical Theory of Art' (DP170102206), where I am working with the philosopher Moira Gatens, and 'Other Worlds: Forms of World Literature' (DP170101002), where I have been privileged to work alongside literary critic Ben Etherington and four distinguished novelists, Alexis Wright, Gail Jones, Nicholas Jose, and J. M. Coetzee himself, in considering their creative engagement with the world.

I acknowledge the Harry Ransom Center, the University of Texas at Austin, for permission to quote from unpublished archival materials in the J. M. Coetzee collection. I further thank J. M. Coetzee for permission to cite from these unpublished materials. I am grateful to Sharon Zwi for granting permission to use her wonderful 'life portrait' of J. M. Coetzee as the cover image to this book.

Some chapters of this book have been built out of earlier versions that were published in academic journals. I acknowledge *Textual Practice* which published an earlier version on Chapter 3, entitled, '*Dusklands* and the meaning of method', 2016, Vol. 30, No. 3, 399–415; *Texas Studies in Literature and Language*, which published a version of Chapter 4, entitled, 'Process and Method in *Waiting for the Barbarians*', Vol. 58, Issue 4, 2016; Edinburgh University Press, which published an earlier version of Chapter 5, entitled, 'Deleuze, Ethics, Ethology and Art' in *Deleuze and Ethics*, edited by Daniel W. Smith and Nathan Jun; *The Comparatist*, which published an earlier version of Chapter 7, as 'Excess as Ek-stasis: Coetzee's *The Master of Petersburg and Giving Offense*', Vol. 31, Oct. 2014, 54–69; and *The Sydney Review of Books* (sydneyreviewofbooks.com) and Bloomsbury Academic, which published earlier versions of Chapter 9 as 'Signs for the Soul', SRB 9/7/2013, and 'Creative Intuition: Coetzee, Plato, Bergson and Murnane' in J. M. Coetzee's *The Childhood of Jesus*, edited by Jennifer Rutherford and Anthony Uhlmann, 2017.

I would like to acknowledge colleagues at the Writing and Society Research Centre of Western Sydney University who assisted in the development of this work, particularly Melinda Jewell, Jason Tuckwell, and Arka Chattopadhyay.

Introduction

Much early criticism of Coetzee's works concentrated on what Patrick Hayes calls 'the vexed and complex question of political responsibility' (Hayes, 1). Hayes goes on to suggest that so much strong work has been done by critics, such as Sue Kossew, Hermann Wittenberg, David Attwell, Peter McDonald, and many others in postcolonial theory and South African literature, that there is now room to evaluate Coetzee's works in other ways, in particular in considering how Coetzee uses formal characteristics of the novel to engage with politics. This kind of evaluation, which considers how the works develop a 'fresh thinking-through of significant aesthetic, ethical and political issues' (Attridge, *Ethics of Reading*, x), was already begun by Derek Attridge with *J. M. Coetzee and the Ethics of Reading*. Since then, a number of works have appeared that read Coetzee's works in relation to philosophy, considering how Coetzee's texts engage with and challenge philosophical ideas (Leist and Singer, Mulhall, Wilm), and how the texture of the works creates effects that push readers to think (Clarkson, Zimblar).

In 2013 a wealth of material was made available in the archives of the Harry Ransom Center at Coetzee's alma mater, the University of Texas at Austin. The most important engagement with the archives to date is David Attwell's *J. M. Coetzee and the Life of Writing: Face to Face with Time* (2015). Attwell characterizes his work as not being an intellectual biography, but rather 'an account of my reading of Coetzee's manuscripts' (Attwell, *Life of Writing*, 17). In effect, Attwell situates the archive as an ur-work, which comprises an extension of the published works.

My book situates itself between this interest in the philosophical provocations of Coetzee's works and how they relate to questions of form on the one hand and a response to a reading of the writing process that is in part set out or staged among the voluminous archives at Harry Ransom on the other. In doing this, I cover new ground, adjacent to but largely untouched by the studies that have so far appeared. I at times agree with and at times diverge from ideas set out in the works of criticism I have cited above.

Provocations

All of the critics cited above agree that Coetzee is not merely someone who makes use of or stages philosophical or literary critical ideas; rather, he is an original thinker. His work is of interest to philosophers or literary theorists not because it comfortingly reflects their own ideas back to them; rather, it is of interest because it is provocative and challenging of their positions.

In his recent study of Coetzee, Jan Wilm makes use of the words 'provoke' and 'provocative' on a number of occasions to characterize the manner in which Coetzee's works are drawn into relation with philosophical thinking. These provocations in turn have had real effects. Cora Diamond, for example, argues that what is at stake in *The Lives of Animals* is not a consideration of how human/animal relations might be solvable by philosophy, but rather the provocative suggestion that philosophy is incapable of coming to terms with this issue in all its complexity. That the horror induced once one takes the time to look at the human treatment of animals squarely cannot be adequately understood. Stanley Cavell, in turn, responds to Diamond offering his own reading of Coetzee in relation to the issue of the capacities of philosophical thinking. It might be argued that many of the responses to Coetzee express this anxiety – the anxiety of trying (and possibly failing) to find effective responses to seemingly intractable problems.

While neither Wilm nor Diamond looks to systematize the idea of 'provocation', I examine this idea further, suggesting that Coetzee's works involve provocations that emerge at both formal and conceptual levels. These levels in turn are tied together by the problem of expression itself. This problem might be posed quite simply: if what we can say or think is determined by the forms within which we think (language itself, and what Michel Foucault calls 'discursive formations'), how is it possible for us to get to the truth?

Is there thought without language?

Coetzee emerged within a period in which proponents of structural linguistics (in the United States and elsewhere) insisted upon the identification of language and thought, and in which continental philosophers, such as Barthes, Foucault, and Derrida, worried at how it might be possible to think outside boundaries imposed by discourses that underpin our cultures.[1] Yet it becomes apparent in attending to his works and his responses that Coetzee does not, in the first instance, concede the point that thought and language are identical.[2] Rather, as I will set out in Chapter 2, which offers a reading of Coetzee's PhD thesis, he questions this hypothesis in remaining open to the existence of an idea of 'content' separate to 'form'.

It is worth underlining what exactly is at stake here by attending to an argument Coetzee himself develops. In 'Isaac Newton and the Ideal of a Transparent Scientific Language' (1982) Coetzee sets out to test Benjamin Lee Whorf's hypothesis, which Coetzee suggests was first stated by Wilhelm von Humboldt in the 1830s, 'that one thinks in forms limited and determined by the forms of one's native language' (*Doubling*, 181). Whorf contends that rather than being natural categories, Indo-European concepts of 'things' and 'events' are related to the grammatical categories implicit within this family of languages. He suggests that within a non-Indo-European language, such as that of the Hopi people of North America, these categories would appear to be cultural constructs rather than 'real' categories. Whorf turns to Isaac Newton as an example, claiming that 'Newtonian space, time and matter are no intuitions. They are receipts from culture and language. That is where Newton got them (p. 153)' (cited in Coetzee, *Doubling*, 183–184).

---

[1] See Coetzee's short paper, 'Is there thought without language?', delivered at a round table on this question in 2006 (Coetzee, 'Thought').
[2] Coetzee, 'Is there thought without language?'.

Coetzee tests Whorf's hypothesis by examining Newton's language, looking for signs that would indicate whether 'we find in Newton's English and Latin the seamless continuity that Whorf predicts between syntax and logic and world view, or, on the contrary, are there signs of a wrestling to make the thought fit into the language, to make the language express the thought' (*Doubling*, 184). Coetzee then highlights a move in Newton's writing away from the use of the active voice towards the use of the passive voice. Coetzee suggests that this strategy is typical of scientific language more generally. The benefit of moving to the passive voice is that the metaphor of animistic agency within nature is eliminated. The use of the active voice in the discussion of gravity and the suggestion that bodies acted with this force led to pointed criticisms of Newton by his contemporaries Huygens and Leibniz, with Leibniz ridiculing the '"inexplicable, incorporeal virtue" possessed by bodies' (cited in Coetzee, *Doubling*, 185).

In short, Coetzee suggests that Newton indeed *does* struggle, in an effort to warp language to accommodate his ideas, in an effort to bridge the gap between the 'nonreferential symbolism of mathematics and a language too protean to be tied down to single, pure meanings' (*Doubling*, 194). This struggle, he argues, contradicts Whorf's hypothesis, although he is cautious about some of the implications of this apparent contradiction. It involves, he suggests, having to embrace a radical idealism: that there could be such a thing as pure thought which an ideal 'transparent language' such as that aspired to by Newton, and groped towards through his stylistic development, might somehow approximate. Although Coetzee tends to the point of view that achieving such an ideal is impossible, I will argue here that the idea of the necessary distortion of a work through textual, stylistic, or rhetorical devices in order to get to something else, some intuitively grasped 'truth', is extremely important to the idea of the capacity or potential of writing that Coetzee both develops through his theoretical writing and makes use of in practice as a novelist. It should be noted that while Coetzee's position (that content and form are in some ways distinct and that there is thinking outside of language) was at the time provocative, recent work in cognitive science has tended more and more towards the position (one long held to by visual artists and musicians) that language is only one part of human thought: that we think through the emotions and feelings as much as we think through logic and reasoning, and this process of sensation sometimes involves linguistic functions and sometime does not (see Damasio, *Descartes' Error*; *The Feeling of What Happens*). It should be noted, however, that Coetzee's position seems equivocal: while he refutes a strong Whorfian view, he recognizes that language and the forms they carry nevertheless strongly inflect and limit our capacity to express.

Coetzee in part implies that there is something other than these forms, some truth or content that can be glimpsed through intuition or insight. He further implies that it is extremely difficult to approach these insights other than indirectly. He responds to problems not by offering immediate solutions, but by developing provocations, which require readers to think. In this sense the idea of the provocation aligns with a Derridian understanding of indeterminancy. It also aligns with Gilles Deleuze's understandings of literary thinking as 'leading to thought' rather than telling us what to think (Deleuze, *Proust and Signs*, 100–101). And further, rather than providing neat answers to questions (such as 'what might an ethical human/animal relationship look like?'), such provocations bring to light what is excluded by the forms of the question one might ask.

Provocation is not merely a loose description of a feature of Coetzee's works but rather a characterization of their method or approach. In general terms, philosophical discourse might be either empirically based and built upon induction from experience or experiment (*a postiori*) or, in the manner of mathematics, metaphysics, or logic, built upon deduction from first principles (*a priori*). Induction moves from the particular to the general, while deduction moves from the general to the particular. In contrast, Coetzee underlines the importance of the *provocation* as the point from which his works of fiction start and the point towards which they tend. If you are arguing *a priori,* you necessarily begin with a postulate, which either establishes or claims the firm ground from which arguments might be built or against which they might be tested. If you are working inductively, from experience or experiment *a postiori*, you are establishing facts that will allow you to predict how materials behave. The provocation, however, makes you think by either questioning the value of an assumed truth (or facts) or requiring the creation of new truths adequate to the provocation.

In this book, I will consider a number of provocations, but all of them will ultimately be drawn back into relation with three key ideas, three key provocations. Firstly, that there is truth in fiction or that fiction can provide valuable understandings of real-world problems. Secondly, that there are fictions of the truth: that we are surrounded, in our everyday lives, with stories we tell ourselves which we wish to believe are true. These two things are by no means identical: they are, nonetheless, inter-involved and confused. Thirdly, that meaning is created and processes and methods of writing can be developed that create a feeling of meaningfulness in texts and that this feeling in turn provokes readers to interpretation.

Truth in fiction

Coetzee underlines the first provocation, that fiction can offer us access to the truth, in a number of places. This statement is provocative because, in data-obsessed capitalist societies, it has become increasingly unpopular to make large claims for the importance of fiction or the arts. It is further provocative because it somehow calls upon the works to justify this claim and critics of those works to understand it.

One of the places Coetzee sets out his ideas is in the first interview with David Attwell in *Doubling the Point*:

> we should distinguish two kinds of truth, the first truth to fact, the second something beyond that; and that, in the present context, we should take truth to fact for granted and concentrate on the more vexing question of a 'higher' truth [...] As you write [...] you have to feel whether you are getting closer to 'it' or not [...] Writing reveals to you what you wanted to say in the first place [....] Writing, then, involves an interplay between the push into the future that takes you to the blank page in the first place, and a resistance [....] Out of that interplay there emerges, if you are lucky, what you recognize or hope to recognize as the true. (17–18)

This takes us back to ancient debates, beginning with Plato and Aristotle, which concern the very foundations of knowledge: that which allows us to recognize or understand some truth.

Fictions of the truth

The second provocation seemingly inverts the first. If there is truth in fiction, there are also fictions of the truth. If 'truth in fiction' relates to content, that is, insights or understandings that are not dependent on fictional expression (since the 'higher truths' exist as intuitively grasped 'content' that pre-exist that expression), 'fictions of the truth' relate to form, that is, they involve *relation* itself, or storytelling, with stories understood to have profound effects on how we behave and we live. These stories are not necessarily true and not necessarily ethical, but the implication is that they can *create* truths and thereby inform or deform ethical understandings. The further implication is that in this capacity stories are the ubiquitous and principal way in which we understand or misunderstand. For better or worse we surround ourselves with and understand ourselves through stories. Again, there is a classical precursor to this idea: Socrates excoriates bad rhetoricians, in Plato's dialogues *Gorgias* and *The Sophist*, as those who convince through passing off stories as true that may not be true. As Nietzsche has shown, however, there is no escaping from rhetoric: one has to simply assume that there are bad rhetoricians (like Gorgias) and good rhetoricians (like Socrates) (see Nietzsche, *Birth of Tragedy*). The idea that forms of expression might be either good or bad depending on how they are used is also at the heart of Foucault's examination of discursive formations, which both enable and limit what we can say (Foucault, 'The Order of Discourse', *The Archeology of Knowledge*).

For Coetzee, the idea that the story is central to our sense of understanding has become so widely accepted as to be a cliché. Our culture (at a time when it seemingly pays less and less heed to the arts) uses the story as a default position for explaining our personal, interpersonal, social, economic, political, and ecological relationships.[3] To put this another way, for Coetzee, with regard to the 'fictions of the truth', there are good stories and bad stories (see *The Good Story* and *Giving Offense*). To be good a story must both be well told – attending rigorously to the processes in which

---

[3]See Coetzee's opening 'provocation' at the Worlds Literature Festival Salon, https://www.youtube.com/watch?v=1EaxNqutqDk.

we are imbedded, choosing the best methods to generate effects and stimulate affects in readers – and true – adequately expressing the insights which have driven the process of expression.

The truth is created through method

The third provocation relates to the need to find a means of expression that might allow one to convey the truth, even though that truth might be obscured by the modes of thought (language, and what Foucault calls 'discourse') that form us. As is apparent in his critical work and in his fiction, and as I will discuss in Chapter 2, Coetzee resists the idea that we are completely constrained by forms of thought. In this study, I will sometimes call these forms 'methods' as disciplines, such as history, politics, philosophy, the sciences, and so on, are in part determined by the methods they are constrained to follow. I will argue that, if it is possible to get outside of our representations or to develop representations that somehow allow us access to the higher truth, there must be a concept which is adequate to this idea. This concept is *intuition*.

Intuition and ethology

If Wilm builds his book around the idea of slowness, Clarkson around countervoices, Attridge around an idea of the 'literal' and Attwell 'life', my study will make use of the concepts of intuition and ethology as a means of drawing my readings of Coetzee's fictions and how they generate meaning into focus. These ideas, and their relationships to the creation of meaning, are critically held to the light in Coetzee's later novels *The Childhood of Jesus* and *The Schooldays of Jesus* but are present in all his works. I will discuss the nature and potential of the concept of intuition in the first chapter. To begin, however, it is important to underline the two components of this concept. Firstly, intuition is that which allows us to think. It offers a point of foundation upon which rigorous thinking might be built (and through which an adequate understanding might become possible). Secondly, intuition is that which allows us to understand. Following Spinoza, in a reading I will set out below, understanding itself might be identified with intuition, because when we understand we are already in understanding. Strangely, this sounds both paradoxical and tautological. I will attempt to clarify these ideas in Chapter 1, in a section that will move away from Coetzee's own readings to a discussion of philosophical concepts.

Rather than attempting a genealogy of the concept of intuition, Chapter 1 will briefly outline how the concept has been used by particular philosophers whose ideas have been highly influential on Romantic and Modernist literature, which in turn heavily influenced Coetzee's writing. In part I am doing this to underline the seriousness of the claims being made here: that is, that intuition in effect is what allows us to begin to think and to understand. Chapter 2 will turn to a reading of Coetzee's PhD dissertation, outlining how Coetzee develops a distinction between form and content and explores the potentials of formal relations in literature. Drawing on close attention to Coetzee's archives, Chapters 3 and 4 will consider elements of Coetzee's creative process and the methods he develops to create meanings in examining *Dusklands* and *Waiting for the Barbarians*.

Chapter 5 works as a companion to Chapter 1, moving back from Coetzee's work to an engagement with foundational concepts that shed light on those works. Drawing on the work of Deleuze and Guattari, Bergson and Spinoza, without claiming that Coetzee himself directly consulted these philosophers in developing his own works, this chapter considers how the concept of 'ethology' allows us to better understand the kinds of representations Coetzee develops in his fiction.

The implications of the concept of ethology, which tie ethics to place, situation, and disposition, are then drawn out in Chapters 6–8 in readings of *Life & Times of Michael K*, *Age of Iron*, *The Master of Petersburg*, *Elizabeth Costello*, and *Disgrace*. Chapter 9 then returns to the concept of intuition, in developing readings of *The Childhood of Jesus* and *The Schooldays of Jesus*. Chapter 10 then works between ideas of intuition and ethology, in considering how ideas are developed in relation to experience via readings of *Boyhood* and *Youth*.

1

Intuition, Knowledge, Truth

The problem of how to ground the truth has been recurrent in philosophy.[1] Plato makes use of the ideal or form to establish the truth and as we will see Coetzee has a strong interest in Plato. Yet Plato's idea depends on belief in a realm above which can only be explained through recourse to myth.

A firmer ground is provided by the concept of intuition, and the concept of intuition in turn has been extremely important to writers, both in the Romantic and Modernist periods. In addition, it is apparent that recent studies in neuroscience have turned to the concepts of insight and intuition. Currently, there are two main conceptual approaches to the concept of intuition in psychology (Hodgkinson et al.). Firstly, it is considered to be 'tacit knowledge' related to associative understanding where information we have processed has become so ingrained as to constitute habit. This information is then accessed unconsciously to aid in decision-making processes (Reber; Dienes and Berry). Secondly, it involves a similarly unconscious process through which, in attempting to solve a problem, one suddenly arrives at a solution, through insight (Mayer; Nisbett and Wilson; Jung-Beekman et al.). Both of these responses presuppose a model of unconscious learning and unconscious processing. Furthermore, such processes are distinguished from instinctual behaviour recognized in non-human organisms (though potentially also residual in human behaviour)

---

[1]This chapter, in part, builds on work I am currently undertaking with Moira Gatens concerning Spinoza and his relation to the arts. While the readings are my own they are deeply informed by our collaboration and the conversations with various interlocutors within this project from philosophy, intellectual history and the arts.

which is considered to not be learnt but rather innate within these organisms (Carlson).

Philosophical traditions differ somewhat from these models of tacit knowledge or unconscious processing by going back to still more foundational processes of understanding, considering how we might understand anything at all. Such philosophical systems have identified intuition with the idea of the foundational premise (Aristotle) which might relate to knowledge of the self (Descartes), of existence (Spinoza), of the perception of time and space (Kant), of consciousness and duration (Bergson), for example.

While these ideas beg the question as to how intuition might be aligned with belief systems, these will be left to one side here.[2] The components of the concept of intuition I will be concerned with are as follows: firstly, it is foundational, involving implicit presuppositions that allow thought to begin. Secondly, it involves the feeling of understanding that occurs when one grasps some idea that has not occurred to one previously (whether it is offered by another or encountered within some process of thinking), which extends the model of deliberation followed by understanding identified through the neuroscientific idea of insight. Thirdly, it involves a forceful feeling of the truth of something which then informs decision-making (as opposed to purely associative understanding).

Here I will set out an overview of some aspects of the idea of intuition. I will begin with Aristotle who is the first philosopher to make use of intuition as both a foundation of knowledge and an explanation of how we come to understand. After briefly discussing the Ancient Stoics and Descartes I will then turn to Kant because of his influence on aesthetic theory since the Romantics. I will also discuss Spinoza, whose concept of intuition remains the most comprehensive and useful and strongly resonates with contemporary theories of cognition. Spinoza too was a major influence on the German and English Romantics, nineteenth-century literature, and Modernism. I will end with Bergson's conception of intuition, which was important to literary Modernism, before briefly considering the work of cognitive scientist Antonio Damasio to underline how the feeling of meaning and intuition are connected.

---

[2]I touch upon some of the implications in Chapter 8.

My claim is that 'the idea', as outlined by Spinoza, explains how one might affirm it is possible to recognize or sense truth and situate it as something which might plausibly occur in literary fiction. While these readings are applicable to Coetzee's works, and Coetzee himself has, particularly in recent times, developed strong interest in the idea of intuition (as will be examined in *The Childhood of Jesus* chapter below), I am not claiming that Coetzee develops a genealogy of the concept or works directly with the philosophers discussed here. Rather, my claim is that the idea of intuition is applicable to thinking in literature in general terms and provides grounding for the claim that there is truth in fiction. There are models for such claims in both Romantic and Modernist literature, and I will touch upon how each of these was influenced by the concept of 'intuition'.

Plato and inspiration

A number of critics have underlined the importance of Plato to Coetzee's work, and this is something I will consider in more detail with relation to *The Childhood of Jesus* below, although it will also be touched on in readings of *Waiting for the Barbarians* and *Elizabeth Costello*. Plato allows a bringing together of the idea of the truth in art and what might ground that truth.

Famously in *Phaedrus* and *Ion*, Plato has Socrates consider, among other things, the truth value of art. Plato has Socrates identify art in these dialogues with knowledge. To be an art something must involve knowledge, and to speak the truth about anything one must have adequate knowledge of what one is speaking about. The charioteer has knowledge of chariot racing, the doctor of the human body.

Socrates wonders, in *Phaedrus*, if rhetoric could be an art and concludes that it can only be where the one speaking has knowledge of this kind about what they are discussing and can readily explain and justify this knowledge. In *Ion*, a dialogue often paired with *Phaedrus*, Socrates explains that artists often do not know how or why they arrive at the truth claims they make. This is the case even of the greatest, even for Homer, but is exemplified in the dialogue through Ion, a performer of Homer who is also a commentator on Homer. The critic Ion, like the artist Ion, seems to work without either absolutely knowing the truth or being conscious of possessing the adequate foundational knowledge on which it must be built.

As Nikolas Pappas argues in drawing together *Ion* and *Phaedrus*, there can only be two possibilities. The first is that the artist is a fraud. This is the case with the one who makes use of rhetoric. That artist has mastered techniques through which he/she might convince others of the truth of something without himself/herself knowing the truth. In this way he/she might convince others that things are true which are not in fact true.

The second possibility, however, is that the true artist might be saved by 'inspiration'. That is, the artist can convey the truth without knowing it himself/herself if he/she is inspired by the gods. The gods give the poet access to the truth; the truth does not belong to the poet, but is spoken through the poet who transmits the truth of the gods (which in turn can be transmitted by the poem to the reader infused with inspired understanding, see Pappas).

Aristotle and intuition (*nous*)

While the idea of inspiration has fallen from fashion and has come to be associated with an idealized notion of artistic process, the idea of an immediate understanding, as that which founds the truth, survives in philosophy through the concept of intuition. That is, both intuition and inspiration involve a sense of understanding that seems to occur unbidden, as something that we know and sense to be true. In what follows I will trace some of the outlines of the concept of intuition as it emerges in a number of philosophers. I do not wish to imply that the concept is identical in each of these thinkers; on the contrary, they each give the concept their own particular inflections, which I will attempt to sketch. What they all have in common, however, is the functional application of the concept of intuition, which, like Plato's 'inspiration', is used as a foundational concept that allows an initial access to the truth upon which knowledge might be built.

While Plato turns to myth to ground or explain the feeling of recognition (the 'a ha' moment that marks any true feeling of understanding, where, to paraphrase Spinoza, we know that we know that we know), others, beginning with Plato's student Aristotle, shifted this idea of recognition onto a concept of intuition (or *nous* for Aristotle) (see Aristotle, Aydede, Lesher). Aristotle's *nous*, like inspiration, involves an immediate understanding of things, an immediate grasping of a foundational truth. One might begin by asking why this is necessary. Why do we need some foundational concept? For Aristotle, and for many who came after, the problem of how one begins to think with certainty is troubling. For Aristotle, one begins with premises, which one knows to be true, and builds from these premises through logical method in order to achieve truths with absolute certainty. This is the kind of method one sees in mathematics or geometry. But how does one start? Aristotle suggests there are (at the time he writes, though one can see similar ideas repeated throughout the history of philosophy) two schools of thought:

> Some hold that, owing to the necessity of knowing the primary premises, there is no scientific knowledge. Others think there is, but that all truths are demonstrable. [...] The first school, assuming that there is no way of knowing other than by demonstration, maintain that an infinite regress is involved, on the ground that if behind the prior stands no primary, we could not know the posterior through the prior [...] The other party agree with them as regards knowing, holding that it is only possible by demonstration, but they see no difficulty in holding that all truths are demonstrated, on the ground that demonstration may be circular and reciprocal. (Aristotle, *Posterior*, 3–4)

The first school might be aligned with the Sophists who held to the idea that all knowledge and truth is subjective. The second school Aristotle describes not only relates to empiricists of Aristotle's times but also brings to mind the failed project of the English philosophers Bertrand Russell and Alfred Whitehead in the early twentieth century, who, taking up the challenge of the German mathematician David Hilbert concerning the foundations of mathematics, sought to prove that mathematical systems could be self-contained and complete. That is, that no prior term was required in mathematical thinking. They were proved wrong by Kurt Gödel, with his famous 'incompleteness' theorems, which show that no mathematical system is complete or self-contained (see Goldstein). That is, one might argue that Gödel confirmed Aristotle's view, which requires something outside the system, to underwrite or found the truth of the system.

Intuition and foundation

It is the moment of immediate understanding that allows us to begin to reason and thereby discover further truths. In *Posterior Analytics* Aristotle sets out his own doctrine opposed to those two set out above:

> Our doctrine is that not all knowledge is demonstrative: on the contrary, knowledge of the immediate premises is independent of demonstration. [...] Such, then, is our doctrine, and in addition we maintain that besides scientific knowledge there is its originative source which enables us to recognize the definitions. (Aristotle, *Posterior*, 4)

He goes on to link this knowledge to intuition (*nous*) stating that, 'by rational intuition I mean an originative source of scientific knowledge' (Aristotle, *Posterior*, 33), affirming that 'rational intuition, science, and opinion [...] are the only things that can be "true"', but that of these three, opinion is concerned with that 'which may be true or false' (Aristotle, *Posterior*, 33). He later extends this idea, further underlining the importance of intuition as that which founds knowledge. He concludes his *Posterior Analytics*, a work that sets out with great rigour his scientific method, as follows:

> From these considerations it follows that there will be no scientific knowledge of the primary premises, and since except intuition nothing can be truer than scientific knowledge, it will be intuition that apprehends the primary premises – a result which also follows from the fact that demonstration cannot be the originative source of demonstration, nor, consequently, scientific knowledge of scientific knowledge. If, therefore, it is the only other kind of true thinking except scientific knowing, intuition will be the originative source of scientific knowledge. And the originative source of science grasps the original basic premiss, while science as a whole is similarly related as originative source to the whole body of fact. (Aristotle, *Posterior*, 54)

The Ancient Greek Stoics:
The truth of perception

Aristotle is not alone in developing intuition as a kind of foundation. The Ancient Stoics, who followed him, sought to modify his understanding by tying the grounds of knowledge more explicitly to our perception. The link between intuition and perception is something that returns, in differing ways, in Descartes, Kant, and Bergson. It is apparent that the ideas of intuition, and its connections to perception, relate to art and literature more or less directly, because art and literature are concerned with perception, feeling, and understanding. It is not difficult to see why some of the ideas of philosophers who affirmed the importance of immediate understanding might be attractive to artists, then, as they offer explanations, precisely, of how art might access the truth (via intuition and heightened moments of perception).

It is worth pausing to consider the Stoic understanding of the 'comprehensive image', which they see as founding truth. In *Chrysippe et l'ancien stoïcisme*, the French philosopher Émile Bréhier offers an overview of the comprehensive image.

Bréhier underlines how for Plato the 'truth' was available to a few. For the Sophists, however, appearance was identified with the truth. For the Stoics there is an immediate apprehension of the truth, anyone can find it, but they cannot find it anywhere, that is, not every perception will lead to the truth (Bréhier, 80–81). The Stoics define representation, or perception, as 'the image of the real produced in the soul by the action of an exterior object' (Bréhier, 82).

The Stoics turn from the Sophists in two ways. Firstly, the Sophists claim that truth comes to us through perception, but that it is relative, it is 'my truth' alone, and so neither contestable nor universal. Secondly, the Sophists claim that all representations or perceptions lead to this kind of personal truth. For the Stoics, however, in *certain cases* the truth of my representation is not relative to me, but absolute. Therefore, there is the possibility of a science of the immutable truth, a science of the sensible (something that is not possible with the relative worldview of the Sophists). This knowledge is not found in general laws, but rather, as with

Aristotle, relates to singular propositions which can then be linked together through a chain of reasoning to build certain knowledge (Bréhier, 86).

The special case, which allows an immediate understanding of a premise or proposition, is called the 'comprehensive image'. For the Stoics not all appearance is of equal value; the comprehensive image carries the mark of its own truth. The comprehensive image itself is an act of understanding, that is, it is active, whereas some images (or representations or perceptions) are passive. The action has its origins in the soul, whereas the passion comes to us from outside (Bréhier, 87–88). The comprehensive image is active, grasping the nature of things; it is intimately tied with assent, the rational action (Bréhier, 89). The comprehensive image is so evident it compels assent (there can be false assent but this can be refuted by wisdom). In this it resembles the 'clear and distinct idea' later put forward by Descartes (Bréhier, 90–91). 'Assent' for the Stoics involves the action through which we grant the truth of some perception or image. It is a key term related to our freedom and our ability to negotiate between what is true and what is false. In most cases assent follows the image: we perceive and then we assent or withhold assent from what we perceive (accepting it as true or rejecting it as false). Yet with the comprehensive image the assent is – somehow – *immediate*. The comprehensive image is 'the representation capable of perceiving or comprehending the real' (Bréhier, 92).

Both the Stoics (whose fragments were collected in the late sixteenth century by Justus Lipsius and so had become available to European scholars) and Aristotle (who had been rescued for the West by twelfth-century Islamic philosophers translators and commentators such as Averroes and Avicenna) were of great importance to the Enlightenment as it developed in the seventeenth century through, among others, Descartes and Spinoza, who both took up the concept of intuition.

Descartes, inference and intuition

Stephen Gaukroger has written a detailed overview of Descartes' conception of inference, which includes a description of Descartes' concept of intuition.[3] Like Aristotle[4] Descartes requires the first premise or axiom of an argument to be founded by something prior to it:

> It is not just a case of axioms being necessary; Descartes clearly thinks that for something to be an axiom it must have special intrinsic properties, such as self-evidence and indubitability, which enable it to play the role it does. Propositions meeting these requirements are grasped by intuition, not deduction, and form the basis for any subsequent deduction. (Gaukroger, 51)

For Gaukroger Descartes goes still further, underlining how this intuitive understanding forms a ground on which true knowledge can be built.

> Although *intuitus* disappears from Descartes' vocabulary in his later writings, this general conception does not, and indeed its crowning achievement is the *cogito*. The *cogito* is effectively an intuition of a basic premiss which, because of its indubitability and self-evidence, can be grasped independently of anything else, including rules of inference. It forms the starting-point for knowledge and the paradigm for knowledge in that, while it is a grasp of a single proposition, to get to other propositions one grasps necessary connections between this and the others, remembering that, in the limiting case, this grasp should itself take the form of an intuition. (Gaukroger, 51)

Here then, we get an example of an intuition: the intuition that 'I think (therefore I am)'. In Aristotle's terms this is an example of a knowledge that founds all knowledge, and which, for Descartes, is both undeniable and able to act as grounds for knowledge that is certain.

---

[3]Thanks to Joseph Hughes for pointing me to this work. Also see Joseph Hughes, 'Cold Quietness'.
[4]Although Gaukroger also points out how they make somewhat different use of the concept (see Gaukroger, 44).

Spinoza's third kind of knowledge (intuition)

Spinoza too offers an example of the process of intuition, although it differs somewhat from Descartes. Spinoza describes three kinds of knowledge, which ascend from the weakest to the strongest, with the third kind, intuition, being the strongest.

That is, while the first kind of knowledge is a knowledge of the imagination or the perception of the senses and the second kind of knowledge is knowledge based on logical reasoning, the third kind of knowledge involves an immediate adequate understanding of things. The most powerful kind of knowledge develops from the linking of an adequate idea to another adequate idea through the third kind of knowledge (i.e. one moves deductively, or through reason, from point to point, but the strongest method of doing this occurs when each point is also grasped via a powerful feeling of understanding made possible, in the first instance, by intuition). The first example of an adequate idea emerging from the intuitive third kind of knowledge in Spinoza occurs in Part 1 of the *Ethics*, where he argues that we recognize immediately, before we know anything else, that existence, which he calls the one substance, God (which is identified with Nature), necessarily exists (Part 1, D8; P8, Schol. 2). This in turn connects Nature's power to Nature's essence (Part 1, P7): that is, what Nature *is* essentially is identical with what Nature can, and does, *do* (Nature's essence is identical with its existence, and it is the only thing whose essence involves existence). We recognize this truth – existence exists – and therefore that (God or) Nature's essence necessarily exists.[5]

It is important to set out how Spinoza differs from both Descartes and the Ancient Stoics in developing what remains the most compelling definition of intuitive understanding. In Part 2

---

[5]While not seeming to be thinking directly of either Descartes or Spinoza, Coetzee contemplates a thought experiment, which he recounts to Paul Auster in *Here and Now*, arguing that while he can imagine a world without J. M. Coetzee he cannot imagine a world without 'me' or 'I'. There seem to be two implications of this intuition for Coetzee: first, it is necessary to imagine existence (and the existence of one witnessing that existence) but that this does not equate to the necessary existence of one's own particular self (see Auster and Coetzee, *Here and Now*, 208).

of the *Ethics*, 'Of the Mind', Spinoza examines the nature of understanding itself. Proposition 43 concerns the truth and our understanding of the truth and states: 'He who has a true idea at the same time knows that he has a true idea, and cannot doubt the truth of the thing' (Spinoza, *Ethics*, Part 2, P43, Schol. 479)

Spinoza's God is identical with Nature and reveals its logic through the laws of Nature. These laws in turn are legible to us since we are part of Nature, part of God, and so partake of the reason which inheres within Nature. The Demonstration of Part 2, Proposition 47 clarifies that we have ideas with which we perceive ourselves and our own bodies as actually existing, and since these ideas are adequate we have access to 'an adequate knowledge of God's eternal and infinite essence' (*Ethics*, Part 2, P47, Schol. 482), that is, we immediately know and sense the existence of existence itself.

The feeling of understanding

This knowledge of the existence of existence is achieved through intuition. Below I will touch on how the contemporary neuroscientist Antonio Damasio reads Spinoza, finding an acute prescience in Spinoza's theories, which Damasio considers to fit remarkably well with our best current knowledge of the workings of the brain. Damasio sets out a concept of feeling, which he opposes to emotion, and argues that feelings (which are the highest point of the emotional system developed through evolution) involve maps of body states which allow us to understand (through feeling joy or sorrow, for example) the state of our bodily system. Intuition is a felt understanding: it allows us to begin to think as it situates us or grounds us within the world; it allows us to understand because grasping something is both a knowledge and a feeling at once. Spinoza states this clearly in Part 5 of the *Ethics*, where he states: 'For the mind *feels* those things it *conceives* in understanding no less than those it has in memory' (Spinoza, EVP23, Schol. My italics).

There are some implications of Spinoza's system that align with the formulations Coetzee develops in his PhD dissertation, which asserts a distinction between form and content. Spinoza too insists upon the immaterial nature of understanding. For Spinoza the idea, or that which is meaningful, cannot be identified with words or images; rather, the idea is 'the very act of understanding' – it is the feeling we get when we understand something.

In turn, the process of understanding itself is immediate. The true idea is recognized immediately, like the comprehensive image of the Stoics. Intuition is what allows us to begin to think; it is also that which allows us to understand.

This also explains the power of misunderstanding in art and life. When we misunderstand, for Spinoza, it is not because we cannot grasp a particular idea; rather, it is because we associate the wrong ideas, the wrong contexts, with the words on the page (Spinoza, EIIP29). So we can find understanding emerging between or among words and images but the meanings we feel are not identical with those words or images. This explains how a work of art might be able to lead us to truths. What needs to be conveyed are relations of ideas, what needs to be conveyed are relations of understandings. Yet while science or logic or mathematics might convey relations through clear deductive method, art works differently: it seeks to convey or translate the feeling of understanding itself. Once such a feeling of understanding is conveyed, it is up to readers to interpret the feeling to examine what it is in the work that has struck them as being true. As Deleuze suggests in his reading of Proust, rather than setting out a clear line of thought, art leads to thought.

Kant and Bergson, intuition, Romanticism, and Modernism

Although there is little evidence Coetzee studied much of Kant's work,[6] Kant's theories have been significantly influential in social, aesthetic, and linguistic theories, including the work of Noam Chomsky (in which Coetzee was well versed).[7] Furthermore, Kant's aesthetic theories, along with Spinoza's concept of intuition, were

---

[6]Coetzee mentions Kant in passing in *White Writing*, 54; *Doubling the Point*, 341; *Inner Workings*, 31; and *Stranger Shores*, 14.
[7]On the links between Kant and Chomsky, see Williams. Coetzee's interest in Chomsky is set out in his dissertation.

extremely important to the development of German and English Romanticism in the late eighteenth and early nineteenth centuries and remained influential into the Modernist era.[8] Equally, literary Modernism and elements of linguistic theory (such as Russian Formalism) were influenced by Henri Bergson's understanding of intuition (see Fink), and Coetzee, again, had studied Modernism and linguistic theories in detail. Coetzee mentions Bergson in passing in his PhD thesis and in his notes to *Waiting for the Barbarians* (Attwell, *Life in Writing*, 95). In turn, as well as heavily influencing the Romantic and Modernist traditions, which feed into Coetzee's works, Bergson, Spinoza, and Kant were important points of reference for French poststructuralist theorists, such as Lacan, Deleuze, Derrida, Barthes, and Foucault, with whose work Coetzee engaged throughout the 1970s and 1980s.[9] It is worth considering Kant's particular take on the concept of intuition, and that of Bergson, in order to develop some depth of understanding of how somewhat different philosophical conceptions of intuition have entered into literary Romantic and Modernist understandings.

Kantian intuition

In reading Kant's early work the 'Inaugural Dissertation' of 1770, Lorne Falkenstein shows how Kant develops his distinction between two cognitive capacities of 'intuition' and 'intellect' from categories derived from Aristotle and the Scholastics. These categories align with sense perception (intuition) and conceptual understanding (discursive intelligence or reason).

Falkenstein considers that Kant, here, in insisting on the distinction between sense perception and intellect, is moving against the spirit of the times, which had shifted, since Descartes, to attempts to bring these two faculties together (168). Yet Kant's predecessors Alexander Baumgarten and Georg Meier too had

---

[8] See Bell, Förster, Hooton, Levinson.
[9] A detailed list of the literary critical and theoretical readings Coetzee undertook in the 1970s and 1980s can be found in the Coetzee archives in the Harry Ransom Centre, which includes a 'Record of Reading, 1970s–1980s' (Coetzee Archives Container, 99.4).

insisted on a distinction between things perceived (or the aesthetic) and things known (or reason), and Werner Pluhar argues that Kant was influenced by this distinction in their work (xlix–l), which among other things involved the coining of the term 'aesthetic'. Following Falkenstein one can trace a line that relates intuition to the body and intellect to the mind in a tradition that separates body from thought, or, to use Kant's terms nature from freedom. Following Pluhar one can trace a line that considers sense and reason to be two aspects of cognition: two powers of thought.

Both lines are important to an understanding of Kant's concept of intuition. As Jennifer Mensch shows, Kant develops two concepts of intuition. The first is termed 'sensible intuition' and the second 'intellectual intuition'. In her reading Mensch concentrates on what Kant calls 'the formal principle of our intuition' (434), the overarching intuition of space and time that fundamentally determines our relation to the physical world that appears to us. Yet intuition is also understood in relation to 'empirical intuition' or perception itself: that is, the data given to us by our senses. As Kant sets out in the *Critique of Pure Reason*:

> Our cognition arises from two fundamental sources in the mind, the first of which is the reception of representations (the receptivity of impressions) the second the faculty for cognizing an object by means of these representations (spontaneity of concepts); through the former an object is **given** to us, through the latter it is **thought** in relation to that representation. (Kant *Pure Reason*, 193, B: 75, A: 51, *emphasis in original*)

Both conceptual thought and intuition are '**Empirical** if sensation [...] is contained therein', but they are '**pure** if no sensation is mixed into the representation' (Kant, *Pure Reason*, 193, B: 75, A: 51, *emphasis in original*). So the intuition of time and space is pure or formal, whereas the experience of being in the world and interacting with things involves empirical intuition mediated by empirical concepts.

As Mensch underlines, 'intellectual intuition', for Kant, is not something that we possess (also see Pluhar note to 289, xci–xcii); rather, it is something that we can conceive of (through judgement rather than conceptual reasoning) as being possessed by God (or the supersensible basis for the reality of Nature). Such an understanding, unlike ours, involves access to things in themselves rather than simply appearances.

In her essay Mensch sets out how denying the faculty of intellectual intuition to human cognition unsettled and disappointed artists and thinkers who followed Kant. In seeking to respond to Hume's scepticism, she argues, Kant set strict limits on human knowledge, prescribing that we cannot know 'the material content of our sensible intuition', that is, we can only access the appearances of things and cannot understand things in themselves. Furthermore, we are also unable to fully understand 'the moral objects of an intellectual intuition'. While Kant in part was attempting to set bounds on human reason in order to make room for faith (446), the denial of intellectual intuition to human cognition, Mensch contends, 'lies at the heart of Kant's rejection by his successors' (438). In consequence, they turn to Spinoza, who allows such a concept, to quote Mensch:

> It is within this context, therefore, that Spinoza's *vis intuitiva* can arrive as a specific solution for thinkers looking to put an end to the many borders – between sense and intellect, nature and freedom, knowledge and thought – demarcating Kant's work. (438)

In one way, then, we can understand the denial of intellectual intuition in Kant as something that provoked revolt in his readers, both in the philosophers that followed him and in Romanticism. As Mensch shows, Goethe, having made the radical move to Spinoza in the mid-1780s, aligns himself with the project of Kant's *Critique of Judgment* in the 1790s, although in doing this he insists on retaining the concept of intuition he understood from his reading of Spinoza. This revolt, then, casts something of a shadow over Kant, as if his denial of intellectual intuition were a mistake (an argument Falkenstein attempts to make in claiming that such a rejection is inconsistent with the conceptual genealogy Kant draws upon in developing his ideas). Paradoxically, then, Kant is connected, through his rebellious readers, to a concept he explicitly rejects. The shift away from Kant involves an insistence that art *can* get to the truth, that it *is* capable of adequate understanding.

That there is truth in fiction means that fiction can provide ways of understanding truths and stage processes through which truths might emerge. Truth itself is a feeling of understanding, and such feelings are our experience of the meaningful. So when we say that fictions can help us to create meaning, we mean they provide a way in which we can access this meaningful feeling.

It is possible to see the shadow of a non-empirical feeling of understanding operating elsewhere in Kant's system. To simplify, the concept of beauty developed in the *Critique of Judgment* involves a non-conceptual feeling of harmony between human cognition and nature. The feeling of beauty is the sensation of this harmony, which can only be arrived at through judgement rather than reason. This sense of the purposiveness of a thing without understanding its purpose is crucial within the overarching system developed in Kant's three Critiques, as it is set out in the *Critique of Judgment*. Furthermore, while not conceived of as (intellectual) intuition, it in many ways functions in a manner similar to (intellectual) intuition.

Kant has three components to cognition: Firstly, *understanding*: this relates to the order of nature and is quasi-passive, as it involves extracting laws from the appearance of nature. It is fully developed in the *Critique of Pure Reason* and works through concepts. Secondly, *reason*: this relates to the moral order and involves a more or less active approach to practical questions of behaviour and ethical deportment. This also involves laws, or imperatives, which must be obeyed, for example, the categorical imperative. It is set out in the *Critique of Practical Reason*. It too proceeds through conceptual thought. Thirdly, *judgement*: this involves a non-discursive, or non-conceptual quasi-understanding. It is set out in the *Critique of Judgment* and has two aspects, aesthetic and teleological judgement. The first concerns the judgement of beauty, both in nature and in art. The second links to theology and concerns the idea of purpose.

The third Critique proceeds through *ideas*, not concepts. Ideas might be aesthetic or rational, but unlike concepts they do not supply a 'cognition' or adequate understanding of something. To quote Kant:

> An *aesthetic idea* cannot become cognition because it is an *intuition* (of the imagination) for which an adequate concept can never by found. A *rational idea* can never become cognition because it contains a *concept* (of the supersensible) for which no adequate intuition can ever be given. (*Judgment*, 215: 342)

Nevertheless, this kind of thinking, which involves incomplete relations to intuition, allows for a bridge to be built between understanding and reason in aesthetic judgement and involves or allows a conception of (if not access to) intuitive understanding with regard to teleological judgement (see Kant, Introduction to *Critique of Judgment*).

In short, then, intuition, in the sense of access to an immediate understanding of things, haunts Kant's works to such an extent that its denial stands and in some senses acts in its place. This short reading of Kant might allow us to glimpse the importance of intuition as a concept, and how important it seemed to artists, at least from the Romantics on, as a way of exploring how art might somehow both grasp and express truths that are not necessarily available to pure reason. That is, that art could sense or feel truths and convey them to readers. In the early twenty-first century, however, we have all been acutely made to feel how loaded the word 'Romantic' has become, even among those with an interest in cultural history. With it comes a scepticism with regard to the possibility that art might somehow reveal, create, or uncover truths.

Coetzee might be seen to accept certain implications of Kant's views: that our experience is largely mediated by the forms of understanding and expression available to us. Yet like Goethe Coetzee continues to claim that art can allow us to glimpse the truth.

Bergsonian intuition

Intuition and the idea that art can access the truth does not die with Romanticism; on the contrary, it is reimagined for the Modernist artists of the early twentieth century, who influenced Coetzee profoundly, and the French philosopher Henri Bergson was a major influence on Modernist writers.[10] Bergson also offered a detailed definition of the nature of intuition, and so it is important to turn to him now.

---

[10]For Bergson's influence on Anglo-American and Russian Modernism, see Douglas, Ferguson, Fink, Gillies, Ardoin et al. For Bergson's influence on Samuel Beckett, see Uhlmann, *Philosophical Image*.

In *Creative Mind* Bergson underlines how he develops intuition as a method in his philosophy, having been led towards it through a consideration of the nature of time, which in turn resulted in the identification of the concept of duration. Following and attempting to improve on the work of Herbert Spencer who Bergson felt to be the first to fully draw questions of life and evolution into a philosophical system, Bergson came to understand that the concept of time had been systematically overlooked in both the history of philosophy and science. Time was never considered through its own nature – movement, change – rather, it had always been understood as a different kind of space, and so, in effect, rendered immobile.

'Duration' as Bergson understands the term attempts to conceive of time from within as a continuous flow that is coextensive with consciousness. Through close attention to experience it is possible, Bergson argued, to become aware of this flow, even though it is hidden behind the concepts developed by the human intellect, which have a natural tendency to divide and fix things at will so that the body might act more effectively upon those things and use them to its advantage. Duration as he understands it is strongly linked to intuition. Reminding us of Descartes' intuition of the *cogito*, he states:

> The intuition we refer to then bears above all upon internal duration [...] It is the direct vision of the mind by the mind. (*Creative Mind*, 34)

In turn, then, both duration and intuition are strongly linked, even identified with, consciousness. Yet here he seems to connect Descartes and Spinoza: it is not just 'I think' or 'I am conscious' but 'I am conscious of something' (existence). To quote Bergson further:

> Intuition [...] signifies first of all consciousness, but immediate consciousness, a vision which is scarcely distinguishable from the object seen, a knowledge which is contact and even coincidence. (*Creative Mind*, 34–35)

While duration, consciousness, and intuition are tied to the self that experiences, Bergson suggests that these concepts are capable of reaching beyond the self. That is, intuition opens itself to all that is capable of conscious perception and beyond this to all of life:

It may be that intuition opens the way for us into consciousness in general. – But is it only with consciousnesses that we are in sympathy? If every living being is born, develops and dies, if life is an evolution and if duration is in this case a reality, is there not also an intuition of the vital, and consequently a metaphysics of life, which might in a sense prolong the science of the living? (*Creative Mind*, 35)

So on the one hand Bergson, like Aristotle, Descartes, Spinoza, Kant, and others, establishes intuition as a foundation as that which allows us to begin to think in the first place. And on the other, like Spinoza, Bergson sees intuition as having an ongoing function as that which allows us to understand. Yet Bergson goes still further, as he claims that intuition (of duration in consciousness) opens up the possibility of understanding the spiritual realm.

Intuition is what attains the spirit, duration, pure change. Its real domain being the spirit, it would seek to grasp in things, even material things, their participation in spirituality, – I should say in divinity were I not aware of all the human element still in our consciousness, however purified and spiritualized. (*Creative Mind*, 36)

As well as being identified with his particular concept of consciousness, which he is able to extend to the Absolute, though he only briefly gestures in this direction (see *Creative Evolution*, 299), duration is identified with intuition. This in turn leads Bergson 'to raise intuition to the level of a philosophical method' (*Creative Mind*, 32). This is important to our concerns here, as, while others turn to 'intuition' as a foundational term that allows them to ground and validate the propositions they build upon, Bergson seeks to mobilize intuition more extensively by thinking intuitively: 'There is [...] a fundamental meaning: to think intuitively is to think in duration' (*Creative Mind*, 37).

Intuition, then, is a felt, sympathetic, or antipathetic understanding of what is essential to some or other situation: a truth that relates to that situation. This understanding is prior to representation, and the process of composition involves working towards that truth. Yet this truth is not necessarily an answer; rather, it might be better expressed to be a problem. Bergson suggests that rather than truth already being well known and so recognized, 'the truth is that in philosophy and even elsewhere it is a question of finding the problem and consequently of positing it, even more than of solving it' (*Creative Mind*, 57). Yet it is true of literature as much as philosophy that 'stating the problem is not simply uncovering, it is inventing' (*Creative Mind*, 57).

The process of inventing, or creating the truth, is something Bergson discusses in an essay on the philosophy of William James. Here he concludes that:

> [James] does not deny that reality is independent, at least to a great extent, of what we say or think of it; but the truth, which can be attached only to what we affirm about reality, is, for him, created by our affirmation. We invent the truth to utilize reality, as we create mechanical devices to utilize the forces of nature. (*Creative Mind*, 255)

So a work of fiction might find a method or way of staging a problem field, a problematic situation, or connected set of situations and, in inventing this problem field, allow us to understand what it is that we will need to come to terms with. The insights are still more useful, as Bergson contends that the invented truths, which come to us through fiction as much as through philosophy or other forms of creative work, including science, in turn shape our understanding of the world.

> Truth, according to pragmatism, has come little by little into being, thanks to the individual contributions of a great number of inventors. If these inventors had not existed, if there had been others in their place, we should have had an entirely different body of truths. (*Creative Mind*, 255)

This conception of 'truth' (invented in the sense that a form has to be found that will allow the expression of this particular problem or truth) would be adequate to the kind of truth given to us by fiction. An invented truth that allows us to perceive situations that pertain to us, problems that surround us, that are drawn into focus by the work of fiction, with that focus being manually corrected and maintained through an intuitive understanding of essential elements of those problems in the process of composition of that work. This conception too aligns with insights Coetzee brings to bear in his essay 'Isaac Newton and the Ideal of a Transparent Scientific Language' (1982), discussed above.

Knowledge too emerges from forms of understanding. On the one hand, this is physical and might be used to describe the human brain and how it interacts with its environment. On the other hand, it is conceptual and might be used to describe the systems that we build which, for Bergson, 'create' the truth.[11] Coetzee is formidably engaged in attempting to understand the processes and methods (the schemes)[12] that cause these forms to emerge and become truths, and this is something I will treat in detail throughout this book, in considering the construction of meaning.

While it is not controversial to claim that Coetzee's work has been influenced by both Romanticism and Modernism, these links alone are not sufficient to situate his own work. Rather, as we will see in the next chapter, in his PhD dissertation Coetzee confronted the problem of how to escape from or exceed the limitations upon expression set by cultural and intellectual forms by considering the problem of literary expression in relation to language and linguistic theory. Here, in closely reading the works of Beckett, he uncovers a method of getting beyond language through language, by setting A against B.[13]

Cognitive science and intuition

As I have touched upon above, neuroscientists have begun to take an increasing interest in the idea of intuition and how it might be thought to underlie decision-making processes. It is important to note that some of these scientists have been influenced by philosophy

---

[11]This point might be related to Coetzee's claims related in particular to autobiographical writings, which he suggests are 'constructions' or 'empowering fictions' (Coetzee, Good Story, 3). Also see his discussion of confession in *Doubling the Point*, 251–293.

[12]To use a term from Donald Davidson, adapted from Kant, see 'On the Very Idea of a Conceptual Scheme'.

[13]This method in turn aligns with that developed by Jacques Derrida in deconstruction where texts are turned against themselves to reveal gaps through which otherwise inexpressible truths might be glimpsed.

and in particular the theories of Spinoza. Writing in 2003 Heidi Morrison Ravven has set out the extent to which Spinoza has influenced neuroscientists and cognitive psychologists. In *Looking for Spinoza: Joy, Sorrow and the Feeling Brain*, Antonio Damasio claims to have been inspired by the prescience of Spinoza.

In *Looking for Spinoza*, the distinction Damasio makes between emotion (which involves preconscious cognitive activity as the brain reports without conscious reflection on the condition of the body) and feeling (which emerges after this initial preconscious appraisal has been made and involves conscious reflection on this initial appraisal) is provisional and, while speaking too simply he does equate emotions with the body and feelings with the mind (28), the detail of his argument demonstrates that the two processes are part of the same system (57–65).

Damasio insists that the triggering of emotions always involves appraisal, both in the initial moment of triggering and in the further associations that come into play (including memories of previous encounters) through the initial triggering (62–65). That is, before one consciously reflects upon what is taking place (what Damasio calls feeling), there is already appraisal; in effect, appraisal, and so meaning, is or should be present at every step of the emotion-feeling continuum Damasio describes. The appraisal mechanism is coextensive with the emotion mechanism, then, at each step. When they are disconnected, which Damasio argues is possible, the consequences for the subject unable to appraise due to brain injury are devastating (79). Such 'appraisal', which is preconscious and felt as understanding, might be aligned with intuition.

Thought, for Spinoza, is not identified with human consciousness; rather, it is the idea of the body and thinking is everywhere parallel with extension. It is not inconsistent with Spinoza, then, to claim, as Damasio does, that certain kinds of human cognitive processes are preconscious; indeed, it is difficult to see how any other claim might be accurate. This only becomes problematic if one exclusively identifies such preconscious cognition with the body alone and conscious thinking with the mind alone, which Spinoza does not do (as thinking is not reducible to consciousness for Spinoza). Damasio remains an important figure in contemporary debates because he has helped to open a dialogue between data being collected in contemporary cognitive science and the powerful theories of affect and understanding developed by Spinoza.

2

Meaning: Coetzee's Dissertation

Content and form

In the late 1960s Coetzee wrote his PhD dissertation, which included an analysis of the archival material to Samuel Beckett's *Watt* at the University of Texas, at Austin.[1] In *Doubling the Point* David Attwell asks Coetzee what drew him to the Beckett manuscripts. Coetzee replies:

> The Beckett manuscripts were in Texas, and I was there. A coincidence. I didn't know they were there before I arrived. But I became quite absorbed in them, particularly the *Watt* papers. It was heartening to see from what unpromising beginnings a book could grow: to see the false starts, the scratched-out banalities, the evidences of less than furious possession by the Muse. (Coetzee, *Doubling*, 25)

As I will set out below, Coetzee was, ultimately, highly sceptical of the benefits of the stylostatistical methods he adopted in developing his thesis; yet, they did lead him to some interesting

---

[1] A number of critics have written on relations between Beckett and Coetzee; see for example Hayes *Coetzee and the Novel*; Veres, Tajiri 'Beckett, Coetzee' and 'Beckett's Legacy'; Marais 'Incurious Seeker'; Meihuizen, Ackerley, Attridge 'Sex, Comedy, and Influence'; Yeoh. For an important discussion of how Coetzee's style differs from Beckett's, underlining that, while engaging with Beckett, Coetzee's works are not determined by Beckett's works, see Zimbler, 25–55.

ideas. In particular, the understanding of the relation between form and content in fiction, and a particular idea of dualism, remained with Coetzee from this period, and these ideas have maintained their generative potential throughout his own career as a writer.

In order to clarify some of these distinctions, I will turn to a reading of some ideas Coetzee sets out in his dissertation. Coetzee examines the question of what might be expressed in language. The dissertation sits within what would be a larger project: Beckett is seen as a prime example of an artist shifting between English and French. In order to determine whether there are different potentials for expression in the two languages, one would need to examine his last works in English, then examine his first works in French. Coetzee's dissertation only attempts the former.

Here, however, I will begin with his understanding of form and content which is crucial to the analysis he is attempting. Coetzee clearly underlines that there is a difference: that content and form cannot be collapsed into a single concept, as has been done twice in the twentieth century – firstly by the Russian formalists, who see content as an element of form and secondly and more influentially by structural linguistics. Coetzee summarizes his position in the final chapter of his dissertation under a subheading entitled 'Forms of thought and language'; he states:

> The opposition of structural linguists to a dualism of idea and word is too well known to need exposition. 'Linguistic features do not reproduce ... meaning', writes one of them, 'they produce it'. Recently, however, there has been something of a philosophic revolution in linguistics, led by Noam Chomsky, against logical empiricism and in favor of a revived Cartesianism in which the 'mental act' is distinct from the verbal act. The implication of the Chomskyan position for stylistics can conveniently be seen in a series of articles and books by Richard Ohmann. Ohmann began in 1958 as a Whorfian: if a speaker's language is itself an interpretative screen between him and his experience, then a writer's 'primitive choices' from the 'Heraclitean flux' of experience must reveal the 'very roots of [his] epistemology'. Therefore 'a pattern of expression' is a sign of 'a habit of meaning, and thus a persistent way of sorting out the phenomena of experience'. (Coetzee, *English Fiction*, 156–157)

Coetzee goes on to take issue with the precision of Ohmann's position that develops a complete identification between the form of the sentence and the form of the thought that is expressed. That is, Ohmann, though in a manner that is different from the structural linguists, returns to a position of monism. Coetzee's own position maintains a dualistic distinction between content and form, though recognizing a nuanced and complex interaction between them. In this Coetzee's position is much closer to Spinoza than that of Ohmann and structural linguistics. Whereas for structural linguistics thought is identified with language, as we have seen, for Spinoza, the idea cannot be identified with the word or the image; rather, the idea is the act of understanding. So too, the attribute of thinking is not identical with human consciousness let alone language; rather, the attribute of thinking involves the idea of extension. That is, the mind is the idea of the body (see Deleuze, *Spinoza*, 17–22). In insisting on the existence of 'content' here, Coetzee is making a similar distinction, one that implies that while there is meaning that cannot be adequately expressed by language, the forms of expression available to it nevertheless strive to make this meaning emerge.

In Chapter 1 of his dissertation Coetzee turns to definitions of kinds of interactions between form and content set out by Morris Weitz in *Philosophy of the Arts*. Weitz describes five uses and Coetzee states that his position is 'closest to (b) but not identical with it' (Coetzee, *English Fiction*, 15). Weitz's position (b) is: 'Content is the aggregate of elements, form the relations among them'. Coetzee goes on to clarify this:

> The form of a literary work is that conception of it which enables the reader to comprehend its entire structure of interrelationships and references. But not all elements of the work are parts of its content. The narrator of *Watt*, for example, is in the novel for formal reasons, and is thus a formal element. (Coetzee, *English Fiction*, 15)

These relations then allow us to develop a fuller understanding of what Coetzee means by 'style'. Earlier in Chapter 1 he sets out the hypothesis behind the larger project of which this dissertation is a fragment:

> The hypothesis I suggest we must ultimately test is that in Beckett's English works form somehow becomes autonomous

and determines content, while in his French work form remains subordinate. I therefore imply that there is in literary work a content which exists in some sense prior to its expression, that the expression can be adequate or inadequate to the content, and that in the latter case one can perceive disjunction between expression and pre-existent content. I imply that there is a general area of literary study which investigates the determination of each other by content and form – content by content, content by form, form by content, form by form – and that the investigation of the last three, but not the first, includes the study of *style*. (Coetzee, *English Fiction*, 5)

Note how, while Coetzee considers them to be dual and not two parts of the same thing, they nevertheless are always understood in relation: with content now being determined by form, form now being determined by content, and form now being determined by form. The distinctions between and interrelation of form and content Coetzee develops illuminate his own works as well as how he understands Beckett.

Dualism and residue: A against B

In 'Eight Ways of Looking at Samuel Beckett' (2008), Coetzee begins with the premise that Beckett is a philosophical dualist – that he is drawn to the idea that we are made up of a mind and a body, rather than being monist. This emphasis on philosophical duality echoes the content/form relation. Content/form implies that there can be meaning prior to its expression. Mind/body implies that there is some remainder, something other than the purely material, something incorporeal, like the meanings that are attributed to the material words we speak or write.[2] The dualisms are not simple; rather, they necessarily involve what Derrida calls supplementarity. Another way to understand their complex relation is in terms of what the American-Indian intellectual Anne Waters

---

[2]This example is taken from the Ancient Stoics (see Bréhier, *La théorie des incorporels*).

calls 'nondiscreet nonbinary dualism', whereby the dualist terms are in complex interrelation rather than understood as static and oppositional.

The two dualisms are isomorphic in that they provide a shape that can account for a meaningful exchange. It is an exchange that is not zero sum. That is, because the mind does not equal the body, because content does not equal form, something remains or else is lacking when the two are drawn into relation, and it is this remainder or deficit which is the site of meaning. To put this another way, ideas or a feeling of understanding emerges between, or among, or behind the words on the page. This feeling of meaning, in turn, can be aligned with intuition: it is the sense of meaning the writer gropes towards and endeavours to express in the writing process, and the reader feels towards in the reading process.

The shape involved can be expressed as '$a \approx b$, yet, $a \not\equiv b$' (with a representing content and b form), or to put this another way, it offers a problem that does not contain its solution. In *Creation and the Function of Art*, Jason Tuckwell explains how mathematics develops two kinds of problem: the first is the exact relation $a \rightarrow b$, which involves the understanding that a problem (such as $2 + 2$) already implies or contains its solution ($= 4$). The second involves the function ($a \rightarrow f \rightarrow b$) where the problem does not presuppose the solution but derives the solution through the process of calculation. This functional relation, which Tuckwell considers the *techné* that generates creation or *poesis*, works through the kind of problematic that is presupposed by a non-identical relation of nevertheless strongly interconnected elements, such as that in the content/form, mind/body relations Coetzee identifies.

This residue interests Coetzee as much as Beckett, but each has different points of emphasis. This is in part demonstrated by Coetzee in 'Eight Ways of Looking at Samuel Beckett', where he focuses on the absence of the Whale in Beckett. The White Whale, in Coetzee's essay, from *Moby Dick*, points us to both whiteness or the incapacity to immediately understand on the one hand, which he sees in Beckett, and the idea of the animal and the possibility of non-human thinking, on the other hand, which he does not see in Beckett. The first, whiteness, is an emblem of the residue or remainder I have alluded to here.

Yet this brings us back to a reading of *Watt* and the Beckett archives at Texas. In his study of the *Watt* manuscripts, which was among the first detailed analyses of Beckett's archival material, Coetzee examines three kinds of changes made to the text by Beckett during the course of composition. The first kind involves changes related to the plot of *Watt*. The second kind involves changes related to the structure of the work. The third kind involves changes related to the style of *Watt*.

All three come together around the idea of 'A against B' which Coetzee considers to be central to Beckett's method as it is revealed in the manuscripts to *Watt*. Coetzee sets this out briefly in his essay 'Samuel Beckett and the Temptations of Style'. Citing an example, he explains:

> The paragraph grows out of a rhythm or pattern of A against B. This rhythm infects most of *Watt*, extending to the logic of Watt's discourses. The process of his reasoning pits question against proposition, rejoinder against question, objection against rejoinder, qualification against objection, and so on until an arbitrary stop is put to the chain of pairs. (Coetzee, *Doubling*, 47)

For Coetzee, this method can be found in Beckett at the level of the sentence, where a phrase will answer another phrase, often with a sentence of two parts involving a proposition and a negation, for example. Beckett himself spoke of admiring the 'shape of ideas', such as in a sentence he attributed to Saint Augustine: 'Do not despair: one of the thieves was saved. Do not presume: one of the thieves was damned' (Worton, 76). Yet it is also apparent in the structure of Beckett's *Watt* as a whole and the way in which elements or sections within the work are used to echo or counter-balance other sections. This is also seen in the narrative of Molloy and the narrative of Moran in *Molloy*, although Coetzee does not refer to this novel in his dissertation. Coetzee traces this kind of movement of sections in the process of composition of *Watt*, showing how it is possible to trace the writing process Beckett adopts, which involves moving sections in line with the A against B stylistic logic also apparent at the level of the sentence (Coetzee, *Doubling*, 39–42).

What is even more apparent in Coetzee's longer discussion of this process is that the [non]-relation of A to B in Beckett is often primarily a matter of rhythm, that is, it is quasi-musical, with the form or shape of repetition carrying a feeling of meaningfulness with it that cannot be precisely defined in terms of connotation. Coetzee offers an example in his dissertation, with 'AB' being a draft version and 'W' the final published text of *Watt*:

AB   I, as I am now, can never get into Erskine's room, as it is now. For me to get into Erskine's room, I should have to be another man, or Erskine's room another room.

W   I, as I am now, can never get into Erskine's room, as it is now. For me to get into Erskine's room, as we are now, I shall have to be another man, or Erskine's room another room. (Coetzee, *English Fiction*, 107)

Coetzee concludes, carefully, that the kinds of revision that move from the AB draft version to the final W published version is one of balance (109) and that with regard to the revisions 'when it is not a matter of connotation, it is often a matter of rhythm' (112).

Stylostatistics, method, and the archive

While this evidence and Coetzee's interpretations add to our understanding of what Beckett himself said about the importance of the 'shape of ideas' to his works, I think Coetzee's dissertation adds a still stronger emphasis on the importance of rhythm and its capacity for generating a feeling that something is meaningful that does not depend on the content or connotations of the sentence. That is, making use of the methods he applies Coetzee comes as close as anyone has to demonstrating how Beckett uses purely formal elements to create sense, a feeling of understanding, in the reader. Yet the quantitative analytical methods can only point to a site of meaning, rather than underlining the nature of that meaning. Furthermore, Coetzee himself does not consider this insight to be profound. Nor does he consider that a stylostatistical method is necessary to its discovery. At best, Coetzee suggests, the stylostatistical method can only confirm what has already been grasped intuitively through close reading.

In developing his dissertation Coetzee begins by wishing to work with and thereby test some of the benefits of the quasi-scientific or at least quantitative method of stylostatistics. He finds that, in the end, these methods are limited and, even after long labour of the kind required in a PhD dissertation, he complains that the method itself does not lead to major critical insights into the work:

> If we investigate the features that stylostatistics traditionally investigates – sentence length, word length, etc. – we find precious little about Beckett that we might not have guessed. It is no consolation to be told that our guesses have at least received numerical confirmation. We have a right to demand that a quantitative statement, in however disguised a form it might occur, should be susceptible of quantitative verification. But we also have a right to at least hope that a clue to a single new critical insight that might otherwise not have occurred to us will be thrown up in the mass of figures. In Beckett's case the figures do indeed throw up a single clue, the slight variance in sentence length in Murphy. But that is all: the rest we already knew. (Coetzee, *English Fiction*, 148)

Later, in *Doubling the Point*, Coetzee goes even further, dismissing his interest in statistical stylistics and generative stylistics as 'a wrong turning, ... a false trail' (*Doubling*, 22). Yet it is apparent that from the point of view of his work, the submersion in stylostatistical method did give Coetzee thematic insights into the nature of method itself that were then developed in his own works. Furthermore, one might argue that the very idea of the archive entered Coetzee's own work through his engagement with Beckett's archive. Coetzee openly acknowledges the influence of Beckett on his work, particularly in the development of style.

> Beckett has meant a great deal to me in my own writing – that must be obvious. He is a clear influence on my prose. Most writers absorb influence through their skin. With me there has also been a more conscious process of absorption [...] The essays I wrote on Beckett's style aren't only academic exercises [...] They are also attempts to get closer to a secret, a secret of Beckett's that I wanted to make my own. (*Doubling*, 25)

The archives to Coetzee's own work have recently been deposited at the University of Texas at Austin and sit alongside the Beckett manuscripts Coetzee worked with. Coetzee's archives are extensive and well organized. Coetzee dates each entry and even many of the insertions and corrections that are indicated in different coloured pens. While this no doubt assisted him in many ways in the composition process, it also now allows critics to easily follow that process. It might be argued that the drafts which trace the writing process were always a potential extension or continuation of the work, or the processes of interpretation that might accompany the work at some future point, offering materials that might exceed the published texts, thereby opening further sites of potential meaning. In offering his archive to view, then, Coetzee might be seen to be entering into dialogue with Beckett, whom he understood through the close study of his manuscripts to *Watt* not simply as a writer of finished texts, but as a writer who struggled with processes of composition.

The uses of research

It is possible to offer a further example of how a partially failed quasi-scientific engagement with Beckett's archive led to less predictable outcomes (as material that Coetzee himself might develop in his fiction). In his dissertation Coetzee suggests making use of a table of random numbers 'such as those prepared by the RAND Corporation' (Coetzee, *English Fiction*, 233) in order to follow through a quantitative analytical argument. The RAND Corporation were at the time involved in a quasi-scientific humanistic analysis of the causes of the Vietnam War, publishing, among other works, the book *Can We Win in Vietnam: The American Dilemma* (Armbruster et al.) and Coetzee would quote Herman Kahn from this book in the epigraph to the first part of his first novel, *Dusklands*.

So too, the kinds of stylostatistical methods Coetzee adopted in writing his dissertation have come to be of ongoing use to the attribution of authorship, not purely in literary contexts, but also with regard to establishing the identity of people in criminal matters and for the purposes of gathering intelligence and as an adjunct to methods of surveillance (Argamon et al.).

For example, during the 2016 American Presidential campaign the emails of the United States Democratic Party were hacked and their contents, showing that the Democratic Party hierarchy sought to actively support candidate Hilary Clinton over candidate Bernie Sanders, were then published by WikiLeaks. While the hacker called himself or herself 'Guccifer 2.0' (making explicit reference to the hacker Marcel Lehel Lazar who used this moniker) and claimed to be from Romania, methods from stylometry were used to establish that the author of the emails claiming responsibility for the hack was a native speaker of Russian, and so the hack was likely the work of Russian agents (BBC News).

The method, then, provides markers that have the characteristics of a signature and not much more. In Coetzee's *Dusklands*, the first section, 'The Vietnam Project', parodies the efforts of social analysts to develop quantitative humanities research methods in order to conduct war by other means.

From lies to truth

I want to suggest here, following Coetzee, that, paradoxically, methods can be useful or generative within works of literature even if they are based on frameworks that are fictitious or untrue. Coetzee identifies an example of this in his dissertation when he criticizes the quasi-scientific claim made by Donald Davie, C. S. Lewis, Erich Auerbach, Leo Spitzer, and others that 'syntactic structures can be explained in terms of processes of thought' (84). He heavily criticizes this idea (89); yet despite thinking that this idea is held to in error, he underlines how it nevertheless has had a positive effect on writers in allowing them to proceed and create works of significance. In a footnote to his objections, he states:

> Whether or not there is a discoverable relation between syntax and thought, a number of poets in this century, notably Ezra Pound, have followed Ernest Fenollosa in regarding the sentence form as 'a reflection of the temporal order in causation' which is not man-made but 'was forced upon primitive man by nature itself,' and have written poetry in which certain syntactic structures are intended to imitate certain structures of thought

or modes of perception. By arguing that the relation of syntax to thought is a matter of experience and convention I do not mean to claim that the experiments of these poets are valueless. However dubious their theory might be, it is they who have created and are creating the new conventions by which our generation relates·syntax to mental experience. See Fenollosa, *The Chinese Written Character as a Medium for Poetry* (San Francisco, n.d.), p. 12. (Coetzee, *English Fiction,* 247)

In sum, the apparently dry method Coetzee used did not, in his view, provide significant insights into the nature of Beckett's work. That is, they did not provide insights on their own terms: precise, quantifiable insights with predictive force. They could help confirm suppositions but they did not point towards new insights. Yet they nevertheless opened the door for Coetzee into unquantifiable insights into the writing process and left him with methodological ideas he could pursue. This is not done so much in his dissertation, however, but rather in his own writings, which engage with the legacy of his approach to Beckett's works. That is, as set out in the previous chapter, out of a feeling or intuition of meaning (which might in fact be wrong), one might nevertheless create a truth.

How might this contribute to the mapping of the relation between truth and meaning we have begun to set out? Clearly, meaning can be generated through fictional form. Clearly, forms are important to the generation of meaning. It is further possible that through these forms (however dubious their foundations might be) elements of truth might be made to emerge. But something here remains troubling, because, following Spinoza, while models or exemplars of how to behave (which are fictitious; see Gatens, 'Spinoza on Goodness and Beauty') need to be invented, not just any will do. The form will produce effects and these effects should be subject to critique, as not all effects are equally beneficial.

Meaning and intention

The distinctions between form and content Coetzee develops illuminate how the concept of meaning operates in his own works. One of the key elements of the concept of meaning relates it to intention. It is possible to think of meaning emerging in two ways. The first way to meaning involves 'intention': what I want to say, what I mean. The second involves 'interpretation': what I understand by what has been said. Both involve a feeling towards, a groping towards, a meaning just out of reach through intuition.

In 'Art as Technique' the Russian formalist critic, Viktor Shklovsky, developing an argument he also sets out in 'The Resurrection of the Word', uses his concept of *ostranenie*, or defamiliarization.[3] Shklovsky's concept of defamiliarization is now so familiar that we no longer see it; that is, the concept itself seems to exemplify the argument he puts forward; that once things become too familiar they are recognized through habit and we do not see them anymore. The idea of making the familiar unfamiliar, of course, underpins most definitions of modernist aesthetics.

> If we start to examine the general laws of perception, we see that as perception becomes habitual, it becomes automatic. Thus, for example, all of our habits retreat into the area of the unconsciously automatic [...] In this process, ideally realized in algebra, things are replaced by symbols. (Viktor Shklovsky, *Art as Technique*, 3–4)

This in turn involves an unexpected or new perception that parallels an expected description, or naming. Two things are involved: a concept or idea that is too well understood and an endeavour to make us think about it again. It is possible to identify two distinct ideas in Shklovsky's essay. On the one hand, there is a kind of meaning that might be called *technical*. This would be a mechanical meaning or a tautological meaning. While such meaning, which involves habitual recognition without any feeling, might be understood to be a truth of facts, it is lifeless. On the other hand, there is a kind of meaning, which Shklovsky is seeking to promote, which would involve *technique*. This deeper meaning is built on feeling. It is generated by form, or technique, but it allows those who engage with it to convey a feeling of understanding.

In talking of habit, Shklovsky is drawing on Bergson, from *Matter and Memory*, where Bergson develops a distinction between

---

[3]Clarkson, 110–111, also considers Coetzee's interest in Shklovsky.

habitual or voluntary memory and spontaneous memory. To function most efficiently, Bergson argues, we have had to develop voluntary memory, which is built on habit. Spontaneous memory, which he opposes to voluntary memory, occurs in the ill-disciplined, in children, say (*Matter and Memory*, 83–85). Yet Marcel Proust would invert these categories to show the potentials of such memory in art in *In Search of Lost Time*.[4]

Contemporary psychology uses different terms, but it is possible to recognize points of similarity. In *The Good Story: Exchanges on Truth, Fiction and Psychotherapy*, Coetzee enters into dialogue with Arabella Kurtz, a psychotherapist from the famous Tavistock Clinic in London. She explains the current received view of memory in psychology, which distinguishes between procedural memory (a kind of habit or reflex through which we engage with the everyday) and episodic memory (*Good Story*, 23).

Episodic memory is similar but not identical with Bergson's spontaneous memory as Bergson's ideas privilege images, while episodic memory privileges language: in short, it is posited that we have no real trustworthy memories earlier than, say, our fourth year. This is because, the argument goes, we are only able to fortify our memories when we can tell stories about them, that is, when we have developed a sufficiently complex grasp of language and its capacities. This might allow us to teach ourselves what we remember by imposing the form of narrative on our experiences.[5]

Following Shklovsky I want to develop a distinction here between the *technical*, which involves precise meaning or an exact relation between a sign and its referent, and *technique*, which involves imprecise meaning that in turn requires interpretation. That is, the story, or at least a certain kind of story, is open to interpretation.[6] Yet there is a paradox in play because this openness is generated, following Shklovsky, through technique, or form or what below we will call method (which combines techniques into a formal whole). We only 'see' those things which have become deadened by habit if a form is applied that makes those dead things strange to us. This

---

[4]I have written in more detail on Bergson and Proust and habitual and spontaneous memory in *Beckett and Poststructuralism*, 65–69.

[5]On episodic and procedural memory, see Hutto.

[6]For a detailed reading of the idea of imprecision or vagueness in relation to Modern fiction, see Quigley.

form in turn requires an interaction with content (or the intuition or feeling of understanding a writing seeks to convey) as content seeks that form adequate to its being felt or sensed as understanding. That is, a feeling of understanding that is available to the reader or viewer must be generated by the form, and this is part of what is intended by the work, even though that feeling of understanding requires an interpretation in order to be situated as a meaning for that reader or viewer.

3

Method: *Dusklands*

In the previous chapter I discussed the related terms 'form' and 'technique'. While form is an overarching term that concerns the arrangement of elements within a work, and the overall shape of a work, technique refers to particular formal elements. One might speak of the novel as a form, for example, and this form will involve techniques (genre, mode, voice, the style adopted, the use of rhetorical figures). In this chapter and the next I will be using the term 'method'. Method involves the deliberative application of particular techniques to generate meaningful effects for readers.

If methods can be used to create understanding, the question remains as to the nature of those methods: their potentials and their limitations. Clearly, some method is required to generate meaning; yet, this does not mean these methods are innocent. This chapter considers the idea of method in Coetzee's works, both in terms of how Coetzee makes use of methods to generate a meaningful work and in terms of Coetzee's focus on the limits of method. That is, this chapter examines questions of method in J. M. Coetzee's first novel *Dusklands*. My interests are not purely formal, not simply concerned with processes of composition. Rather, I will argue that the question of method itself emerges as a site of concern and as a subject of critique in *Dusklands*.

I have touched upon Coetzee's interest in the work of Samuel Beckett above, and this was at its height when he wrote *Dusklands* in the early 1970s. A second important literary influence Coetzee has acknowledged at this time was Vladimir Nabokov (Coetzee and Attwell, *Doubling*, 27–28). While the stylistic flourishes of Nabokov and his efficacy in developing a first-person voice immediately strike readers of his works, Nabokov's narrative method, which differs from Beckett's, is clearly equally important to Coetzee at this time.

Nabokov's method involved choosing a genre which might then be subjected to parody: he terms this the 'springboard of parody' in *The Real Life of Sebastian Knight*, a novel that outlines some of the artistic methods adopted by Knight, an avatar of Nabokov.[1] He made use, for example, of the genre of biography, *The Gift*; the detective novel, *Despair*; the romantic novel, *Lolita*; and various other genres throughout his career, with the method being used most transparently in *Pale Fire* (a novel about which Coetzee wrote at the time of completing *Dusklands*).[2] The idea for this novel occurred to Nabokov while he was working on a scholarly edition of Pushkin's poem *Eugene Onegin* (Boyd, *American Years*, 425–456). Here the genre of the academic scholarly edition is parodied, with the novel being the work of an 'editor' Charles Kinbote, who provides a delirious Introduction and critical apparatus to the long-poem 'Pale Fire' by the Robert Frost-like poet John Shade. The poem, the poet, the editor, the scholarly apparatus that tells the story of Kinbote's alter ego King Charles Botkin of the kingdom of Zembla in a perverse dialogue with the actual poem, are all, of course, composed by Nabokov. The methodological similarities here are self-evident: in *Dusklands* Coetzee offers two parodies of academic work: Eugene Dawn's mythographic readings of Vietnam in 'The Vietnam Project' and J. M. and S. J. Coetzee's historiographic and translational endeavours in 'The Narrative of Jacobus Coetzee'.

The form of *Dusklands*

As noted above the archives left by Coetzee to *Dusklands*, and all the subsequent works, are extensive and well organized, and it might be argued along these lines that the drafts which trace the writing process were always a potential extension or continuation of the work, or the processes of interpretation that might accompany the

---

[1]Nabokov, *Real Life*, 'As often was the way with Sebastian Knight he used parody as a kind of springboard for leaping into the highest region of serious emotion', 76. See Appel. I discuss this method in more detail in *Thinking in Literature: Joyce, Woolf, Nabokov*.
[2]See Coetzee, 'Nabokov's *Pale Fire* and the Primacy of Art', also see Panza's discussion of this essay.

work at some future point. In offering his archive to view, then, Coetzee might be seen to be entering into dialogue with Beckett.

The idea of the writing process[3] is important to Coetzee and is crucial to his understanding of the kind of truth that can emerge in fiction, which as we have seen differs from the simple truth of facts (Coetzee and Attwell, *Doubling*, 17–18). So too, as Carrol Clarkson has admirably demonstrated Coetzee's critical methods echo through his creative methods. The interest in stylistic and compositional methodology Coetzee developed in his dissertation emerges in *Dusklands* and sheds light on it. After Beckett, A answers B, or at least A should answer B. 'The Vietnam Project', which Coetzee composed last in order to develop a work of sufficient length to pass for a novel (and word length is an ongoing theme within the Coetzee archives: the number of words are obsessively counted as the author struggles to fill the space necessary to enable the work to exist within the publishing industry), must answer 'The Narrative of Jacobus Coetzee'.[4]

The form of *Dusklands* highlights that the challenges it will pose to its readers relate to the question of interpretation itself. The two sections, 'The Vietnam Project' set in the early 1970s (corresponding in time more or less precisely to the time of composition) and 'The Narrative of Jacobus Coetzee', are not obviously connected; yet, the idea that the sections are completely separate as some have suggested is clearly unsatisfactory. Rather it is apparent that the clear gap between the sections requires a relation of interpretation that brings them together. Yet this is only one of a set of such relations between texts that require an intensive degree of interpretative relation. The nature of the relation between history and fiction and the nature of the relation between literature and politics and literature and its own form have provided much of the focus of the existing criticism of *Dusklands*.[5] Connecting these problems is the relation between

---

[3]The term 'process' will be discussed more fully in the next chapter. Here it loosely refers to facing the blank page through the process of composition of a work.

[4]See Coetzee Archives, Container 1.1, 'Lies' second sketch for 'The Vietnam Project', handwritten draft with revisions and notes, 11 June–13 February 1973; Container 1.3-4, 'The Vietnam Project', handwritten draft with revisions and photocopy, 4 April–24 May 1973.

[5]See Attridge, *Coetzee and the Ethics of Reading*; Attwell, *South Africa and the Politics of Writing*; Gallagher, *A Story of South Africa*; Easton, 'Coetzee, the Cape and the Question of History'.

literature and its purpose: that is, the extent to which literature
might be thought to enable an understanding or insight into the
meaning of things and ideas.

So critics might examine questions of history, and the political
and social questions involved with history, in relation to *Dusklands*,
or they might consider the nature of the literary text itself. Yet in
each case, in attempting to confront these problems, our attention
is overtly drawn to relations between the texts presented and those
texts and contexts to which, in various ways, they refer. What is the
meaning, and what are the consequences of the methods adopted by
history, or by politics, or by literary fiction? What understandings
do these methods render possible? What kinds of understanding
do they render obscure or efface? What are the consequences of
acting upon these methodically produced possibilities or failing to
act on understandings that cannot be accessed because of them?
That is, whether or not intended by the author, the novel examines
and critiques the process of creating the truth described in Chapter
1 in relation to Bergson and William James.

Questions of writing method are brought to the surface. That
is, a logic of gaps or significant absence is in play. The question of
interpretation is the question of what is not said as much as what is
said; or rather, how what is not said relates to what is. In his notes
to *Dusklands* in 1971 Coetzee writes: 'Lacunae in the sense of the
text, e.g., X is there, then in the next [illegible symbol] X is not
there' (Coetzee Archives Folder 1.6, 'Narrative of Jacobus Coetzee',
19 August–11 December 1971).

This point can be clarified by citing a note Coetzee makes over
twenty-five years later within his preparatory notes for the Tanner
Lectures at Princeton, which were to develop into the short work
The Lives of Animals and then into the novel *Elizabeth Costello*.
Here moving from the interests of his character to his own interests
as a writer Coetzee writes:

How does the Princeton essay relate to my other work? Answer:
interest in suppressed speech – cf Carol Adams.[6]

---

[6]Coetzee Archives, Container 30.1, 'The Lives of Animals', typed notes for Princeton
lectures, 1995–1997, 22 August 1997, p. 9.

Carol Adams, whose work he was reading as background to the *Lives of Animals*, develops an interest in how language can be used to hide its true objectives, and the assumptions that underlie the workings of power structures, with regard to both the eating of meat and the treatment of women. For example, she highlights

> the *objectification of consumption* through language, so that meat's true meaning is cast out. Behind every meat meal is an absence, the death of the animal whose place the meat takes. With the word 'meat' the truth about this death is absent. (Adams, 92)

The meaning of the archive

The draft versions of *Dusklands* have been available to scholars since the late 1990s when they were deposited by Coetzee along with other materials at Harvard University. Kai Easton was among the first to consult them in 2006. In addition, by attending to archives Hermann Wittenberg has outlined the publishing history of the novel that examines the correspondence between Coetzee and his publisher Ravan Press (Wittenberg, 'Archaeology'). The archives were transferred with a large quantity of additional material to the Coetzee archives in the Harry Ransom Center at the University of Texas, Austin, in 2013.

Just as the novel poses problems to the areas with which it engages – history, politics, and fiction – and to the form it makes use of, so too the extension of the work comprised by the archive poses questions to archival and genetic criticism. It is not enough to merely point to the changes made in the development of the work; rather, the question becomes one of interpretation: what do these changes mean? That is, the question that is central to this work is the question of interpretation itself, and this question re-emerges at every stage of critical endeavour. Whether one examines it from a historical or socio-political or literary methodological perspective, the work returns focus upon the 'meta-': on the means of interpretation itself. This is because the meaning that is generated within the text occurs through juxtaposition: through incomplete relations, vagueness, juxtaposition. These are underlined in the genesis of the work where the ordering of material becomes central.

The archives order the draft material in relation to the finished form of the novel. Yet the order of sections does not correspond to the order of composition. The second section, 'The Narrative of Jacobus Coetzee', was written first, and the first section, 'The Vietnam Project', was written second. This much is obvious and already well known. Looking closer, however, it becomes apparent that the order of composition of the four subsections of 'The Narrative of Jacobus Coetzee' (the 'Translator's Preface', the 'Narrative', the 'Afterword', and the 'Appendix') also differs from the published order.

As has been noted by Easton, Attwell, Kannemeyer,[7] and others, Coetzee begins *Dusklands* on 1 January 1970, clearly as a new year's resolution, while he is working at SUNY Buffalo. The text that he begins, however, is not the narrative proper, but what becomes the 'Afterword' of the mock scholarly re-edition of Jacobus Coetzee's journal, purported to have been written by 'the late Dr S. J. Coetzee', the father of the editor 'J. M. Coetzee', for the first edition in 1951. So far so fictitious, of course, as J. M. Coetzee's real father was still living at the time, did not have a PhD, and was called Zacharias or Jack for short. This point is underlined in *Summertime* where the character John Coetzee confesses to inventing this father figure in *Dusklands* among other deliberate errors of fact (Coetzee, *Summertime*, 54).

The meaning of error

The ordering of the work, which moves the introductory text to the end, takes place later. First, in the third draft on 11 October 1971 J. M. Coetzee composes a [Translator's] 'Preface' to the mock edition by 'S. J. Coetzee'. It is only with the third draft that the introductory text is moved to the end as an Afterword. At this point too Coetzee decides to include as an Appendix 'a translation of Coetzee's official 1760 deposition'.[8] While the 'Translator's Preface', the 'Afterword',

---

[7]See Easton, 'Coetzee, the Cape and the Question of History'; Attwell, *Life of Writing*; Attwell, 'The Problem of History'; Kannemeyer.
[8]Coetzee Archives, Container 2.1, 'Narrative of Jacobus Coetzee', handwritten and typed draft with revisions and notes, 11 October 1971–2 January 1972.

and the 'Narrative' are all works of fiction, this translation draws closely on an original and authentic deposition dictated by a historical figure, Jacobus Coetsé, copied by a scribe of the Castle of Cape Town in 1760 in Dutch. J. M. Coetzee's translation of this deposition differs sufficiently from E. E. Mossop's 1935 translation of the deposition of Jabobus Coetsé to be clearly J. M. Coetzee's original translation rather than a variation of Mossop. Yet Coetzee's 'Appendix' also includes a number of important omissions from and additions to the original, which I will return to below.

The deposition attributed to Jacobus Coetzee[9] is a real, if bowdlerized, historical source.[10] However, within the context of the novel most casual readers would be likely to think that it too is probably fictional. For their part, scholars of Coetzee had believed, with Knox-Shaw, that the 'Appendix' was not fictional, but faithfully reproduced in *Dusklands*, until Attwell corrected this error and pointed out some of J. M. Coetzee's subtle changes to the historical deposition in 1993 (Attwell, *Politics of Writing*). The ground, then, is treacherous, and what is at stake is not only the precise points of relation between texts and intertexts, but the effects of instability brought to bear through a method that exploits error (through both deliberate distortion on the part of the author and implied misattribution on the part of readers).

We are being led into potential error, then, it would seem, deliberately. This move is emphasized elsewhere in the published Translator's Preface, where the 'translator' 'J. M. Coetzee' claims to have changed nothing in the Afterword or the Narrative except to restore 'two or three brief passages omitted from my father's edition' (*Dusklands*, 55). In the 11 October 1971 draft of the [Translator's] Preface, however, Coetzee adds that this is done 'because of internal inconsistencies in the [illegible word] Relaas'[11] [that is, in the 'Narrative' rather than in the 'Appendix']. While it would not be possible to identify the allegedly omitted passages from the [fictional] published edition, then, the further evidence provided by the draft indicates that it must relate to the well-known

[9]I will use from here the form of the name used by J. M. Coetzee rather than that in Mossop, except when referring specifically to Mossop's translation.
[10]See Jacobus Jansz Coetsé in Mossop.
[11]Coetzee Archives, Container 2.1, 'Narrative of Jacobus Coetzee', entry for 11 October 1971.

inconsistency in the novel where Jacobus's faithful Hottentot servant Klawer dies twice: once by drowning and then immediately after through illness (*Dusklands*, 93–95) (see Kannemeyer on this point). This error requires interpretation, and this, perhaps, along with acting as a sign of the author, is the *function* of the method of error here (which is developed further throughout his works).[12] The incongruity involved also often leads to playful humour, as the reader is invited to compare the narrator's view of his own integrity with evidence of its failure. Here the manner of Klawer's death is called into question: while we are unable to choose between alternative versions, we also become disinclined to believe either: that is, our attention is drawn to the fact that Jacobus may not wish to recount the real manner of Klawer's death.

Yet other errors and omissions are equally important. Kai Easton, working from the archives, has developed an interesting argument related to the intertextual use Coetzee makes of the work of the nineteenth-century British explorer (and one of the sources consulted by Coetzee) William Burchell, in this part of the novel, and was the first to underline that the historical Jacobus Coetzee was illiterate. This is affirmed by the original historical deposition of 1760 where Jacobus Coetzee makes a mark 'X' to affirm the truth of the deposition he has narrated to the Political Secretariat of the Castle rather than signing his name (see Coetzee, *Dusklands*, 125; Mossop, 289–291). This is further acknowledged in the first draft of the Preface (later the Afterword) by 'S. J. Coetzee' who, in a subsequently deleted passage, states with regard to Jacobus that: 'we may imagine that in that desert he might have reproduced Western civilization, at least that part of it which is available to the illiterate' (Easton, 11).

The status of both the Afterword and the Narrative is therefore, with absurd humour, called into question: 'S. J. Coetzee' (who Attwell relates to a real Nationalist critic, N. A. Coetzee, writing about the genuine deposition in 1958; see Attwell, *Politics of Writing*, 45) promises us 'a more complete and therefore more just view' (Coetzee, *Dusklands*, 108) of its subject Jacobus Coetzee and disparages the deposition that had been copied by 'a Castle hack' (Coetzee, *Dusklands*, 108). Yet in effect S. J. Coetzee makes

---

[12]I discuss this idea in detail in relation to Coetzee's *Summertime*. See Uhlmann, 'The Uses of Anachronism in *Summertime*'.

no mention of the status or the provenance of the first person 'Narrative', or how it came to be written by an illiterate man. Furthermore, he makes no mention of the content of the 'Narrative', which is comically dismissed as irrelevant:

> His journey and sojourn north of the Great River, his return, his second expedition with Hendrik Hop, full of incident though they are, are nevertheless somewhat of an historical irrelevance. (*Dusklands*, 120–121)

Errors (omissions and interpolations) of translation

This section of the novel points us directly out to historical sources and, in the first instance, to the original historical deposition of Jacobus Coetzee. In comparing the actual text in Mossop's edition to Coetzee's version in *Dusklands*, we are alerted to the strategic nature of the omissions and interpolations, and many of these have been noted by other scholars, with Attwell offering the most precise reading of how *Dusklands* engages with its sources. Attwell does so, however, in emphasizing the relations of power brought into focus rather than considering the method of composition.[13]

In J. M. Coetzee's version of the deposition in the Appendix to *Dusklands* Jacobus Coetzee departs with one rather than two wagons and six rather than the twelve servants of the historical deposition. These servants are also identified in the original source as coming from the Griqua nation. Coetzee deletes the early reference to the hunting of elephants, which explains why Jacobus Coetzee pushes further on (i.e. in search of elephants). Coetzee also lengthens the trip to the Great River from twelve days in the historical text to forty days. He deletes the mention of the hippos that line the river at the crossing point. Interestingly, he adds the editorial interpolation '[*sic*]' to the statement that Jacobus Coetzee

---

[13]See also Gallagher, *Story of South Africa*; Attwell, *Politics of Writing*; Knox-Shaw; Easton; and Canepari-Labib.

brought golden sand back with him (suggesting that this is an error and that nothing was brought back with him).

Coetzee alters the first meeting with the Great Namaquas in omitting the statement in the original that Jacobus Coetzee sends a Hottentot servant as an envoy to meet with them and ask them for permission to explain his purpose. Furthermore, Coetzee changes the original by adding the detail that Jacobus Coetzee convinces them 'upon making demonstration of his weapons'. In the next paragraph, he adds several lines to the passage that concerns his meeting with a different tribe of Namaquas who tell him of the Damroquas natives of European appearance and dress. J. M. Coetzee adds the following in *Dusklands*:

> The Envoy of the Damroquas had not long ago met a treacherous end at the hands of servants afflicted for lack of pursuits with the Black Melancholy; that these servants had fled the Namaquas he the narrator had first met and dwelt yet among them; wherefore he should treat warily with the lastmentioned and look always to his Person. (*Dusklands*, 124)

He then cuts a section that describes Jacobus Coetzee giving gifts to his hosts and seeking to discover what objects interest them. In the final paragraph J. M. Coetzee adds the phrase 'being on his return journey deserted by his servants' (*Dusklands*, 125). He then deletes the final sentence of the deposition. In Mossop's translation, this states:

> The narrator furthermore has brought with him one of the above-mentioned Great Amacquas [Namaquas] who desired to travel hither with him. (Mossop, 289)

The alterations, then, have the effect of changing the character of Jacobus Coetzee. The revised deposition emphasizes his belligerence and constructs the abandonment by his servants and an ongoing enmity with the Great Namaquas. It further deletes the evidence of friendly exchange with them through bringing one of their number with him as a travelling companion.

The altered deposition fits better with the events narrated in the first person 'Narrative' Coetzee invents and it works with the fictional Afterword by S. J. Coetzee in establishing further context for the second voyage in which he returns to exact revenge on the Great Namaquas and the servants who have abandoned him. Mossop provides a footnote to the original deposition, which indicates that Jacobus Coetzee's story of the European-like Damroquas brought about the subsequent expedition of Henrick Hop. This is taken up in S. J. Coetzee's Afterword where Jacobus Coetzee is seen to be naïve in believing this story. Yet in the 'Narrative' proper it is reimagined as a pretext that allows Jacobus Coetzee to return and extract his revenge.

To summarize: in developing the first part of his first novel Coetzee makes use of methods borrowed from Nabokov and Beckett. From Nabokov he takes the idea of parody of forms from other genres (here 'historical' texts). The form of parody both works with the generative principles of a given genre and holds those generative principles up for ridicule. Meanings emerge from the generic form, then, but are immediately bracketed off as something that cannot be taken at face value.

From Beckett he learns the compositional method of setting A against B, moving elements of the work during the process of composition to create feeling. This method of A against B also involves juxtaposition, which leaves gaps between sections. These non-relational gaps in turn both urge us to interpret and ensure that our attempts to find meaning will always remain incomplete. Here the play between the feeling of understanding (an intuitive recognition on behalf of the reader that something here is felt to be significant, even deeply so) and the endeavour to fix meaning (the purpose of the text, its exact sense) is established by the form.

In addition, what will become a signature of Coetzee's style also begins to emerge in the process of composition, as he makes use of the trope of 'error'. This error is at times deliberate and obvious to the reader and at times is somewhat submerged. In each case, however, error has two effects. Firstly, it draws our attention to the process of composition and the existence of the author, making us ask what the author's purpose might be in including errors of this kind, since it becomes clear that they are not simple mistakes. This effect in turn is complex, as on the one hand it makes us consider things which we cannot hope to understand (it is well known that any exact understanding of authorial intention is out of our reach) and on the other hand it requires us to interpret, to seek fixed meanings which must remain out of reach. This effect, then, echoes that of A against B – indeed, the effects of all three methods, A against B, parody, error, resonate. Each of them helps to create a feeling of understanding which emerges between elements (between A and B, between the standard genre and the parody of that genre, between what is said and what is contradicted by error). Each of them requires readers to interpret in order to find a clear meaning or purpose; yet, each of them holds that clear meaning just out of our reach. The second effect is to force us to think about the issues raised, rather than telling us exactly what to think. We are forced to think precisely because the work succeeds in generating a feeling of understanding, an intuition for readers, that is, the form of the work generates the sense that something here is meaningful and needs to be considered.

A against B, again: *Dusklands* and *Molloy*

Coetzee works with slightly different methods in the other section of *Dusklands*, 'The Vietnam Project' which was written after 'The Narrative of Jacobus Coetzee' but is placed before it in the novel. The early drafts of 'The Vietnam Project' differ radically from what is finally developed.[14] A first draft exists that is recounted as an interview between Eugene Dawn's wife Marilyn and her psychotherapist. This version is completely abandoned with Dawn installed as narrator in the subsequent versions.[15] At one time Coetzee considers placing his main character not as a scholar in the mythography department of the Kennedy Centre but as a creative writing student in one of 'Coetzee's' classes.

The protagonist begins by indicating an interest in philosophy, something that is further underlined by typed working notes that Coetzee used in developing the work. At one point it is explained that Dawn's overseer, Coetzee, is himself overseen by a shadowy figure called Gaber.[16] This is a direct (too direct and so cut) reference

---

[14]On Vietnam in the novel, see Ng 'Violence of Forgetting' and Masterson.
[15]Coetzee Archives, Container 33.2, 'Discarded first sketch of Vietnam Project,' handwritten draft, 11–27 May 1972.
[16]Coetzee Archives, Container 1.1, 'Lies' second sketch for 'The Vietnam Project,' entry for 11 June 1972.

to Beckett's novel *Molloy*, where Gaber is a functionary who comes to see Moran who in turn is overseen by a shadowy father figure called 'Youdi' who is Godot-like in his invisibility (Beckett, *Molloy*, 95–115).

While the direct reference is cut, it alerts us to some of the initial thinking involved in the design of the work and in particular underlines what is already apparent to readers of *Dusklands* familiar with Beckett's work: that the structure of the whole and elements of the characterization echo *Molloy* and in particular the character of Moran. The first section of Beckett's novel recounts the adventures of the vagrant Molloy hopelessly attempting to travel to see his mother. In the second section of *Molloy* Moran, a spy, sets out in pursuit of Molloy, a vagrant who is identified as being of interest to Moran's master Youdi. Following the structure of A against B Moran heads out on his journey from his home and then returns home, coming to resemble the other he pursues more and more through the journey. For his part, in the first section of Beckett's novel, the character Molloy is drawn momentarily in towards what would be his home if he could recognize or find it (his native village, his mother's room) and ends *both* outside and far from that room in a plain on the edge of a forest (as the events recounted in the narrative end)[17] and inside that room writing (as he affirms as he begins his narrative).[18]

Jacobus Coetzee

In 'The Narrative of Jacobus Coetzee', Jacobus moves out from home on a journey towards an other: the Nama. He returns first towards his own home while seeming to come to resemble his idea of these others, in shedding all the trappings of his Western identity, becoming naked and armed with a bow and arrow. There is a point at which he might embrace this new identity or be overcome by it:

> My retrogression from well set up elephant hunter to white-skinned Bushman was insignificant. What was lost was lost, if

---

[17]Beckett, *Molloy*, 182, 'Molloy could stay, where he happened to be.'
[18]Beckett, *Molloy*, 3, 'I am in my mother's room, it is I who live there now'.

it was irretrievably lost, for the time being. Even the white skin could go. What dismayed the heart about those three hundred miles was the same road back, the old footmarks, the familiar sights. Would I be able to translate myself soberly across the told tale, getting back to a dull decent farmer's life in the shortest possible time, or would I weaken and in a fit of boredom set out down a new path, implicate myself in a new life, perhaps the life of the white Bushman that had been hinting itself to me? I must beware. In a life without rules I could explode to the four corners of the universe. (Coetzee, *Dusklands*, 99)

There is a Moran moment, then, but unlike Moran, who chooses to embrace his new life without boundaries and rules and go out into the garden (Beckett, *Molloy*, 181), Jacobus Coetzee turns decisively back. He does so at first not by returning to his own understanding of his essential self (the white superior to his environment and the inferior others that he must act upon within it) but by embracing the limited understanding he has of the other, the Bushman, an understanding based solely on violent exchange. He makes himself his own idea of a Bushman, slaughtering a settler's cow and shooting the herder himself with an arrow in the leg before stampeding his herd: an act he knows will be attributed to Bushmen who will in turn be punished for it. The essence of violence he finds in his reading of the other allows him then to easily translate himself back into his old position of power. Within the very same paragraph he returns home, slaughters a lamb on his property, and stalks back into his house carrying its liver. A final section answers the main body of the narrative as he returns with the expedition led by Hop and slaughters his errant and rebellious servants.

Eugene Dawn

A answers B within the two parts of *Dusklands* as we necessarily compare Eugene Dawn and Jacobus Coetzee. Whereas Jacobus Coetzee is a man of action, but one who depends upon a robust interpretation of the world (one which sees violence as the essence of being, and all interactions as relations of superior and inferior violence), Eugene Dawn is a man of interpretation. Moreover, he is a man of unstable interpretation as he seeks those understandings that might be imposed on the other, in this case the Viet Cong.

In the early drafts of the second version of 'The Vietnam Project' (initially entitled 'Lies'), Eugene is imagined spending at least one month in Vietnam familiarizing himself with the conflict and problems that need to be understood and mastered through techniques of propaganda that will successfully apply the right understanding upon the enemy. Yet as the writing process proceeds Coetzee cuts those sections that involve direct interaction within Vietnam, removing them and leaving them only as residue in a set of photographs that Dawn examines.[19] In the final work Dawn does not go to Vietnam; rather, he stays at home in his library and sees this wholly imaginary engagement with Vietnam as a strength rather than a weakness. He is, at first, a man of ideas and interpretation, one capable of finding and fixing meaning and purpose, the opposite of a man of action like Jacobus Coetzee who proceeds, for the most part, without understanding. Eugene states:

I discovered all the truths in my Vietnam report, by introspection. Vietnam, like everything else, is inside me, and in Vietnam, with a little diligence, a little patience, all truths about man's nature. When I joined the Project I was offered a familiarization tour of Vietnam. I refused, and was permitted to refuse. We creative people are allowed our whims. (Coetzee, *Dusklands*, 14)

The Vietnam Project and the Vietnam War

Other elements that emerge in the drafts shed light on the writing process. Dawn is imagined as working for a group similar to the RAND Corporation; yet, it becomes clear that the target for critique here is not the conservative think tank, as we might now assume from the distance of several decades. Rather, the think tank in which Dawn works is clearly aligned, through its name,

---

[19]Coetzee Archives, Container 33.2, 'Discarded first sketch of Vietnam Project,' handwritten draft, 11–27 May 1972.

the Kennedy Centre, and the Harry S. Truman library in which Dawn works, with the United States Democratic Party, who after all initiated and prosecuted the Vietnam War under Presidents Kennedy and Johnson until Richard Nixon took over from 1969. What is subject to critique is the idea that meaning and purpose can be clearly identified and fixed and that once fixed can be used as a foolproof means of control. If such were the case, intentions might not only be clearly determined; they might be completely realized.

So too, the intertextual references to Herman Kahn (through the epigraph at the beginning of 'The Vietnam Project') implicate the Hudson Institute not just imagined as a right-wing think tank emerging from the RAND Corporation (as it is now mostly pictured) but as a consultant to the Department of Defense between 1966 and 1968 when the book from which the epigraph is taken, *Can We Win in Vietnam: The American Dilemma*, was published. While Kahn's views and theories are rightly considered to be more aligned with what are now conservative positions, it is clear that liberal discourse is a target for Coetzee's critique in *Dusklands*. That is, it is a certain kind of distanced, apparently rational discourse, that might emerge from humanities and social science disciplines such as psychology and branches of philosophy and history and that has the capacity to enable and or justify atrocity in the name of realizing a stated intention. *Can We Win in Vietnam* is addressed to an intelligent reader who might well be to the left as to the right of politics. It makes use of systematic methods in order to convince people of reason as to the validity of the positions it sets forth, which are complex and multifaceted, but have in common a pragmatic engagement with the problem of how America might best manage the war to achieve its desired outcomes.

We would be wrong, then, to read *Dusklands* as simply taking aim at what, for the left, are easy targets: the other that is the right-wing think tank. Rather, the entire edifice of the Western enlightenment tradition is held up for ridicule and scrutiny, and no one can hide from being implicated within it and subject to its apparently rationally derived interpretations. This, no doubt, is the reason that J. M. Coetzee the author implicates himself within both narratives, with 'Coetzee' as the overseer of Dawn and 'J. M. Coetzee' as the editor of the work of his father and ancestor. He is, like all in the field and not least the readers of the work, the product of a system of understanding and interpretation that has the tendency at least to violence both on the Left and the Right.

The book succeeds, then, in generating a feeling of understanding that is not simply amorphous. Rather, we feel we understand some of the ways in which the forms that surround and make us also limit us and drive us towards outcomes and actions that are grotesque.

Eugene Dawn's itinerary

If Jacobus Coetzee has twin journeys out and back, Eugene Dawn has a different itinerary. He begins wholly in the mind in developing his Introduction for 'The Vietnam Project'. This is then presented to his superiors and clearly fails to win their approval. Dawn's flaw seems to be that he wishes to trace the rational method of pragmatic engagement to its logical conclusions. Working with 'mythographic' images he develops theories of the 'father voice' and the 'brother voice'. A logic emerges which aligns America with the father that must impose its will and the Viet Cong with a rebellious son, who might be influenced by a brotherly voice to be commanded by the father. Yet the rebellious son instead chooses to hide from the father by returning to the mother (who symbolizes the earth or nature). Dawn's logical conclusion is to destroy the earth, to leave the rebellious son with nowhere to hide:

> Our future belongs not to the earth but to the stars. Let us show the enemy that he stands naked in a dying landscape. (Coetzee, *Dusklands*, 29)

One assumes thermonuclear war is meant – the destruction of the earth on both sides – with an idea of escape into outer space suggested. The slip from logic to insanity is marked by a move from rational argument to personal motivation, and in this way Coetzee shows the influence of Nabokov's *Pale Fire*, but the argument that becomes generalized is that an insane outcome rests coiled as a potential of following to its conclusion a logical pragmatic argument that affirms violence as a legitimate method.

Eugene Dawn then plays out the logic of his mythographic scenario in his own life: he takes on the role of the father reclaiming the son from a mother who coddles him, removing his own son to a motel. Here the influence of other Nabokov novels becomes apparent: *Lolita*, *Despair*, where characters are holed up in motels or hotels awaiting the consequences of causal chains they have put in place. In each case they act logically, but only after accepting a lie or a mystification as true: for Hermann in *Despair* it is the idea that he is a great artist of life with a power over his own identity and that this allows him all licence, including the licence to murder. For Humbert in *Lolita* it is the idea that there is equality of some kind in the relations he undertakes with Lolita. For Dawn, it is the lie that some natural order exists, built into our language our culture and our very relations to the natural world, which provides an incontrovertible method through which power might perfectly express itself so as to be necessarily answered by compliance and universal agreement. This 'natural order' is expressed in a simple mythical formula through which the father (the seat of power, or the State) must control the son (the seat of rebellion, or the other) against the coddling of the mother (the realm of protection to which the son flees, or nature).

Eugene Dawn, however, is undone by the very instability of his interpretations. He harms his son and is captured, but unlike Humbert and Hermann whose narratives end with their being, in some way, run to ground, Dawn is brought back into the bosom of the systems of interpretation that help to create and drive the world in which he exists. He is being cured through interpretations that involve the imposition of signs. He seeks an understanding that will be right, will be in accord with what he is supposed to think (Coetzee, *Dusklands*, 47–49). Here again Spinoza's ideas add clarity: the adequate idea is not a matter of signs; rather, it involves a feeling of understanding, which he links to the highest form of knowledge, intuition. This is something that cannot be forced upon anyone: we understand that we understand. If we are taught in the manner Dawn is taught here, it cannot be with understandings or truths but with signs which are simply obeyed and not understood.

At the heart of the writing process and the themes of *Dusklands* there is the problem of method itself. What are the implications and consequences of particular methods? Methods of action and methods of interpretation are equally held to the light. The real might not only be misapprehended through the distorting lens of personal desire; such misapprehensions of the real might further enter into logical chains of understanding, which, in a feedback loop, recast these desires. So too, *Dusklands* shows us that insofar as violence is affirmed as central to the methods of creation or manipulation of meanings which one attempts to fix in place, such methods have the potential to move towards unsound or insane outcomes.

4

Process: *Waiting for the Barbarians*

I have no interest in telling stories; it is the process of storytelling that interests me.

(J. M. Coetzee, Container 33.03, Notebook 1 to Waiting for the Barbarians, 17 October 1977)

Like the previous chapter this chapter considers how, through the writing process, Coetzee seeks out a method adequate to conveying a feeling or intuition of understanding in the work he is composing. It has two parts. The first part is introductory and involves adding further ideas related to process and method, considering how they might shed further light on Coetzee's claim that fiction can offer us access to the truth. The second part describes some of the processes and methods of composition that are apparent through paying close attention to the manuscripts of Coetzee's third novel, *Waiting for the Barbarians* and develops a reading of some of these materials and elements of the finished novel.

Process and method

Here I am working with a distinction between process and method. The rough distinction that will suffice for our purposes is that process is understood as involving everything that happens, both systematic and unsystematic, both conscious and unconscious, both internal and external that allows the work, in the end, to emerge.

The term 'process' carries with it a number of connotations: it points towards process philosophy, a metaphysical standpoint that opposes the idea that Being can be understood as eternal and unchanging (instead emphasizing becoming, and how the world unfolds or comes into being, moving forward through time and being created and recreated). This relates to Bergson's description of intuition set out in Chapter 1 and involves a school of thought including thinkers such as Pierce, Whitehead, and Deleuze.

'Method' on the other hand, as above, is understood to involve the deliberative deployment of formal techniques through which meaning is generated. The word 'method' derives etymologically from the prefix 'meta' (after, along with, beyond, among, behind) and 'hodos' (way), and in Greek 'methodos' involves the pursuit of knowledge. That is, it is specifically connected to the manner in which knowledge is established or generated.

In a paper delivered in 1967 called 'The Method of Dramatisation', Gilles Deleuze considers how our methods of understanding involve dramatized scenarios. Conflicts, or dynamic relations, are at the heart of all activity. He states: 'Dynamisms, and all that exists simultaneously with them, are at work in every form and every qualified extension of representation' (Deleuze, 'Method', 98) and here he includes the physical world (both animate and inanimate) as well as our means of representing it, including science and the arts and everyday psychic representations, such as the dream. He continues by arguing that 'these abstract lines constitute a drama which corresponds to this or that concept, and which also directs its specification and division' (Deleuze, 'Method', 98). In order to clarify this, he uses the example of the concept of the truth to illustrate how both philosophical and scientific knowledge work with concepts, which involve abstract dramatic scenarios. He concludes that

the concept of truth in representation is divided in two directions – the first according to which the true emerges in an intuition and as itself, the second according to which the true is always concluded from indices or inferred from something else as that which is not there – we have no trouble discovering beneath *these traditional theories of intuition and induction,* the dynamisms of inquisition or admission, accusation or inquiry, silently and dramatically at work, in such a way as to determine the theoretical division of the concept. (Deleuze, 'Method', 99)

Deleuze's ideas are useful here because they allow us to see two tendencies in the concept of truth, which play out in Coetzee's *Waiting for the Barbarians*. One typically approaches the truth from one of two angles. The first approach follows intuition through which an idea (a feeling of understanding) precedes what is made to emerge through a process of interrogation (such as the dialectic). This involves the interactions described in Coetzee's dissertation where content engages with form. A mythological representation of this process can be found in Plato's *Phaedrus* where true ideals exist in the realm of the gods and are glimpsed by mortals who, on returning to earth, carry a memory of this truth with them that they recognize in the material processes they suffer on earth. The second approach involves an engagement with signs that call upon the observer to interpret inductively – to find or extract precise meaning from the concatenation of these multifarious signs.

False and true intuition

The intuitive and the inductive forms further carry with them dramatic qualities. The intuitive method leads to the interrogation or trial that seeks to extract the truth. One version of this method extends from the intuition of truth and seeks to extract signs that correspond to that truth. As such, given the readings I have developed so far one might guess that this is a good thing. Yet, as we will see here, and elsewhere in Coetzee's works, it becomes apparent that one might claim an intuition, that is, one might claim an understanding, where no such understanding exists. It is for this reason, in common usage, the word intuition has a dubious history. That is to say that this method of so-called intuition might be perverted. This becomes apparent in the manner of Colonel Joll in *Waiting for the Barbarians*. Here, while the process of interrogation remains central, the so-called intuition of the truth is left to one side as something that is absent. In short, the trial seems to mimic the form of intuition or felt understanding while discarding the idea of a prior insight necessary to discovering truths. Rather, the 'truth' is purely formal, empty of real understanding. The Magistrate asks: 'What if your prisoner is telling the truth ... yet is not believed? ... How do you ever know when a man has told you the truth?'

(*Barbarians*, 5). Joll responds, 'A certain tone enters the voice of a man who is telling the truth. Training and experience teach us to recognize that tone'. Pressed as to how this might be possible, and whether Joll is capable of recognizing this tone at any given moment, it becomes clear that Joll in effect is relying on the method rather than bringing with him an intuition of the truth. The method of torture has a shape and this shape, Joll contends, *ends* in the truth. That is, it is not at all like genuine intuition, which *begins* with a feeling of the truth. Joll states:

> I am speaking only of a special situation now, I am speaking of a situation in which I am probing for the truth, in which I have to exert pressure to find it. First I get lies, you see – this is what happens – first lies, then pressure, then more lies, then more pressure, then the break, then more pressure, then the truth. That is how you get the truth. (*Barbarians*, 5)

Rather than involving intuition, then, as that which guarantees an understanding of what is true, the method of torture is purely instrumental and is stripped of understanding. Susan Gallagher has underlined that in order to properly represent torture, without falsifying it, or aiding the oppressor, Coetzee needs to develop strategies that undermine fixed meanings (Gallagher, 'Torture', 280). The tone of the broken one that Joll listens for no longer signifies anything but pain. It might be that he mistakes this for the truth, or it might be that he has, in effect, broken through to something beyond subjective understandings without knowing it. The Magistrate, however, recognizes this when, following Joll's speech, he addresses the reader stating, 'Pain is truth; all else is subject to doubt' (*Barbarians*, 5).

This process contrasts with that which the Magistrate describes late in the book when he reflects upon his previous function as the legal authority in the border outpost he administers. The Magistrate recognizes that human law is flawed and that it is flawed precisely in relation to our understanding, or intuition, of what is just. That is, again, our fixed meanings or laws are limited and do not always concur with what we know or sense to be true. He recalls a particular case whose imperfect outcome nevertheless involves the proper administration of the legal system and reflects on how the most correct outcome might nevertheless remain imperfectly just. He addresses the one he condemns, saying, 'You think you know

what is just and what is not. I understand. We all think we know.'
He then turns again to the reader and continues:

> I had no doubt, myself, then, that at each moment each of us,
> man, woman, child, perhaps even the poor old horse turning
> the mill-wheel, knew what was just: all creatures come into the
> world bringing with them the memory of justice. 'But we live in a
> world of laws,' I said to my poor prisoner, 'a world of the second-
> best'. (*Barbarians*, 152)

That Coetzee is here thinking of Plato and the concept of
intuition I have outlined is confirmed in a notebook kept during
the process of composition of *Waiting for the Barbarians* where he
states: 'I discover that the man is straight out of Plato. "memories
of justice"' (Coetzee Archives, Container 33.03, Notebook 2, 20
September 1978).

The inductive method

For its part, the inductive method involves the interpretation of
signs through the association of ideas in the light of experience.
Yet experience fails when one encounters what is outside one's
experience, some system of signs of which one is ignorant. While
such alien systems are not difficult to find, they carry with them
little clue as to how they might interrelate and how they might be
understood. So, the Magistrate traces the signs of torture on the
body of the girl, or those left on strips of wood by the ancient
barbarians, but is uncertain as to what the meaning might be. He
is certain, however, that there is something to be understood and
that examining signs is the only way to understand. At the very end
he expresses the frustration that this carries with it: 'I think: "There
has been something staring me in the face, and still I do not see
it"' (*Barbarians*, 170). That is, it surrounds him but remains beyond
his experience. That Coetzee is equally conscious of this inductive
method of finding meaning, and its limitations, is also apparent in
the notebook kept while writing the novel. He states: 'Idea of world
as conflict between world as labyrinth of signs and the notion of
the Truth' (Coetzee Archives, Container 33.03, Notebook 2, 10

September 1978). So too, in considering the representation of the torture of the barbarian girl in this novel Jennifer Wenzel underlines the importance of maintaining the autonomy of the novel from the disciplines of history and politics (Wenzel, 61–63): since literature, precisely because it does not depend upon fixed meanings, is able to examine questions that are left to one side by more 'exact' disciplines. Here the magistrate's uncertainty carries with it a fuller understanding than the affirmation of an exact solution would allow.

Method and process

Following insights developed by Bruno Clément, it is apparent that methods can be identified through paying attention to process. In *Le récit de la méthode*, Clément points to the importance of stories (invented after the fact) to explain the real intuitive foundations on which any method is built. That is, those who talk about or explain their methods, such as Descartes for example, can be shown to have discovered that method through a process of composition in which the correct method reveals itself intuitively as a process or becoming. Describing method, then, involves recounting a story of its emergence, but paradoxically the method that leads to understanding is only recognized after the process has begun rather than preceding and determining the exact nature of the process. Process in art is a story of composition and that story has, for its themes, the methods that emerge to force that meaningful thing into being. The next section will attempt to follow some aspects of this process by following the archives step by step, in the process of composition of *Waiting for the Barbarians*.

A difficult process

When you examine in detail the several containers of material that make up the manuscript and typescript material to Coetzee's third novel *Waiting for the Barbarians*, it is clear that writing the book was a painfully difficult process. Coetzee filled two notebooks while writing the book, which he used to add to while working on the various drafts of the novel. He dates each entry to both the notebooks and the drafts. His habit was to write every day of the year, no matter how little, although there are a few gaps here and there of dark silence lasting a few days as Coetzee struggles with his material, for example, on 3, 4, and 5 November 1977. The dates, then, allow us to witness the process as it unfolds in a way that is unusual with the manuscript material left by most writers.

In the first notebook, which began on 11 July 1977, Coetzee sets out a detailed overview of the plot of the novel and its major themes before beginning the first draft on 20 September 1977. After this, however, he commences and abandons no less than six versions before he finally begins version G, which is the real first draft of the novel, some seven months later on 28 April 1978.

Versions A–C (which are not named) tell the story of a 40-year-old Greek man, Manos Milis, who falls in love with a younger woman whom he meets in one version in a refugee camp on Robben Island in Cape Town (the famous prison at which Nelson Mandela was held) and in another version on a ship docked in Cape Town docks where he waits among other refugees for the fuel that will allow them to depart. He will either be executed or commit suicide. The versions involve different narrative techniques: third person and heavy dialogue.

Abandoning this entirely at last, he casts about somewhat for a new idea and begins a version D. This echoes Marguerite Duras and Alain Resnais and their film *Hiroshima Mon Amour*, although it involves two women rather than the man and woman of the film, with one woman, a nurse, recounting a story of the past and the other countering with the refrain 'No, I remember nothing of that'. This too is abandoned. After this, versions E ('The Disposal of the Dead') and F ('Exile') move closer to the world we see portrayed in *Waiting for the Barbarians* but are set in a Chinese outpost fort on the Silk Roads. I will discuss these versions in more detail below. Yet once G is begun the novel at last begins to emerge in the form we recognize, with version H revising G, version I involving red pen insertions and corrections in H, before the first typescript, version J, is begun, concurrently with the corrections of I. The final major corrections are completed on 25 May 1979 and the first typescript on 1 June 1979.

The process itself is part of the method, as the abandoning of versions is not arbitrary but follows the logic of either contradiction (where the story fails under its own weight) or incapacity (where the author does not consider himself suited to or interested in continuing in a given mode). He underlines this point in Notebook 1 on 26 April 1978 where he states: 'Where the narrative founders on contradictions or incapacity, new versions are tried' (Coetzee Archives, Container 33.03, Notebook 1).

Process *as* method

While this quick overview gives some sense of the difficulty of the process, it is more fully brought home through confidences offered in the notebooks. Writing on 30 May 1978, at a time when he had already made major breakthroughs and had begun the true first draft, version G, 'Waiting for the Barbarians', he writes in parenthesis:

> (An experience of revolt this morning. Every morning since 1 Jan 1970 I have sat down to write. I HATE it.) (Coetzee Archives, Container 33.03, Notebook 1)

Yet some of the expressions of frustration point to methods that can be seen to emerge through the process. In *Phaedrus*, asked what it takes to attain the art of a true rhetorician, Socrates replies:

> If you have an innate capacity for rhetoric, you will become a famous rhetorician, provided you also acquire knowledge and practice, but if you lack any of these three you will be correspondingly unfinished. (Plato, *Collected Dialogues*, 515)

The daily discipline of writing itself is a process, which becomes method if the right form can be found. While working on version E, on 25 December 1977, he states:

> It is a wholly unreal enterprise I am engaged in. No matter what, this is a book that could have been written a hundred years ago. Exoticism, nothing more. There is no pressure of form on me, hence the lack of any emergence of feeling. The book comes straight out of the Western long-knives and Redskins. (Coetzee Archives, Container 33.03, Notebook 1)

Again, the process of daily writing can become method if a narrative flow can be found. On 24 June 1978, he writes:

I spend so much time agonizing because I can't get a narrative going. Narrative is a means of facilitating writing. Narrative is a way of knowing where you are going from one day's writing to the next. (Coetzee Archives, Container 33.03, Notebook 1)

Themes and method

Yet more can be made of the idea of method even in the rough sketch I am able to offer here. It is clear from the notebooks that a number of ideas are present from the very beginning and that they, to use Plato's terms, 'inspire' the book.

Coetzee sets these out clearly in a note on 14 January 1978:

The trouble is that the various passions out of which the story grew are no longer with me: (a) love of woman, (b) tenderness towards a daughter, (c) anger at political torture. (Coetzee Archives, Container 33.03, Notebook 1)

Elsewhere in the notebooks, these elements are referred to again and again. He wants to write a love story related to some recently past feeling of being in love. He wants to explore the idea of father–daughter love based on his strong feelings for his young daughter Gisella ('children, one would die for them', he says at one point). Perhaps above all he wants to express his outrage at the political torture and murder of Steve Biko.[1]

David Attwell in *J. M. Coetzee and The Life of Writing* offers an important insight with regard to this by underlining that the torture of Biko becomes known *after* Coetzee has already begun the novel. In effect, Attwell shows how the shock of Biko's death and the light it shone on the torture methods then being used by the South African apartheid regime of the late 1970s changed Coetzee's thinking and the structure of the novel. After Biko's death Coetzee moves away from the story of Manos Milos in the refugee camp or on a boat waiting to flee the country to stories that involve torture and border conflict (see Attwell, *Life of Writing*, 113–119).

---

[1]For discussions of this novel in relation to the question of political torture, see Kelly Adams, Wenzel, Moses, Gallagher, 'Torture', Spencer.

This underlines the point made by Bruno Clément with regard to method: the method is discovered through the process of composition, and here this process involves, necessarily, an interaction with the socio-political world that surrounds Coetzee and the new revelations about its hidden nature. This theme then joins with the others so that by the time Coetzee writes the note of 14 January 1978 he thinks of it as being there from the beginning (rather than arriving belatedly and changing everything as Attwell shows through his reading of the archive).

Nevertheless, Coetzee's creative desires, which are described in the note of 14 January 1978 and elsewhere in the notebooks, can now be set out under a number of headings. He wants to develop a relation to life that addresses what he calls 'his own situation'. Yet this cannot be confronted directly: rather, he seeks to approach it through kinds of knowledge. These kinds of knowledge in turn are also desires, theoretical desires that speak to the inchoate desires of the living self. He wants to develop a relation to politics and history that allows his story to confront the ugliness of the present in South Africa. So, he needs a method that will allow such a representation, that is, a set of situations that do some justice to the idea of torture and injustice. He wants to develop a relation to psychoanalysis (love in all its complexity, linking a father–daughter–lover relation). So, he needs a method that will allow such a relation, that is, a set of situations that pair an older man with a younger woman, young enough to be his daughter. He wants to develop a relation to philosophy that allows him to pair ideas of love and justice with the truth. So, he needs a situation that allows for dialogue: the wise old man and the student, who might also be the lover and the beloved of Platonic dialogues.

Yet none of these desires are simple to realize. They have to be given existence – a method that is adequate to them has to be uncovered. There are many elements to this method and I will only touch upon a few here.

Elements of method

One element involves a relation to other books and literary form (on this point see Attwell, 84). On 13 October 1977, he writes: 'Must do more reading. So much of the other books [*Dusklands* and *In the Heart of the Country*] was sparked off by concurrent reading'. A few days later, on 18 October 1977, he writes: 'Perhaps there is a liberation from realism' (Coetzee Archives, Container 33.03, Notebook 1).

He then moves from the realism of the first attempt to a number of versions that move within different formal terrain, bringing with them symbolic resonances, finally turning to the borderlands of China before making these borderlands still more equivocal by adding a South African resonance to the names but keeping an exoticism to the setting and time frame. I am in disagreement here, then, with Attwell, who argues that the overall form of *Waiting for the Barbarians* is realist (128). While elements of the realistic mode are in play, the dominant mode of the novel is symbolic.

Yet Coetzee's major breakthrough comes by thinking of other books that have represented such a situation. On 10 November 1977, he writes:

THE BARBARIANS. All the men who have guarded the borders of civilization against the Barbarians. No actual state of warfare exists, only a state of vigilance.

There are all kinds of literary stereotypes associated with Border stories. Millions of stories have been written. It is a matter of moving with ease among the stereotypes. (Coetzee Archives, Container 33.03, Notebook 1)

About this time, he mentions for the second time (it was first mentioned a month before on 19 October 1977) the work of the Italian author Dino Buzzati, who wrote the novel *The Tartar Steppe*[2] about a guard at an old border fortress, and a long poem by Pablo Neruda, *The Heights of Macchu Picchu*.[3] Rather than look at these two texts and their intertextual relations to Coetzee's novel, I will turn to others. That is, I will turn to something that was there at the beginning and after the end.

---

[2]On links between Buzzati's novel and *Waiting for the Barbarians*, see Knaller, Pugliese.

[3]While little has been written to date on Coetzee and Neruda, Boletsi, among others, has written on the relation between the novel and C. P. Cavafy's poem 'Waiting for the Barbarians'.

Plato and Kritoboulos

In 2003, some 25 years after he was working on *Waiting for the Barbarians*, Coetzee received news that he had won the Nobel Prize for Literature while teaching with Jonathan Lear at the Chicago Committee on Social Thought. That year they were co-teaching a course on Plato's *Phaedrus*.

As touched upon above, the untitled first draft of *Waiting for the Barbarians* set on the docks of Cape Town (which resembles in many ways the setting for Coetzee's *The Childhood of Jesus*) involves an older Greek man, Manos (a Greek name derived from Emmanuel, a name linked to Jesus in the Gospels) Milis.

The older Greek man becomes the lover of a younger woman (whose age reduces at last to 17) and at one point is offered oral sex by a 10-year-old boy, and in the notebooks he is mentioned as seeking such contact out (see Container 5.1, 12 October 1977). A perversion of the Greek wise man/beautiful youth model of Plato's dialogues seems to announce itself in these choices.

There is a further link to Greece, however, in the first drafts. Manos is imagined to be translating a text by 'Kritoboulos' (Coetzee Archives, Container 33.03, Notebook 1, 28 August 1977). The name brings Plato to mind because one of Socrates' favoured young students went by that name (although spelled in most English translations with a C rather than a K); furthermore, 'Critobulous' is the name of the beautiful young boy at the centre of Thomas Mann's *Death in Venice* which also makes reference to Plato and the wise man/beautiful youth motif of the dialogues. Yet Coetzee is clearly referring to Michael Kritoboulos who wrote the *History of Mehmed the Conqueror*, a work in five volumes that details the fall of Constantinople at the hands of the invading Ottoman Turks.

On 28 August 1977, he writes: 'The Kritoboulos translation ceases to be a nihilistic welcome to the Barbarians' (Coetzee Archives, Container 33.03, Notebook 1). Kritoboulos' book and the translation of it are about the fall of one civilization at the hands of another. This idea, then, is the first seed for the idea that becomes *Waiting for the Barbarians*, and this is underlined in a note on 13 November 1977, where Coetzee writes:

If we are to link this [Chinese setting] with the decay of Constantinople, the problem is that, by an inevitable extension, South Africa becomes another in a series of doomed civilizations. (Coetzee Archives, Container 33.03, Notebook 1)

The figure of K(C)ritoboulos seems to perfectly knit together Coetzee's early themes of (perverse) Platonic love, and the fall of empire. Yet he does not seem to know how to work with it. Writing in his notebook on 30 August 1977, he states:

Precisely what role Kritoboulos will play is not yet clear. The text is the one thing the man is allowed to take with him to the camp. (Coetzee Archives, Container 33.03, Notebook 1)

As Attwell contends, what is lacking is the light shone on the true nature of the South African apartheid regime of the late 1970s by the murder under torture of Steve Biko and the subsequent inquest into it. This process is somewhat belated. Biko's death is first reported on 14 September 1977 and Coetzee followed the reports closely (see Kannemeyer, 326; Attwell, *Life of Writing*, 114). Coetzee abandons draft B relating the story of Milis, the girl, and the translation of Kritoboulos on 16 October 1977, beginning a new draft C (otherwise untitled) on 18 October 1977, a draft which continues with the story but attempts it by using long sections of reported speech, as if in interview form. This version is abandoned in turn the next day and with it the story of Milis and the girl and Kritobulos. A new version D is now attempted, which, as touched upon above, is reminiscent of the work of Marguerite Duras and involves two women in conversation.

This version too is abandoned, with version E, 'The Disposal of the Dead', begun on 30 October 1977. There is a significant gap in Coetzee's notebook at this time, with no entry made into it between 23 October and 2 November 1977. The latter entry is cryptic:

See the grass as kindly grass, the earth nourishing it. Then seeing the earth as a chemical bed for decomposing oneself. We are only a body. (Coetzee Archives, Container 33.03, Notebook 1)

Seeking the way

Version E begins with a series of letters from the Border camp, written in the first person by a figure not unlike the Magistrate, although there is still much work to be done to discover his real voice. Attwell is right, then, to link the importance of Biko's death, and the nature of that death, to shifts in the composition of what would become *Waiting for the Barbarians*. Indeed, the point could be made still more specific, because while Attwell says that 'there is no single moment of crystallisation' (114) of the shock caused by Biko, it is possible, following the dates of the manuscripts, to closely link the date of reading about Biko with a completely new scenario – one that for the first time had come to resemble what would emerge as the final version. The revelations surrounding the death of Biko have led to some kind of understanding that was not present before some intuitive understanding of the relations at play in the situations Coetzee is trying to imagine.

The meaning of Kritoboulos

Yet the process does not end here, as version E remains a long way from the finished novel. While it is not possible to adequately address what takes place, it is still possible to sketch arguments for how method emerges from the process after this point. Method is what allows one to organize and portray the intuitions one has felt. A first question that arises is whether the figure of Kritoboulos completely disappears from subsequent versions or whether it is somehow translated.

Coetzee had originally planned to insert excerpts from Kritoboulos into his narrative. Yet this would have significantly changed the focus of the work and the kinds of meanings it would be capable of generating. Reviewing the English translation of Kritoboulus by Charles T. Riggs, which appeared in 1954, Downey offers some background; he states:

> Michael Kritobulos was a member of a prominent family of the island of Imbros who, after the fall of Constantinople in 1453, entered the service of the conqueror … he composed, in

Greek, a history ... which related, from the Turkish point of view, the events of the years 1451–1467, notably the capture of Constantinople, the subjugation of other parts of what was left of the Byzantine empire. (Downey, 122)

Kritoboulos provides a unique insight into the fall of Constantinople for two reasons. Firstly, he is writing from the Turkish point of view: 'The work is of real interest as a sympathetic portrait of Mehmed II and is a specimen of the point of view of a "collaborator"' (Downey 122, also see Costas 30). Secondly, however, Kritoboulos himself, like Coetzee, in attempting to give meaning to his subject matter, is engaged in a kind of stylistic rewriting. As Downey explains:

A curious feature of the book is that it is written in the style, and often in the very words, of Thucydides – testimony to the strength of the classical tradition at Byzantium – and it is odd to read of the deeds of the Turks in terms of the Peloponnesian War, complete with speeches and description of the plague. (Downey,122)

Kritoboulos himself is aware of the difficulties of his task, as he was not present at the final siege of Constantinople; rather, he had to rely on the testimony of witnesses to reconstruct his account. His problem is the same as Coetzee's problem. How to do justice to the immense themes he is grappling with, in his case, through the genre of history that he has inherited from the classical Greek tradition. He states:

I have already labored hard, for I was not a witness of the events, to know the exact truth about these things. In writing the history, I have at the same time inquired of those who knew, and have examined carefully into how it all happened. (Kritovoulos, 60)

Yet the kind of truth Kritoboulos recounts differs markedly from what occurs in *Waiting for the Barbarians*. Alongside the panegyric to Mehmed Kritoboulos offers a harrowing description of the fall of the city, with the invading forces urged on by Mehmed to take the girls, women, and boys of the city as part of their prize before demolishing it. Kritoboulos goes on to describe with horror and dismay the widespread rape, murder, and brutality that accompanies the sack of the city (Kritovoulos, 60–75).

There is a marked difference between this kind of situation – an event that has taken place that involves awful injustices perpetrated by the conquering forces – and the situation ultimately described in *Waiting for the Barbarians* where the invasion is more imagined than real and the injustices occur among those awaiting an event that might not take place as they imagine it. Rather than injustice being something that might be externally attributed, which would be a tendency that would be difficult to avoid, had Coetzee gone on to use excerpts from Kritoboulos as planned, the focus shifts inward to those who fear being overthrown. This is what is at stake in the shift that is urged by events surrounding the murder of Steve Biko, which remove Coetzee from the formal association he had planned with Kritoboulos, and instead bring him into contact with the realities of the moment in which he writes, that carries with it the immediate and compelling horror of torture.

Finding the way

Version E begins to involve first-person narrative, although this is couched in letters. It is clear that Coetzee wished to avoid using the first person which he had already worked with in his first two novels and this is something he underlines in his notebooks. Yet the situation in version E resembles that which occurs in the finished novel and some scenes (such as discovering the boy with cuts all over his body after undergoing torture) are 'recovered', with these being marked by red lines in the manuscript. The epistolary form falls away after twelve pages, although it is possible to read what follows as part of one long letter. Yet the first-person form has taken over at this point. On Christmas day, 25 December 1977, thirty-one pages into version E, Coetzee reverts to the third person and continues in the third person (recounting the story of the girl and the story of voyage into the desert to meet up with her people). At this point Coetzee seemed to be thinking the work would break into two parts: the first involving the first-person narrative, and the second being 'Notes and Commentary' (Coetzee Archives, Container 33.03, Notebook 1, 26 December 1977). Version E is broken off during the story of voyage into the desert on 19 February 1978.

He writes in his notebook on this day: 'It is difficult to believe in this ridiculous story. My only hope is that some transmutation will occur to me'. He then continues with some thoughts: 'The sexual alienation of the man had better be linked to the torture ... This means that he will have to live through what is going on in the torture room more intensely'. He begins to bring his themes together, and this is an example of how method might create meaning adequate to the initial intuitive understanding. The bringing together of themes involves relations between them, and meaningfulness resonates across the gaps between these themes, requiring the reader to draw them more fully together in interpretations.

Before beginning version F on 13 March 1978, he develops a new idea (which while soon abandoned nevertheless exemplifies this method of trying to draw relations between the main themes). In his notebook, he writes:

Perhaps the whole thing can be saved by telling it from the point of view of X's secretary right hand man .... The narrator is a spy on the girl and X. He accompanies them to the barbarians. He himself is immune to the harms that befall everyone else. Like those twins in *The Castle*. But he is also a kind of double to K. (Coetzee Archives, Container 33.03, Notebook 1)

F indeed proceeds in this manner, again in the third person with this new Kafkaesque narrator. Yet this too fizzles out after just fourteen pages on the 28 March 1978. Again, a period of reflection follows as Coetzee waits for some method capable of drawing together relations between themes to occur to him, and he does not begin the first complete draft until a month later on 28 April 1978. There does not seem to be a clear understanding in Coetzee's mind that he has, at this point, solved the problems he needs to solve and so yet more ideas are considered.

He considers returning to some of the methods he used in *In the Heart of Country*, where he makes use of a filmic form that works with photographs rather than moving images. He mentions Robbe-Grillet and Chris Marker's *La Jettée* (the latter is explicitly mentioned with regard to the earlier novel in *Doubling the Point*, 60). He thinks of some photographs and imagines describing items as if they are artefacts in a museum. The first he pictures is a pair of 'dark glasses'. On 26 April 1978 he writes, 'Centre becomes the dark glasses (home made), plus perhaps one or two other strange artefacts'. In the same entry he writes, 'Translate the story out of Asia into contemporary S. A.' Again, these relations (the image of the unfamiliar but eerily modern object and the closeness to the present situation made possible by the South African names) help to make the final version possible.

Then, on 28 April 1978 he writes: 'Have begun, in desperation, on a new version. As I "imagine" it, it is now set in a vaguely 18th–19th century Africa; but soon it is going to be snowing!' (Coetzee Archives, Container 33.03, Notebook 1). So, strangeness is paired with the familiar, rendering the familiar symbolic and allowing Coetzee to apply the power of symbolism to the banality of the contemporary evils he must confront. The new version, G, is eventually given the title 'Waiting for the Barbarians' on a day noted in the notebook as 2 May 1978. Interestingly, after the note of 28 April 1978 Coetzee writes less in his notebook and more in his draft, with days going by where no notebook entries are made. The work is now completely in the first person with 'X' becoming the narrator/Magistrate. The scene of the glasses develops a mixed symbolic/realistic space and from this the work gathers momentum which is apparent not only in the comparative ease with which Coetzee begins to write at this point, but also for the reader, as that striking opening scene moves quickly to the themes of torture and the idea of the truth (as problems of existence that are at once general and particular), that open in turn to the vain attempts to understand the signs left on the girl, the girl herself, her people, and his own people (as problems of interpretation that are at once general and particular, symbolic and real). It is difficult to explain the shift that takes place between the earlier drafts and the sudden breakthrough to the new way forward. As one reads the previous drafts and moves to this point of breakthrough, the writing is suddenly gripping when before it had been workmanlike. It is as if something has suddenly been grasped and now that it has been grasped, the relations between elements within the work are somehow aligned. From here, in the manuscript, the work seems to tumble forth.

While it is only possible to roughly sketch the idea of how the process of writing, which mixes discipline with the pressures of an everyday need to establish some meaningful or truthful relation to the world in which the writer writes, with methods of writing

PROCESS: *WAITING FOR THE BARBARIANS*   85

(formal techniques that allow meaningful relations to be posed in the work and interpreted by readers). Yet it is apparent that finding the setting, the situation, images, and the voice of the Magistrate in first person are crucial to constructing the method through which the novel is completed and that paying attention to the process allows insight into these methods.

5

Ethics and Ethology

Numerous recent studies have underlined how Coetzee's work engages with ethics.[1] This chapter sets out a series of concepts that examine how Coetzee's works engage ethically with their subjects. I will focus in particular on the idea of an engagement with disposition place and environment. This chapter looks at philosophical concepts implicated by Coetzee's works, rather than claiming that Coetzee was directly influenced by the philosophers discussed. The following chapters will draw out some of the implications of these ideas through close readings of his works. If Coetzee provokes us to consider the nature of truth, and meaning, he further provokes us by suggesting that works of art, through 'sympathy' and feeling or sensation, can offer access to ethical understandings, and by suggesting that the writer has an ethical duty to answer their situation.

Ethics is that aspect of philosophy concerned with how to live. The Greek understanding of the word 'ethikos' involves 'the state of being', that which is manifest in the soul or mind. Ethics is etymologically linked to ethology, through the Greek word root, 'ethos'. The original meaning of 'ethos' is 'accustomed place', or

---

[1]See, in particular, Leist and Singer's edited collection, *J. M. Coetzee and Ethics*; Attridge, *Ethics of Reading*; Hämäläinen, Nora, 'The Personal Pilgrimage of David Lurie — or Why Coetzee's *Disgrace* Should and Should Not Be Read in Terms of an Ethics of Perception', *Partial Answers: Journal of Literature and the History of Ideas*, vol. 11, no. 2, June 2013, pp. 233–255; Ciobanu, Calina, 'Coetzee's Posthumanist Ethics', *MFS: Modern Fiction Studies*, vol. 58, no. 4, Winter 2012, pp. 668–698; McDonald; Baker; Spivak, Gayatri, 'Ethics and Politics in Tagore, Coetzee, and Certain Scenes of Teaching', *Diacritics: A Review of Contemporary Criticism*, vol. 32, no. 3–4, Fall-Winter 2002, pp. 17–31.

'habitat', and by analogy it was quickly associated with 'custom, habit'. It evolved however to be understood as the 'character', 'disposition', or core values of individuals or groups. Ethology, then, links ethos and 'logos' (which might mean reason or expression), that is, it links disposition and understanding in naming the scientific study of the behaviour of animals within their natural habitats. A secondary meaning is the study of the formation of human ethos. Linking ethics and ethology, then, underlines how forming an understanding of one's disposition within one's habitat enables the proper living of one's life.

The word 'art' is often associated with human relations to nature (often through ideas of the 'representation' or 'imitation' of nature, but also importantly with regard to 'creation' understood to analogically correspond with natural creation). As such it is an understanding both of nature and of dispositions within nature. Working in what Michael Hardt calls a 'minor tradition' of philosophy, Gilles Deleuze shows us not only how life is linked with nature, as ethics involves ethology, but how life and nature express dispositions as understandings, and how such processes of expression involve art and its necessity. To put this another way: Deleuze shows us how art is necessarily concerned with the same fundamental questions which concern ethics and ethology: living.

In *What Is Philosophy?* Deleuze and Guattari muse on that time of life when a philosopher feels compelled to reflect upon the question of the nature of her or his practice. The desire for such reflection, they argue, comes with age. It involves self-reflection, something that concerns one's disposition, and one's place in the world. As such it is properly an ethical process. The idea of reflection, however, is also fundamental to both thought itself and artistic practice or the practice of creation. In considering the nature of philosophy, then, Deleuze and Guattari turn, through logical necessity, to the nature of thought and the thought of nature: that is, they also consider science and art. As I will argue in this chapter, this interrelation is at the heart of their understanding of natural being and links in with the minor traditions of thinking that they trace and prolong in their own work.

Yet the connection between art and how we should live also occurs in the dominant tradition of thought: rather than ethics, however, this tradition links artistic practice to morals, and the 'moral' (or the lesson or specified meaning). There are a number of distinctions, then, which involve not so much binary oppositions as differences of perspective, and these are crucial to an understanding of the interrelations Deleuze and Guattari and Deleuze develop between art, ethics, and ethology. These distinctions assert an ethics over a morality; thought over (human) consciousness; creation over mimesis.

In *Difference and Repetition*, Deleuze describes a negative image of thought, a dogmatic image of thought which, rather than opening up potentials for thought, closes them down. It does this in part by standing as a shared assumption: the idea that all reasonable people will think in the same way. This habit of mind involves a logic of imititative identities: in art, it involves the idea that art imitates nature; in moral philosophy the idea that morality involves imitating set modes of behaviour; in philosophy that there is one true thought that each will follow. In *Proust and Signs, Nietzsche and Philosophy,* and *A Thousand Plateaus*, however, we are shown a new image of thought which challenges our idea of what it means to think and opens up possibilities for thinking. This line of argument is consistent with ideas Deleuze and Guattari and Deleuze develop elsewhere: art does not imitate, it creates; ethics involves living in accordance with one's nature, rather than imitating rules of behaviour; philosophy involves engaging with that power of thought which opens possibilities which are coming into being, rather than describing forms or categories that seek to fix meaning or being.

In considering the question of art, ethics, and ethology, then, Deleuze and Guattari repeat three gestures: they look to the kind of ethics developed by Spinoza, which they characterize as an ethics developed around ethology; they return to the idea of the animal in its habitat as a reflection of ethology; they consider the nature of art via this ethological understanding. In each case the three terms, ethics, ethology, and art are linked through the idea of affect.

Spinoza, ethology and ethics

In 'On the Difference between The *Ethics* and a Morality' Deleuze argues that Morality was founded upon the traditional principle that consciousness (or the mind) must master the passions (or the body)

(Deleuze, *Spinoza Practical Philosophy*, 18).[2] It is not a matter of referring to a moral code first, which specifies an action as Good or Evil, and then acting on that advice; rather, it is a matter of seeking to be joined with that object which agrees with your nature and avoiding that object which disagrees with your nature: 'good and bad have a primary, objective meaning, but one that is relative and partial: that which agrees with our nature or does not agree with it' (22, see also 30–43). The distinction between ethics and morality, then, is as follows. Morality works through static rules or defined terms. According to a moral code a specific behaviour (homosexuality, for example) might be marked as 'evil' and followers of that moral code are asked to affirm this judgement. For Deleuze following Spinoza, however, ethics involves determining what is good for you and what is bad for you and seeking out what is good and avoiding what is bad. In the case cited here, homosexuality is central to the disposition of a homosexual individual, and so is good for them.

As we have seen, ethology is that which links an animal's behaviour to its relationships within its habitat. Spinoza's understanding of ethics in effect does much the same. In 'Spinoza and Us', Deleuze states, 'studies [...] which define bodies, animals, or humans by the affects they are capable of founded what is today called *ethology*' (Deleuze, *Spinoza Practical Philosophy*, 125). He explains that every thing in Nature selects those other things in the world that correspond to it; those things which affect it, or which it affects, 'what moves or is moved by it' (125). The ethical question related to any animal then becomes: what affects this animal and what does not affect it (125)? For Deleuze, Spinoza is a philosopher of ethology because he develops an ethics which functions through an idea of good and bad, in terms of what is good for you and what is bad for you in what affects you and what you affect, rather than a moral system based on rules which designate specific things as 'good' and 'evil'.

Deleuze and Guattari turn to Spinoza in defining how ethics and ethology might be linked. This is not their only strategy, however. They also move back from ethology, or an understanding of animal behaviour, to ethics, while in the process linking both to art. This is a complex manoeuvre, which involves viewing Spinoza's *Ethics*

---

[2]I discuss these ideas in relation to Samuel Beckett's *Malone Dies* in *Beckett and Poststructuralism*.

from a different angle and relating these ideas to others drawn from Henri Bergson's *Creative Evolution*. Something of the nature of this approach is revealed in the two main plateaus of *A Thousand Plateaus* that connect art, the animal (ethology), and ethics: '1730: Becoming-Intense, Becoming-Animal, Becoming-Imperceptible ... ', and '1837: Of the Refrain'. In '1730: Becoming-Intense, Becoming-Animal, Becoming-Imperceptible ... ', Deleuze and Guattari offer a number of 'memories' in counterpoint, among which are 'Memories of a Bergsonian' and 'Memories of a Spinozist, I and II'. Developing a reading of important passages from Bergson and Spinoza through the lens of Deleuze and Guattari and Deleuze allows a better understanding of how art, ethology, and ethics might be linked.

I have touched upon how Deleuze and Guattari turn to the image of the animal to explain those processes of ethological interrelation that might be understood to be ethical. They also, however, turn to art for three reasons: firstly these ethological interrelations are *expressed as affects*, and for Deleuze and Guattari, art itself involves the expression of affects and percepts. Secondly, art allows for transversal processes through which relations might be made between objects that are only apparently incompatible (and that are in fact connected): that is, art imagines, or creates, the possibility of becoming something other – of becoming animal, for example. As such art enables us to be moved by a feeling of understanding of this other, and our place in a larger environment. Art, then, not only shows us how *one* is affected (thereby expressing an ethics that might pertain to our own lives), it can also show the interrelated processes of affection that comprise habitats. Third, following on from this, art is capable of building passages which both construct or create territories and build networks of interrelations between territories: that is, art can create the consistency necessary to understand interrelations that are real but difficult to conceive. Art, in effect, expresses an ethology that is coextensive with ethics.

Art and animals

The connections between art, ethics, and ethology are consistent, then. In helping us to see this consistency, Deleuze and Guattari and Deleuze return to images of animals taken from ethology, on the one hand, and create a theory of expression capable of encompassing the consistency they perceive between art, ethology, and ethics on the other. Spinoza allows one way of doing this; yet when one reads the *Ethics* separately from Deleuze and Guattari's readings, Spinoza seems an odd choice for developing the connection between ethics and animals, as he has little to directly say about this issue. However, he can logically be read to understand the universe as a whole as a composite animal.

Bergson, on the other hand, does turn directly to animal behaviour in developing his own interrelation between instinct (intuition) and logical thought. In doing this he draws us towards a concept that has become unfashionable, but which, if conceived in his terms, allows us to understand how affect might permeate an environment and link participants within this environment transversally. The word he uses is 'sympathy'.

In *Elizabeth Costello*, J. M. Coetzee has the eponymous character state that there is a faculty – sympathy – which 'allows us to share at times the being of another' (Coetzee, *Elizabeth Costello*, 79) and she goes on to claim that literature has the capacity to develop this faculty to an extremely high level: 'If I can think my way into the existence of a being who has never existed, then I can think my way into the existence of a bat or a chimpanzee or an oyster, any being with whom I share the substrate of life' (Coetzee, *Elizabeth Costello*, 80). Many other voices are raised to disagree with Elizabeth's views on this and other questions and we are given no direction, from a narrator, for example, which might affirm whether or not we are supposed to believe what she says, or what those who disagree with her say. We are asked to think, rather than told what to think.

Elizabeth Costello, an Australian novelist who has been invited to give a talk on 'The Lives of Animals' in an American university, takes issue with and enters into dialogue with the philosopher Thomas Nagel, who argues that it is not possible for us to understand what it is to be a bat, because our minds are inadequate to the task (76). She disagrees, arguing that we can enter into relation with the bat, share, in a sense, something of its existence, through the faculty of sympathy:

> The heart is the seat of a faculty, *sympathy*, that allows us to share at times the being of another. Sympathy has everything to do with the subject and little to do with the object, the 'another',

as we see at once when we think of the object not as a bat ('Can I share the being of a bat?') but as another human being. [...] there is no limit to the extent to which we can think ourselves into the being of another. There are no bounds to the sympathetic imagination. (Coetzee, *Elizabeth Costello*, 79–80)

Geoffrey Baker has argued (Baker, 27–49, also see Durrant), in comparing *Elizabeth Costello* with *Disgrace* (*Disgrace*, 33–34), there are *limits* to sympathy. As I will set out below I consider (reading *Disgrace* and following Coetzee in *The Good Story*) that there are not limits to sympathy; rather, there are limits to the imagination that cause us to fail to access this sympathy.[3]

Bergson and sympathy

Elizabeth Costello is a follower of literary Modernism: the work that makes her famous enters into dialogue with James Joyce's *Ulysses* in extending the monologue of Molly Bloom. Her understanding of sympathy, then, enters into relation with Modernist understandings of the term, which were strongly influenced by the work of Henri Bergson (on this influence, see Douglas, Fink, and Gillies).

In *Creative Evolution* Bergson considers three means through which life has developed its capacities to interact within the world, both responding to and creating the environment of which it forms a part: torpor, instinct, and intelligence. Torpor largely concerns Bergson's understanding of plant life. Of most interest to us here is the interaction between instinct and intelligence, which allows us to understand how a relation to the material real both differs from and relies upon a relation to ideal forms.

The terms instinct and intelligence are not held in opposition; rather, they are complementary, and can and do co-exist. Yet instinct is most highly developed in certain parts of the animal kingdom. Indeed, it is, for Bergson, the dominant means through which animals, from the simplest to the most complex, interact within their environment.

---

[3] A number of critics have considered different aspects of the concept of sympathy in Coetzee; see Lamey, Graef, Heister.

It is only more highly developed animals which make use of 'intelligence' and the animal which makes most use of intelligence is the human. For Bergson all life must answer the question of how it can act on the material world. For animals, he argues, nature has developed two responses (though these are interconnected) – two ways in which they might have an effect on the environment. Both of these might be understood to involve some kind of 'thought', but they are different in nature. Both involve a response to the world.

Instinct involves an organism using those tools that are a part of its body to effect a task. An insect, working purely through instinct, makes use of tools that have already been organized for it by nature: the wings that allow it to fly, the proboscis that allows it to suck nectar, the camouflage that allows it to avoid its enemies, and so on. It has, for Bergson, been organized, or, if you prefer, it has evolved, in order to perform this task among other tasks. It makes use of instinct in performing this task. Instinct, then, is a kind of organized thought. Intelligence, however, is that capacity which allows certain animals to find or invent tools within their environment with which they might act on that environment. Human beings, making use of their intelligence, are able to fabricate tools from materials that have not been specifically organized by nature for this purpose, such as axes and knives and spears, or cars and aeroplanes. If instinct is thought which has already been organized and is coextensive with the organism it inhabits and comprises, then intelligence is organizing thought: thought which allows for the development of instruments which will serve to affect the environment in a certain way (Bergson, *Creative Evolution*, 139–142).

There is another way of looking at the difference. Instinct involves acting on material things: seeing the world in terms of those actual particular things upon which we might act. Intelligence, however, concerns itself with the abstract forms we use to organize our understanding of things in a general way.

Intelligence, then, is a knowledge of forms or ideals, whereas instinct is a knowledge of matter. When one starts to think in terms of knowledge and knowing our place in the world, however, there is a paradox for Bergson:

> *There are things that intelligence alone is able to seek, but which, by itself, it will never find. These things instinct alone could find;*

but it will never seek them. (Bergson, *Creative Evolution*, 151, italics in original)

This is because instinct excels in fitting itself to reality: reality for Bergson is movement (155). Intelligence, however, works by fixing things in place, rendering them artificially static, or abstracting them from movement. That is, intelligence conceives of the living as if it were lifeless (165). Intelligence by itself, then, is incapable of fully comprehending reality. Instinct fully comprehends the movement of reality, but it simply acts, it does not reflect. For Bergson, then, *'The intellect is characterised by a natural inability to comprehend life'* (italics in original, 165).

How, then, is it that we feel that we can comprehend life, at least intuitively, at least instinctively? This is because we, like those organisms that act through instinct, have a sympathy with the world, with our environment. Bergson compares life to a musical theme: there is an original theme that has been played into an immense variety of variations in life on earth. How can we grasp the original theme?

As for the original theme, it is everywhere and nowhere. It is in vain that we try and express it in terms of any idea: it must have been, originally, *felt* rather than *thought*. (Bergson, *Creative Evolution*, 172)

The link between music, ethology, and ethics is developed to an extraordinary degree by Deleuze and Guattari in '1837: Of the Refrain'. This, in connection with Bergson, allows us to understand how music moves out both from the individual, which is seeking to establish its territory or place in the world and from the world to the individual, allowing passage from the self to indefinite sets of transversal interrelations.[4]

Bergson compares this felt understanding with instinct, using as an example the paralysing instinct of certain wasps. He draws on the work of the entomologist Fabre in describing how the Scolia

---

[4]Among other terms Deleuze and Guattari use the concept of the 'Dividual' to account for this interaction among and between (intra- and inter-) that occur in 'group individuation' (*A Thousand Plateaus*, 341).

Wasp attacks the larva of the rose-beetle: it 'stings it in one point only, but in this point the motor ganglia are concentrated, and those ganglia alone: the stinging of other ganglia might cause death and putrefaction, which it must avoid' (Bergson, *Creative Evolution*, 172). So the Scolia Wasp stings its correspondent, the rose-beetle larva in the only place which will cause it to be paralysed but still living, something it needs so that its own young might hatch and feed on the paralysed beetle larva.

How are we to understand this level of precision? Bergson argues that we get into trouble because we try and express this knowledge in terms of intelligence. We cannot conclude that the Scolia learns where to sting its prey, in the same way as the entomologist has learnt the make up of the body of the beetle larva (Bergson, *Creative Evolution*, 173). Bergson then concludes that:

> there is no need for such a view if we suppose a *sympathy* (in the etymological sense of the word) between the Ammophila [wasp] and its victim, which teaches it from within, so to say, concerning the vulnerability of the caterpillar. This feeling of vulnerability might owe nothing to outward perception, but result from the mere presence together of the Ammophila and the caterpillar, considered no longer as two organisms, but as two activities. It would express, in concrete form, the *relation* of the one to the other. (Bergson, *Creative Evolution*, 174)[5]

A few pages on, Bergson concludes that the concrete explanation of the 'original theme' is no longer scientific or purely concerned with intelligence: rather, 'it must be sought ... not in the direction of intelligence, but in that of "sympathy"' (176). This kind of thinking is then explicitly linked not only with a philosophical project, which Bergson calls metaphysics, but with certain artistic practices:

---

[5]The etymological definition of 'sympathy' from Le Robert, *Dicitionnaire Historique de la Langue Française*, is as follows: 'from latin sympathia "accord, affinité naturelle" [agreement, natural affinity] taken in turn from the Greek sumpatheia "participation à la souffrance d'autrui" [participating in the suffering of another], "communauté de sentiments ou d'impressions" [community of sensations or impressions], and in the language of Epicurius and the Stoics "rapports de certaines choses entre elles, affinities" [the relation of certain things between themselves, affinities]'.

Intelligence and instinct are turned in opposite directions, the former towards inert matter, the latter towards life. [...] But it is to the very inwardness of life that *intuition* leads us – by intuition I mean instinct that has become disinterested, self-conscious, capable of reflecting upon its object and of enlarging it indefinitely. (Bergson, *Creative Evolution*, 176)

He continues:

That an effort of this kind is not impossible, is proved by the existence in man of an aesthetic faculty along with normal perception. Our eye perceives the features of the living being, merely as assembled, not as mutually organized. The intention of life, the simple movement that runs through the lines, that binds them together and gives them significance, escapes it. This intention is just what the artist tries to regain, in placing himself back within the object by a kind of sympathy, in breaking down, by an effort of intuition, the barrier that space puts up between him and his model. (Bergson, *Creative Evolution*, 177)

The powerful connection, sympathy, which Coetzee appeals to through Elizabeth Costello, involves a natural affinity between ourselves and our environment, an environment understood as being comprised of those relations themselves.

Deleuze and Guattari turn to ethology and the work of Jacob von Uexküll to underline this process. Just as Bergson uses the example of the wasp, Deleuze and Guattari in *A Thousand Plateaus*, and Deleuze in 'Spinoza and Us', use that of the tick which is defined by the affects of which it is capable. To shift from the language of Deleuze and Guattari back to that of Bergson allows us to develop a syncretic interpretation of Deleuze and Guattari's crucial concept of 'affect' – one that involves a correspondence between immediate understanding (i.e. disinterested instinct, or intuition) and ethical action and a *felt* relationship to one's world (sympathy).

While it has been pointed out that the evolutionary science Bergson engages with comes from an earlier period and that things have moved on from here, it is worth noting that here Bergson seems to closely relate to ideas developed by the contemporary neurobiologist Antonio Damasio. In *Looking for Spinoza*, Damasio, who is struck by the prescience of insights developed by Spinoza, underlines how 'feeling', which he distinguishes from 'emotion' (the former being the processing of ideas related to felt experience, the latter being the often visible physiological responses to external stimulus), sits on top of a tree-like felt-bodily system (prior to 'conscious' or intellectual thought) which allows us to adapt to our environment and interact effectively with it (see Damasio, *Looking*). Contemporary neuroscience, then, agrees with Spinoza and Bergson, that feelings, distinct from rational ideas, are crucial to our understanding of the world.[6]

Our connection to the world: Spinoza

The whole of Spinoza's *Ethics* is built upon a logic of relations understood not simply as involving the relations of self within self, but the relationships of all things (see Spinoza, Part II, Lemmas 1–7, 458–462; Part II, Prop. 40, 478; Part IV, Prop. 39, 568), and this in turn reminds us of Bergson's 'sympathy'.

For Spinoza, all interrelations involve relationships of joy and sadness. Relationships of joy draw bodies together into larger bodies (increasing the power of all the connected bodies). A harmonious nation might be understood as forming one, more powerful body comprising a single body, and the same might be said of the world as a whole, the universe as a whole (see Spinoza, Part II, Lemma 7, 462). Relationships of sadness sunder bodies, tearing them apart and decreasing their power.

There is a second aspect of this intellectual system, then, which I feel are of particular importance to a reading of artistic practice. This involves the conception of essence Spinoza develops and the manner in which he relates this to the soul. Rather than drawing us towards what has been a dominant understanding of being, this takes us to another place, one which allows us to recognize the interrelatedness at the core of any 'individual' essence or, if you prefer, a different conception of individuality, linking art,

---

[6]See Damasio, *Descartes' Error*, for a philosophical perspective. On the new position of cognitive science, see Cahterine Malabou, *What Should We Do with Our Brain?*.

ethics, and ethology in the manner of Deleuze and Guattari's 'haeccity' (Deleuze and Guattari, 1987: 262–263).

Of the Refrain

In '1837: Of the Refrain' Deleuze and Guattari trace two movements in images to introduce the conception of the interaction between art, ethics, and ethology. They begin with the image of the child singing, which moves out from the child's fear to interaction with the world. Fear makes the child sing to calm herself; she then builds a milieu about her with her song, until she is sufficiently at home that she might develop links, through her song, from the small circle of her milieu to the great circle of the world. The song is itself an 'ethos' an abode: it is a milieu created by the child in relation to the world in order to live with and within that world (A Thousand Plateaus, 311–312). A 'space' becomes a 'milieu' when the world is translated from space or physical matter to the matter of expression: the song itself is a signature whose meaning is the marking of a milieu (A Thousand Plateaus, 315). The creation of a milieu is linked to expression, not aggression: rather than fighting with rivals over a shared space, it creates a particular milieu in which one might live (A Thousand Plateaus, 316). This marks the conditions of possibility for art, but it is not yet art. Art emerges when the signature is transformed into style, through the variation of motifs and counterpoints which no longer merely offer a placard 'I am', but generate affects which in turn can make others feel. That is, it involves moving from asserting the self to creating an expression of the world into which others might enter. In life the world is composed of the actual interrelations of actual bodies and actual thought and we gauge its meaning by sensing the resonance of multiple points of relation. Art presents those relations that resonate in life, even though the terms of the actual relations (the bodies and minds) are absent: 'The relation to joy and sadness, the sun, danger, perfection, is given in the motif and counterpoint, even if the term of each of these relations is not given' (A Thousand Plateaus, 319). The artist, then, can generate sympathy by creating inter- and intra-relational resonance.

The first image Deleuze and Guattari develop concerns the self faced by the world who expresses milieus which pass into greater milieus. Yet while these circles involve interaction with the world, a further process, which involves the exchange between selves, between and among their milieus, emerges – a process of passage which creates the very territories through which one passes. 'The territory itself is a place of passage' (*A Thousand Plateaus*, 323). It is the territory which allows 'assemblages' to form: 'The territory is the first assemblage, the first thing to constitute an assemblage' (*A Thousand Plateaus*, 323). While the self moves out from the milieu, it moves among territories passing from one to another: the assemblage is this passage from one to another (*A Thousand Plateaus*, 324).

What is the role of art in this process? In short it is crucial to it: crucial to the realization and understanding of worlds and habitats (which have to be imagined to be either realized or understood). Art imagines and expresses dispositions. Deleuze and Guattari offer four classifications of refrains: firstly, there are refrains that create and mark territories; secondly, there are refrains that mark relations (such as love); thirdly, there are refrains that mark shifts between assemblages involving the movement between territories; and finally, there are refrains 'that collect or gather forces, either at the heart of the territory, or in order to go outside it [...] They cease to be terrestial, becoming cosmic' (*A Thousand Plateaus*, 327). If the first set of images – the singing child – relate to the self confronting the world, then the second set of images – the territory, the assemblage, the passage, the cosmos – involve the manner in which matters of expression move through worlds confronting life and forming both worlds and individuals.

Art, like ethics and ethology, emerges in the process of interrelation. Interrelation, however, and the worlds formed through it must be *created*, and this process of creation occurs through expression. The logic of sensation that comprises art is already present in nature and both work to generate an understanding while forming dispositions.

6

Ethology: *Life & Times of Michael K, Age of Iron*

Much of Coetzee's fiction of the 1980s and 1990s is deeply concerned with the particular political crisis then unfolding in apartheid South Africa. The nature of these relations, including the particularities of the exchange between Coetzee and Nadine Gordimer I will touch upon here, is beyond my capacities as a critic to encompass. Much has been written about these questions elsewhere by South Africanists and post-colonial critics. This chapter, which concerns two deeply political novels, while touching upon the particularities of the processes of composition, largely focuses on the formal elements of the relation to the political and the formal solutions Coetzee develops in an attempt to come to terms with what are properly ethological problems.

Coetzee's fourth novel *Life & Times of Michael K* underlined his emergence as a writer of international reputation through the award of the Booker Prize in London; yet, praise for the book was not universal. Famously, in her review of Coetzee's *Life & Times of Michael K*, Nadine Gordimer suggests that Coetzee has moved from allegory in his previous work to an interest in the real events of apartheid South Africa in this novel. Gordimer begins by praising this but then develops a withering critique.[1]

---

[1] On agreements and disagreements between Gordimer and Coetzee see Kannemeyer, 396–400, 413–421. Also see Zimbler, 131–144 and Attwell *Life of Writing*, 141–142, and Szczurek. For a detailed overview of the reception of *Michael K* in South Africa see Attwell, *Politics of Writing*, 88–117.

The main charge Gordimer directs against Coetzee in 'The Idea of Gardening' is as follows:

> The unique and controversial aspect of [*Life & Times of Michael K*] is that while it is implicitly and highly political, Coetzee's heroes are those who ignore history, not make it ... No one in this novel has any sense of taking part in determining that course; no one is shown to believe he knows what that course should be. The sense is of the ultimate malaise: of destruction. Not even the oppressor really believes in what he is doing, anymore, let alone the revolutionary.
>
> This is a challengingly questionable position for a writer to take up in South Africa, make no mistake about it. (Gordimer, 'Idea')

Coetzee himself makes a somewhat similar self-criticism while in the early stages of developing his novel. He states:

> There are two problems, on spiritual, one technical.
>
> The spiritual problem is that I show no advance in any thinking from the position I take in WfB [*Waiting for the Barbarians*]. I am outraged by tyranny, but only because I am indentified with the tyrants, not because I love (or 'am with') their victims. I am incorrigibly an elitist (if not worse); and in the present conflict the material interests of the intellectual elite and the oppressors are the same. There is a fundamental flaw in all my novels: I am unable to move from the side of the oppressors to the side of the oppressed. Is this a consequence of this insulated life I lead? Probably.
>
> The technical problem is that I cannot interpret [Kleist's novel] MK 'into' a recognizable present situation (in fact I don't even know the text well enough). (Coetzee Archives Container 33.5, Notebook MK, pp. 6–7, 16 June 1980)

The approaches Coetzee takes to these problems develop and shift through the process of composition. At first Coetzee imagined a white South African character, who, after a robbery, becomes obsessed with Heinrich von Kleist's novel, *Michael Kolhauss*; yet, this intertextual relation becomes increasingly tenuous as the work progresses, so that, with the finished work, it is difficult to draw clear relations between Kleist's work and Coetzee's.

Gordimer affirms that Coetzee's *Life & Times of Michael K* derives much of its power from the realist portrayal of the plight of coloured and black South Africans under the apartheid regime. Coetzee's Michael K inhabits a clearly identifiable time and place, a possible future near to the present in which Coetzee wrote, aligned with an extremely faithful topographical realism. The situation Michael K finds himself in also closely mirrors the social situation of a coloured South African in Cape Town in 1984. As Gordimer points out, we do not have to be told that Michael K is coloured; the social positions he and his mother hold and their manner of existence announce their status as coloured.[2] Yet as Gordimer also points out, Michael K is not a typical individual:

> He is marked out, from birth, by a harelip ... His deformity distorts his speech and his actual and self-images. He shrinks from the difficulty of communication through words and the repugnance he sees holding him off, in people's eyes; thus he appears to be, and perhaps is, retarded – one of those unclassifiable beings that fascinated Dostoevsky, a 'simple'. (Gordimer, 'Idea')

While Gordimer is puzzled by Coetzee's decision to work with an atypical character, it might be argued that the problem of speaking for the other occurs to Coetzee as a difficulty. That is, the extent to which it is possible, from the position of privilege he occupies, to speak on behalf of the oppressed, is open to question. The same problem recurs in *Foe*, where 'giving voice' to Friday seems all but impossible and is symbolically designated in these terms through the absence of Friday's tongue.

To put this in slightly different terms, while, as Elizabeth Costello contends, it is possible through the imagination to sympathetically engage with any other being, be it a bat or a human of a different race or gender or disposition, fully imagining such beings involves understanding the sets of relations that determine the nature of their experience of the world. While it is always possible for

---

[2]Indeed, there is only one direct reference to MK's race in the novel, when he is arrested as a vagrant in Prince Albert and taken to hospital before being removed to the nearby camp of Jakkalsdrif, the Police note his details as 'Michael Visagie – CM – 40 – NFA – Unemployed' (Coetzee, *Life & Times*, 70), with the initials 'CM' clearly signifying his race and gender.

writers to attempt this – just as, for example, the white American
E. L. Doctorow does in *Ragtime*, where in imagining the African-
American character Coalhouse Walker (in turn derived from Kleist's
Michael Kolhaus) he attempts to set in place some of the causal
relations that lead to his actions – it remains extremely difficult to
do justice to the complexity of these relations. Coetzee's novel in
part deals with this problem by cutting Michael K from normal
relations and relationships.

Forms of relationship

While Michael K is situated by his relations to others, the relations
that serve Michael K and in part determine his actions are strangely
tenuous. He has tenuous family relations: he only knows his mother,
who abandoned him as a child to the 'care' of the state institution
Huis Norenius, where he suffered, and yet he displays unbreakable
loyalty to the idea of her. So too his physical relations to places in
the Western Cape of South Africa (Cape Town and then the Karoo)
are tenuous: the farm on the Karoo is his mother's home rather than
his (though for her too this is mediated by its being the property of
the white masters), and yet he develops a profound bond with it and
wishes to remake it as his own home, through a direct engagement
with it in his gardening.

This logic of fractured and reimagined relations is a formal
power that drives the narrative. Having imagined the outlines of
the character of Michael K (his simple nature, his job as a gardener,
his relations with his mother whom he visits at Sea Point), Coetzee
suggests that 'the basic problem is not how to write this story:
it writes itself, that is the trouble. The problem is to introduce
consciousness into it' (Coetzee Archives, Container 33.5, Notebook
MK, 16 December 1980). The choice of words here is interesting.
Why does Coetzee write 'consciousness' here? One might argue that
in imagining Michael K as simple and cut from normal relational
particularity, he becomes a figure of action rather than of reflection.
The character that is developed is one that *is*, rather than one that
reflects. In the end Coetzee addresses this concern in part through
indirection: K's story is juxtaposed with the failed attempts at
interpretation developed by the medical officer who treats him

in part two. In addition, partly because of the abject failure of the white medical officer to understand him, in Bergson's terms, through the intellect, K's actions take on an emblematic status, opening themselves to ongoing interpretation.

Political truths: The gap

The logic involved in parts one and two of the novel is the logic of A against B, although here the gap occurs within the diegetic story world. There is a disconnect between the life of K and the world of the medical officer which cannot be bridged by intellectual interpretation. Whereas the juxtaposition of elements in *Dusklands* serves to reinforce themes across the two main parts, in *Michael K* the idea of the gap seems to signal a failure of understanding, rather than points of relation. In effect, the story as a whole dramatizes the weakening of relations and the understandings they presuppose and bring into being.

K himself notices the blank nature of the idea of the gap when he explains to himself why he does not go off to fight with the guerrillas rather than remaining to tend to his garden. It is because he is keeping alive 'the idea of gardening' (Coetzee, *Life and Times*, 109).[3] This is the very thing that gives Gordimer pause, and it arises as the response to the possibility that K might join the war. K himself is aware the answer may not be correct. He thinks:

> Between this reason and the truth that he would never announce himself … lay a gap wider than the distance separating him from the firelight. Always, when he tried to explain himself to himself, there remained a gap. (Coetzee, *Life & Times*, 110)

Perhaps because of the overwhelming nature of the task set to a writer to come to terms with the situation of the South African apartheid regime, *Michael K* seems to question the terms we have been exploring throughout this study. Faced with the awesome

---

[3]Coetzee discusses the idea of the garden and gardening in relation to white settlement of Cape Town in *White Writing*, with Cape Town itself being linked to the garden through the Dutch East India Company, which set it up as a garden, and through analogy to the Garden of Eden.

nature of the problems confronted by the book, one might ask what kind of understanding is possible? What kind of 'truth' might be called upon to answer it?

For her part Gordimer at once suggests that Coetzee does express the truth; yet, she excoriates Coetzee for failing to pursue the logical response to it: revolution. She states:

> The presentation of the truth and meaning of what white has done to black stands out on every page, celebrating its writer's superb, unafraid creative energy as it does; yet it denies the energy of the will to resist evil. That *this* superb energy exists with indefatigable and undefeatable persistence among the black people of South Africa – Michael K's people – is made evident, yes, heroically, every grinding day. It is not present in the novel. (Gordimer, 'Idea')

The criticism is pointed; yet, it turns away from the ideas Coetzee chooses to consider. It is built upon the idea that he should have written a different novel. Perhaps it was not possible for Coetzee to write this different novel. Coetzee anticipates some of the criticisms Gordimer makes, pointing again to Pablo Neruda's *Heights of Maccu Picchu*. On 7 July 1981 he asks himself, 'Why shouldn't K – get to voice the people? Read Neruda' (Coetzee Archives Container 33.5, Notebook MK, p. 36). Neruda, in a heroic act of the imagination, calls upon the soul of the representative slave, killed during the construction of Machu Picchu, to re-emerge through the voice of poet. So Neruda imagines these long dead slaves and creates a voice for them. Yet is it so easy to force a voice upon those who are very much alive and struggling to create a new world? What is implied in Coetzee's work is an expression of the limits of understanding. That is, in Bergson's terms it is the intellect not instinct that fails.

Instead of the persistence Gordimer describes, Coetzee chooses to consider the idea of the failure of relations, the failure of logical reason, the failure of the intellect to understand life, the failure to connect, the idea of the gap. The notion of gap Coetzee considers is worthy of consideration. Coetzee alludes to this idea again in his notebook:

> The gap occurs not only when he asks himself why he does not go off with the guerrillas, it arises whenever he explains himself to

himself, for example when he asks why he looks after his mother. … For all the questions K asks there occurs the phenomenon of the gap opening. The fundamental question is one of origins. (Coetzee Archives Container 33.5, Notebook MK, p. 84, 6 September 1982)

This suggests that K has blind spots or is unable to understand certain things, certain actions he seems obliged to undertake through instinct. It further suggests that the lack of intellectual understanding stems from the absence of foundations. The K Coetzee imagines has been removed from his origins; his existence has been fragmented. His response is to attempt to construct meaning, to make a place for himself in a world which has denied him a place. Yet because of the lack of foundation (an intuitive understanding of how one fits with the environment one is situated within), gaps remain. His response is to attempt to ground himself, symbolically and literally.

As we have seen Deleuze and Guattari use the concept of ethology to consider how our ethical relations are determined by the relations of a living being to its environment. This relation is not simply neutral and not simply determined by the environment; rather, it involves the disposition or potential of the being within that environment. Yet why is ethology at stake here? If K has been disconnected from his origins and the understanding a relation to place allows, he in part compensates through the identification of action with thought, that is, K responds to his environments with disinterestedly instinctual or intuitive action. There is a symbolic resonance to his actions, particularly in what Gordimer calls 'the idea of gardening', which makes simple physical actions, burrowing into and toiling the earth, carry meaning that is co-extensive with an idea of place, and create new bonds with place and nature. The focus Coetzee chooses, then, shifts from the persistence of black South Africans to the problem of how to make a new world, possibly from out of ruins.

Coetzee is acutely aware of the distinction between acting and reflecting on action (or intellectual interpretation). Such a distinction is apparent in fictional form through the realist and allegorical modes, although these modal distinctions are rendered unstable in Coetzee's novel. The first form, realism, involves action (without thought or with thought smuggled in), while the second requires thought (through the structure of A against B or tenor against vehicle).

This answers Coetzee's comment that he felt the novel was writing itself but what was needed was to insert some consciousness: while Michael K has moments of insight into his situation and occasionally reflects upon it; he most typically acts without thinking, and thought is often deliberately reduced or held at bay. In Bergson's terms, he acts through instinct rather than intelligence and in so doing manages to achieve the kind of immediate understanding that inheres within instinct that has become disinterested (intuition).

Modal technique: Deforming realism and allegory

As we have seen it is further reflected in the structure of the book where section one, which details Michael K's adventures, is answered by section two in which the medical officer at a camp at the old Kenilworth race course is tasked with 'interpreting' Michael K, something he does with increasing desperation and implausibility; he does not even have his name correct, calling him Michaels, even though Michael tries to correct him (*Life & Times*, 131). Here the novel undermines the terms it is seemingly working with. That is, the terms (realism, allegory) are confused, so that the man of action, K, is understood as a symbolical and not a particular being. The medical officer, who struggles to interpret, sees him in allegorical terms. At the end of his narrative the medical officer imagines himself chasing after Michaels, catching up to him and sharing with him some of the difficulties of interpretation he poses:

> Your stay at camp was merely an allegory, if you know that word. It was an allegory – speaking at the highest level – of how scandalously, how outrageously a meaning can take up residence in a system without becoming a term in it. Did you not notice how, whenever I tried to pin you down, you slipped away? I noticed. (*Life & Times*, 166)

While Derek Attridge critiques the habitual use application of allegorical readings in relation to Coetzee's works in presenting his own ideal of a 'non-interpretative' or 'literal' reading, he also concedes the virtual impossibility of doing so insofar as one is attempting an interpretation – attempting, that is, to relate the work to something outside it (Attridge, *Ethics of Reading*, 32–37). The metaphor of allegory here is complex. Allegories involve systems of relations (whether exact as in traditional allegory, or inexact as with Benjaminian allegory or 'modern allegory') between a symbolic level and a 'real' level. By 'modern' allegory I am referring to the work of Walter Benjamin, Angus Fletcher, Frederic Jameson, and others who do not consider allegory to involve an exact relation between a sign A and a sign B, but rather to necessarily involve a play or inexactness of relations (see Fletcher, Buning). Yet Michael K is seen to offer an allegory of something within a system that is not related to the system (and yet remains meaningful). In short, this involves a logical anomaly that renders the idea of the system itself unstable.

There is not only a distortion of the allegorical mode then, but also a distortion of the realist mode. Writing in his notebook to *Michael K* Coetzee notes he has made progress in understanding the work's relation to realism:

> The passage written today at least provides some kind of indication of where the book might go: in the direction of an arid if rigorous meditation on realism. (Coetzee Archives Container 33.5, Notebook MK, 9 December 1980)

Much of Michael K's story proceeds and is driven by the logic of realism or instinctual action without reflection. Michael K is confronted by problems that he needs to solve and much of his time and, much of the substance of his narrative, is taken up with the need to address these immediate problems. How is he to make a cart capable of transporting his mother out of the city? How are they to escape the city avoiding the roadblocks and check points? How is he to keep her out of the sun? How are they to sleep and eat? To avoid confrontation?

These imperatives are disrupted by her death in Stellenbosch which is followed by a period of idleness that is, nonetheless, curiously non-reflective. Rather than seeking to interpret his situation intellectually, Michael K waits for the moment when he will be able to leave, having swapped the duty of taking his mother to the Karoo with the duty of taking her ashes there. The same kinds of imperatives organize his existence when hiding on the farm in the last section of his narrative. How is he to water the plants while hiding them and himself from the others who threaten them? Yet just as the allegorical mode of meaning creation has been rendered unstable by Michael K's failure to relate within that mode, the realist mode of instinctual action is upset by the anomaly of K's being *meaningful*. As the medical officer sees, K carries meaning; he is somehow symbolic, though within a broken system of symbolism.

Intertextual technique

While the archives prove Coetzee's interest in Kleist's story *Michael Kohlhaas* in the genesis of the work, there is also mention of Kafka[4] – at one point Coetzee contemplates the title 'The Childhood of Joseph K' – as well as of Theodore Drieser's *An American Tragedy* and Richard Wright's *Native Son* (Coetzee Archives Container 33.5, Notebook MK, p. 2, 10 November 1979; p. 16, 19 December 1980). Yet it further becomes apparent that Coetzee struggles to align the story that he is developing with the structure of Kleist's story. As he sets out in his notebook the structure of *Michael Kohlhaas* is clear: confrontation and theft of Michael's property, followed by violent retribution, followed by punishment for daring to take this retribution against the ruling powers.

While we might read the idea of 'theft' as the very condition of existence that confronts Michael K, he however never acts in violent retribution. There are then, in the end, few obvious parallels to Kleist's story. This might be contrasted, again, with the use E. L. Doctorow makes of Kleist's story in *Ragtime*, where Coalhouse Walker is robbed, does seek violent retribution, and is punished in turn.

Rather, almost against the logical relation he has intended to set up between Kleist's story and his own, Coetzee finds himself moving towards a different model: that provided by parts of Daniel Defoe's *Robinson Crusoe*. Crusoe is mentioned in the notebooks

---

[4]Critics have long linked this book to Kafka, see Head for example.

on two occasions (Coetzee Archives Container 33.5, Notebook MK, p. 10, 21 October 1980; p. 49, 28 October 1981) and Michael Marais has written in detail about the idea of space in *Crusoe* and *Michael K* (Marais, 'One of Those Islands'). The idea that Michael K is not 'a castaway' is underlined (*Life & Times*, 115); yet, this assertion seeks to differentiate Michael K from the manner in which he understands his state.

Whereas Crusoe stops and reflects on the necessary actions he performs (described in the realistic mode by Defoe) in order to survive, coming to the conclusion, at last, that his survival has all along depended on the occluded interventions of a providential god, Michael K's understanding is instinctual and intuitive and tied firmly to the place he has made for himself in nature. Yet there are many places in part one of the novel in which Michael K's story mirrors Crusoe's.

He goes to the house for supplies just as Crusoe goes to the ship. He tends his garden and plants and finds seeds. He finds goats, although unlike Crusoe he does not tame them. He builds his shelter and hides it from observation. He watches, horrified, from a distance, at the evidence of others on his island. Just as Crusoe finds the footprint, Michael K finds the door of the house ajar. He watches the revolutionaries just as Crusoe watches the cannibals who have come to the island, although here again the poles are reversed with Crusoe's disgust and horror replaced by Michael K's desire to be among them.

While he mentions Crusoe, nowhere in his notes does Coetzee indicate that the parallels set out here are in the front of his mind; rather, they seem to emerge as if subconsciously, or further, as if in response to the demands of the form: the realist mode that engages, in its most pure form, with those actions rendered absolutely necessary to enable life to persist: instinctive or intuitive action.

The tension provided by this mode, then, in Robinson Crusoe, and here in *Life & Times of Michael K*, comes from the drama of a certain kind of being. While Crusoe sets himself up as a colonial lord, whose lodgings and bearing reproduce his understanding of what it means to be a civilized Englishman alone in a wilderness surrounded by savages, Michael K overtly refuses the trappings of the colonial world (*Life & Times*, 64–65) and seeks instead another way of being, a way that is, controversially for Gordimer, linked to nature and gardening as an end in itself.

Michael K is not a castaway because he does not need to be saved and he is not carrying with him the reflected desires of another state of being. Up to a point the mode of realism drives the narrative through the step-by-step consideration of necessary relations, although these relations fail to hold the story in place because of the unstable symbolism of K within the work. These relations, however, are necessary not to the basic level of survival of the body or the maintenance or establishment of a particular level of comfort, but to some instinctual understanding of his essential needs, which involve his desire to build connections to nature or, to put this another way, his soul. 'This was the beginning of his life as a cultivator [....] It is because I am a gardener, he thought, because that is my nature' (*Life & Times,* 59).

In establishing his garden Michael K develops or creates a particular relation to a territory. The territory of the small field beside the dam is connected to him through the ashes of his mother that are spread there and link back through her to the 'line of children without end' (*Life & Times,* 117), which, like the seeds he plants, are children of the earth (*Life & Times,* 109). The water that waters both his garden and himself comes from the earth, and the only food with any flavour are the pumpkins and melons that he tends that grow from that earth. His connection to that earth and its fruit becomes so strong that he builds a niche to allow himself to live among it, though not in comfort. He further changes in relation to the needs of the overarching relation to the earth and its fruit, becoming nocturnal to better hide from men and drive away animals, changing or augmenting his senses in the process.

Life (instinct)

As we have seen above, in *Creative Evolution* Bergson considers how life has developed its capacities to interact within the world through instinct and intelligence, which both respond to and create the environment of which they form a part. This ethical relation to the environment is what Deleuze and Guattari call 'ethology'.

One can read the ampersand in the title of *Life & Times of Michael K* as, on one level, serving as a gap, pause or full stop. *Life* is made to stand alone as an abstract term. It refers not only to

Michael K's life and his immediate responses to his environment, but also simply to life itself. Understood in this way 'life' is revealed as having a specific structure: capture, escape, flight, hiding, that recurs and loops indefinitely.

Understood in this way 'life' is considered as a purely physical thing, that is both realist and allegorical, or rather, not quite either; a quasi-symbolic thing, that emanates from the earth in relation to the rest of nature; the ecosystem that supports the growth of plants; the sun, the soil, water from the sky or under the earth; wind that allows water to be drawn to the surface by machines that are man-made but able to operate without man for extended periods; and so on. Drawn into relation to this, one way Michael K is able to function in concert with it is as a gardener – one who tends the soil and sees to it that certain kinds of plants grow that in turn sustain the life of the one who gardens.

What renders *Life & Times of Michael K* strange is not this relation, but the anti-relational forces set loose by war: the conflicts determined by violent race relations and the political logics that support them. At one point Michael K thinks about the relation between the host and the parasite, a moment that gives Gordimer pause, as again she questions K's failure to act, and again she counsels (at least within the novel she imagines Coetzee might have written) violent resistance.

(If Michael K is shown to see himself 'like a parasite dozing in the gut,' he can never develop the metaphor by becoming the internal underground rebel who destroys the body of the enemy society he inhabits.) (Gordimer, 'Idea')

The moment is dwelt upon by Coetzee in his notebooks. He notes that the idea is taken from J. Hillis Miller in *Deconstruction and Criticism* (Coetzee Archives Container 33.5, Notebook MK, p. 47, 19 September 1981; p. 79, 1 August 1982). Hillis Miller underlines the fluid and reversible nature of the terms parasite and host. In the end, the inferior element in the relation between host/parasite and parasite/host is that which leads to the disintegration of the whole that has been established.

These ideas concern the so-called parasite that kills the host or the host that, in seeking some higher form of health, kills the 'parasite' that has, unbeknownst to that host, been the very thing that has allowed the kind of life it has to persist. All those that would seek to drive out the 'parasite' Michael K are in effect seeing to it that a relation, between the earth and the gardener who tends it, would come to be broken.

> K knew that he would not crawl out and stand up and cross from darkness into firelight to announce himself. He even knew the reason why: because enough men had gone off to war saying the time for gardening was when the war was over; whereas there must be men to stay behind and keep gardening alive, or at least the idea of gardening; because once that cord was broken, the earth would grow hard and forget her children. (Coetzee, *Life & Times*, 109)

In 'The Method of Dramatisation', Deleuze underlines how conflict subsists within any creative process. More than once in the notebook to *Michael K* Coetzee complains that the drafts that are emerging, while 'writing themselves', lack conflict and that there can be no drama without conflict. Following Spinoza, one strives to preserve one's nature or conatus and to do this at times it is necessary to flee or hide from powers that seek to destroy that nature, and if one is caught again it is necessary to escape again. While Coetzee does not always seem to be aware of it in the notebooks, the processes of life he describes – in which one, in a recurring frame, avoids, suffers, escapes conflict – already presuppose drama.

& times (intellect)

The kind of conflict implied in such drama can be seen in the story of flight itself, the story of the road, which unfolds like Bergson's duration, which involves the intuition or process of becoming in relation to the world that is unfolding. This in turn speaks to the second half of Coetzee's title: 'Times'. In his notebook Coetzee speaks of two 'times' that surround one: firstly, the times of politics, of events outside our control that impress themselves upon us and force us to respond to them for good or ill. Times of this kind are always determined by intellectual interpretations that result in programmes and sets of rules, political or moral orders that are established precisely to capture and control those who live at that given time, and in response there will be organized attempts to oppose those forms of capture.

Secondly, in his notebook Coetzee suggests there is an 'inner time', which is sometimes out of sync with the time of the outside world (Coetzee Archives Container 33.5, Notebook MK, p. 77, 22 December 1982). While he is probably not thinking of Spinoza, or Bergson, the concept Coetzee develops through his own intuitions accords with Bergson's concept of duration. This, in one sense, is the moment of a present lived as fully as possible, life in the process of coming into existence. Furthermore, this powerful experience of living is such that it sets itself outside the interpretations of the times enforced by the various apparatuses of capture.

If part one of *Life & Times of Micheal K* involves the logic of persisting in being through instinct, part two concerns the idea of the intellect. For Bergson, disinterested instinct (intuition) is organized thought, whereas intelligence is that capacity which allows certain animals to find or invent tools within their environment with which they might act on that environment.

As we have seen, for Bergson intelligence conceives of life as if it were lifeless (165) and therefore cannot fully comprehend reality. Instinct understands the movement of reality, but it simply acts without reflection. There is a failure of thought or the intellect set out in relation to the doctor who treats Michael K in part two in Kenilworth Racecourse. Michael K both cannot comprehend himself and cannot be comprehended, through the intellect.

Part three (imagination)

Part three returns Michael K to Cape Town and his mother's room, near to where the narrative began. The book as a whole, then, seems to involve a process of affirmative exhaustion. In his notes Coetzee remarks with surprise that he is writing a book without sex or violence. Throughout the book Michael K, as a quasi-spiritual being, a kind of holy sinner on the model of Thomas Mann, seems to refuse the normal needs of the human body. That is, he refuses, or has no interest in, sexual relations. He refuses, or has little interest in, food. He refuses, or has little interest in, human company or fellowship.

Within the Christian spiritual tradition these refusals of normal needs would equate to an effort to overcome the temptations of the flesh. In other traditions, such as Buddhism, they might be understood as moving beyond the *maya* or the false appearances of things. Yet Michael K also has a strongly material relation to the space he inhabits.

His cave is not chosen because it is the best place to keep him hidden from those who would tempt him from his spiritual path. Rather, his cave is constructed or created in order to allow him to maintain a particular relation with a particular patch of earth. It might be argued that this relationship, with this earth, is adequate to, or replaces, the other three normal needs. In part three, however, removed from the relation to the earth in the Karoo, he is given, as if through charity, all three normal needs again.

Firstly, he is given sex and does not refuse. Secondly, he is again asked to both eat and drink alcohol, and again he does not refuse. Thirdly, he is offered human company, which he does not refuse. In effect, however, none of these relations touch him essentially.

The book ends with him returning to his mother's dank windowless room in Cote D'azur, in Sea Point, Cape Town. He has not been deeply affected by the sex, food and alcohol, or company. He is affected apparently more by the scent of the previous inhabitant, another 'tramp' such as himself, who has recently occupied the space and whose blanket he now wraps himself in.

Realism involves the conflict of survival, like the conflict of the road, or the conflict of staying put. Yet the sense of meaningfulness that needs to be attached to it in order for one to have the will to continue can only be represented if this realism is impurely mixed with some symbol, some incomplete allegory, which attaches itself to the conflict or movement or rest and gives it meaning.

Forms of ethical relation: *Age of Iron*

Like *Life & Times of Michael K*, *Age of Iron* offers strong representations of an ethological ethics. In his notes to *Age of Iron*, Coetzee writes:

The question: How is one to live? The only answer must be: With decency. The complication: that decency implies living as the ancestors lived, and in this case the ancestors did not live well. So one must invent decency. (Coetzee, Container 33.6, Notebooks to Age of Iron, 28 September 1987)

In order to bring this about in this book, the idea of place needs to be somehow related to understanding. The writing process, as set out in the notebooks, indicates difficulties that concern place: the places of white South Africa and black South Africa. The place of the immediate contexts of a political conflict verging on Civil War and the equally pressing conflict brought about by the idea of death, which was at the front of Coetzee's mind due to the recent death of his mother (see Kannemeyer, 439–441; Attwell, *Life of Writing*, 161–176). The problem becomes: how might one understand the relation between politics or socio-political concerns other than through acceding to forced or prescribed views?

The letter

In considering this, questions of formal relations that are in turn character based and thematic come to the fore, and these touch upon questions of ethology or the understanding of one's disposition within one's place. Early on a formal solution to the question of relation emerges through the idea of the letter or epistle: a message that is composed in the present but reaches out to the future – that is sent from one place to another, from one situation within one disposition to another.

In effect, this mirrors the fictional process itself and it is no coincidence that, like the realism of survival that becomes necessary in *Life & Times of Michael K*, this form (the epistolary novel) is also tied to the emergence of the novel in English. It allows a bridge across from one world to another, one place to another, one disposition to another.[5]

If the letter offers a formal solution to the problem of relating ethological views, the thematic solution is the idea of the angel. In an insightful reading, Kay Sulk has written on the idea of the

---

[5]Hogarth's unpublished dissertation concerns epistolary form in *Age of Iron*.

angel in *Age of Iron*, indicating how Coetzee develops a means of speaking both within and outside historical experience by moving between symbolic figures of the witness and the angel.

The angel is the messenger that passes between the realms of the human and the divine, the living and the dead. In considering how to send messages from one disposition to a different disposition (the white and the black, the old and the young, the dying and the living), Coetzee faces the problem of remaining true, not just to the political situation in South Africa but to the integrity of the main character he imagines (Mrs Curren) as well as to the truth to his own disposition as an artist. With regard to the latter he remains committed to writing a certain kind of literary fiction addressed to imagined readers who value layered and subtle texts, texts that require the reader to develop understandings rather than offer trite solutions to intractable problems:

> She [Mrs Curren] insists on her right to think of herself and of people in her own metaphors.
>
> Have been reading interview with Joseph Brodsky. I certainly won't make anything of the current book unless I have the courage to write for that kind of reader. The pressure of so-called relevance re SA too much for me. That is to say, I am capitulating before it.
>
> The book will only work if I work on things like <u>angelhood</u>. And perhaps not even then. (Coetzee, Container 33.6, Notebooks to Age of Iron, 19 November 1988)

The central element of the character-based solution to the problem involves Mrs Curren, who exists in white South Africa but is able to visit the conditions of black South Africa and who in turn is visited by them. She is also moving towards inexistence as she slowly dies of cancer. Like *Life & Times of Michael K*, *Age of Iron* moves between a deformed realism and a deformed symbolism. The character of Vercueil is both a tramp and an angel.[6] Its realism has attracted most critical attention, and all the characters in the work can be understood purely in realist terms. This is of the body (or content or instinct). Yet they all might also

---

[6] Sulk also underlines the allegorical nature of this relation.

be understood in symbolic terms, that is, in terms of ideas (or forms of understanding or intelligence).

Ideas and symbols

In engaging with the everyday reality of the black townships Mrs Curren and Vercueil take on the form of Dante and Virgil entering hell.[7] Both are messengers, or angels, both respond to the problem of how to live well. The black characters can also be understood in symbolic terms. Florence is a kind of Greek goddess, Aphrodite. Thabane is a teacher, linked to Socrates. The boys too are messengers, passing between the two worlds. Their world is of the body because it is political, that is, they are marked by the brutality of the age and harden themselves in the face of it; they engage and so suffer for that engagement, intuitively understanding what needs to be done.[8]

The archives confirm that the title of the novel, *Age of Iron*, is taken from Virgil's Georgics.[9] The boys and their generation are primed to action, to toil, not reflection or play, but behind the action or practice is a hard ideal, the ideal of (what is necessarily indeterminate) freedom.

While all the characters might be understood both symbolically and realistically, there are also points of emphasis. That is, Mrs Curren and Vercueil are more of the spirit than the body; the boys, Florence and Thabane, are more of the material, with their ideas also being material. This accounts for the ongoing misunderstanding between the two sides and this is also reflected in the ideas of place that work throughout the novel as ethological domains.

A primary domain is Mrs Curren's home, which draws Vercueil, Florence and her children, John, and later the police. As mentioned, like Dante and Virgil entering hell, Mrs Curren and Vercueil enter the hospital, a place of dying:

---

[7]On Dante in relation to this novel see Roberts, Hoegberg.
[8]On the difficulties of representing the trauma of the Townships see Attridge 'To Speak of This'.
[9]For details of the connections between the novel and Virgil, see Dooley, 'Hades'; Shapiro, 'Reading on the Edge'.

only place for old to go is hospitals and what are they but museums of ways of dying. (Coetzee, Container 33.6, Notebooks to Age of Iron, 18 May 1988)

The townships are the second exemplar of hell. Again, like Dante, Mrs Curren is drawn into this space, though here with a new Virgil figure, Thabane, leading her. Later in the book the idea of place, linked with the process of dying, takes on new form, as Mrs Curren finds new more tenuous territories wrapped in her quilt out on the streets, lying with Vercueil in the park, and lying with him and his dog in her bed. Her body too is understood as a territory or space, both of life and death, having nourished her daughter and now housing the cancer that is killing her.

A second allusion, reimagined in the twentieth century by Rilke and Barthes, is the story of Orpheus. As well as being understood as visits to Hell, the trips to the hospital and to the township might be understood in the terms of Orpheus visiting the underworld to reclaim his lost love. The logic of Dante's trip to Hell, Purgatory, and Heaven is pedagogical: reform your life, learn to live well. The logic of Orpheus, however, is 'nostalgic'. This is a false step, wanting to reclaim what is lost, or will necessarily be lost, as one looks back in an effort to hold on to it.

Barthes interprets the Orpheus myth as about nostalgia. By looking back on what you love, you kill it. (Coetzee, Container 33.6, Notebooks to Age of Iron, 1 December 1987)

This element of nostalgia is apparent in Mrs Curren's relation to her daughter, although as the book proceeds this tendency is more and more effaced, as she comes to love those she is with rather than those who are related to her, but who through distance have become more abstract. Mrs Curren's car has the capacity to relate, to bring together, as well as itself being a territory, one that connects Vercueil and Mrs Curren, Mrs Curren and Florence, and the people of the townships. So too does the house, which moves or changes as well as standing in place . That is, it moves or changes with the times and those who come to occupy it: Vercueil, the boys and Florence, the police. So too does history, which moves like the car and in which one must live like the house.

The territory which has to be made for Mrs Curren is the territory of living well unto death or dying well. One of the sources here for Coetzee is Cicero's essay 'On Good and Bad Ends'. To end well is to live well. As touched upon above writing itself is a kind of messenger and involves the transference of ethological understanding (of disposition in place) across time and space. The key site, however, is one's own mind or body, because the body and mind are in danger of being colonized by outside forces, which might change one's disposition or relation to place.

The idea of 'ventriloquism' in *Age of Iron* relates to this fear; that one might be inhabited or overcome by discourses foreign to and even hostile to one's own soul.[10] Discourses that might claim or steal the soul. Mrs Curren thinks:

> I have intimations older than any memory, unshakable, that once upon a time I was alive. Was alive and then was stolen from life. From the cradle a theft took place: a child was taken and a doll left in its place to be nursed and reared, and that doll is what I call I. (*Age of Iron*, 109)

Those outside forces might already have stolen the soul long ago, and all that is given to one to somehow understand this is the flash of insight or intuition. An intuitive understanding like a message from the divine passed on by angels. Mrs Curren continues:

> A doll? A doll's life? Is that what I have lived? Is it given to a doll to conceive such a thought? Or does the thought come and go as another intimation, a flash of lightening, a piercing of the fog by the lance of an angel's intelligence? (*Age of Iron*, 109)

As we have seen with regard to *Life & Times of Michael K*, intelligence alone is inadequate to an understanding of life. While one must interpret, intelligence must be mixed with instinct or intuition. The truth is that which emerges as a feeling of the meaningful in being read or interpreted. So Mrs Curren needs a reader, her daughter who will receive the messages carried by the 'angel' Vercueil:

---

[10]My point of reference here is Foucault's concept of discursive formations which enable and limit what can be said (*Archaeology of Knowledge*).

> If Vercueil does not send these writings on, you will never read them. You will never even know they existed. A certain body of truth will never take on flesh: my truth: how I lived in these times, in this place. (*Age of Iron*, 130)

Interpretation is both fraught and crucial because it might be that one only has access to the lie and that the truth can only be found within or behind that lie.

> I say to myself that I am watching not the lie but the space behind the lie where the truth ought to be. But is it true? (*Age of Iron*, 30)

So too, the extraordinary struggle of those black South Africans living in the townships involves not just the fierce material struggle against apartheid but a struggle to break free of ventriloquism, to speak in their own voice. However, this requires a sacrifice that gives Mrs Curren pause, a sacrifice that she is not sure she can condone, the sacrifice of the self to the cause. That is, in order to eventually find a voice for their cause the boys must renounce their own voices, or add them to a greater voice, through their own martyrdom. This opens to the question of knowledge, of understanding, of what any individual life can understand in the face of larger events and the forces that determine one's being.

Struggle

There are several ideas of struggle in novel, but these can be drawn together into two. The first concerns the struggle of history, the struggle to overcome apartheid. The second sees writing as a space of struggle against ventriloquism (*Age of Iron*, 98, 109–111). With the overarching discourses (the force of the apartheid regime that crushes life and the resistance that, in opposing that regime, requires the sacrifice of life) that drive, infuse, and dominate life, the second struggle involves finding a way of understanding what is going on and representing that understanding. This in turn involves moving away from the directions one is given to find another direction. Mrs Curren thinks, 'A way of indirection. By indirection I find direction out. A crab's walk' (*Age of Iron*, 82).

Beyond understanding

When Coetzee wishes to explain an understanding beyond words, an understanding beyond comprehension, he makes use of the metaphor of the eyes. He does this with the sheep about to be slaughtered in *Boyhood* (*Boyhood*, 102): he sees in their eyes that they understand their fate. He also uses the metaphor of the mouth with an absent or silent tongue (as in *Foe*). The scene of Mrs Curren viewing the body of Bheki, who has been shot by soldiers, turns about the image of the eyes and the mouth that can no longer speak for itself: 'His eyes were open and staring, his mouth open too' (*Age of Iron*, 102). The horror conveys itself in turn to Mrs Curren who is given an understanding, although it is one that cannot be expressed or contained. It is a kind of understanding beyond understanding, an intuition unable to be conveyed by words, but one that is immediately felt:

> I was shaking: shivers ran up and down my body, my hands trembled. I thought of the boy's open eyes. I thought: What did he see as his last sight on earth? I thought: This is the worst thing I have witnessed in my life. And I thought: Now my eyes are open and I can never close them again. (*Age of Iron*, 102–103)

Just as she does not understand the weight of the horror that awaits those who confront and resist apartheid, she does not understand how the white boys who defend the regime with violence do what they do, 'You are all too young for this. It sickens me' (107). She asks their captain:

> 'Why don't you just put down your guns and go home, all of you?' I said. 'Because surely nothing can be worse than what you are doing here. Worse for your souls, I mean'. (*Age of Iron*, 107)

Yet the captain she addresses claims an understanding, an understanding also linked to eyes, through a metaphor of sight, but this time the metaphor implies a resignation, a going through the motions.

7

Disposition and Method:
The Master of Petersburg

The Master of Petersburg deals with the potentials of fiction and in particular its ethical potentials. In doing this it deals with the ideas of situation and disposition which are both linked to the idea of the writer. Just as with *Waiting for the Barbarians* and *Foe*, the consistency of situations and dispositions allows a thinking across or between historical periods. If *Waiting for the Barbarians* is linked to apartheid South Africa in part through an indeterminate place and time on an imaginary borderlands of an empire under threat, *The Master of Petersburg* is linked to contemporary concerns through an exploration of the function and role of the writer – the nature of the writer's disposition.

Here the question of limit emerges as a fundamental ethical question. Limits to human conduct emerge from relations of disposition, socio-political situation, and time and place. There are limits to what one can do (in terms of what is good for you and bad for you rather than as universal moral rules) and there are limits to what one should do. *The Master of Petersburg* focuses on the problem of limits by considering the question of excess, which is related to the disposition of the male subject, the father as subject position, and to the disposition of 'the writer'.

This chapter develops a reading of Coetzee's novel *The Master of Petersburg* (1994) alongside ideas that Coetzee examines in *Giving Offense: Essays on Censorship*, which was published in 1996 by Chicago University Press, the year he began teaching as a visiting professor at the Committee of Social Thought at Chicago. That elements of these two books might be related can be inferred from the overlap involved in the writing process of each (the first essay in *Giving Offense* appeared in print in 1988 and Coetzee worked on essays related to the book from then until 1996). *The Master of Petersburg* appeared after *Age of Iron* (1990) and was followed by *Disgrace* in 1999. It might be paired with *Foe*, which appeared in 1986, as a novel that explicitly engages with the work of another novelist: Daniel Defoe in *Foe* and Dostoevsky in *The Master of Petersburg*. This chapter considers how an understanding of excess that involves thinking outside of or beyond reason can be witnessed in both of these books. Excess will further be linked to related ideas of 'offence' and 'refraction' or 'perversion': each of these terms involves elements of 'going beyond' – an already given perspective in order to generate new meanings and new understandings of the 'true'. These processes are revealed through a comparison of themes developed by Dostoevsky in 'At Tikhon's', a chapter that was censored from the original published version of his novel *Demons* (see Dostoevsky, *Demons*, 749–787), because it was considered perverse, offensive, and excessive, and *The Master of Petersburg*, which enters into dialogue with it. Such excess provokes a questioning of disposition, the ethos of what it means to be a writer, and what is at stake for the writer in creating territories that might be shared.

Techniques of intertextuality: Error

As has been underlined by earlier critics and reviewers *The Master of Petersburg* involves a pairing of Coetzee's work with Dostoevsky's novel *Demons* (which was published in earlier translations as *The Possessed*, *The Devils*) and the historical events related to the perversely violent Russian revolutionary Sergei Nechaev and the murder of his student follower Ivanov in 1869 (see Adelman; Attridge, *Ethics of Reading*; Kossew, 'Anxiety'; Lawlan; Popescu; Scanlan; Hayes). In order to first get our bearings, it is necessary to establish the terms of relation between Dostoevsky's novel and Coetzee's novel, and the conceptual ideas, outlined in *Giving Offense*, that offer insight into the kind of thinking through distortion and excess that Coetzee achieves in *The Master of Petersburg*. The main outlines of this relationship have now been well summarized by J. C. Kannemeyer and David Attwell, who set out most of the differences that I will recite again below. Kannemeyer also details the controversies that surrounded the reception of Coetzee's novel, as reviewers including Dostoevsky's biographer Joseph Frank lined up to heavily criticize what they perceived as his distortion of the facts, which were considered arbitrary falsifications (Skow; Frank, 'The Rebel'), while others, including the distinguished critic James Wood, seemed to take offence at the manner in which the novel deals with Dostoevsky and his legacy, by unfavourably comparing Coetzee with Dostoevsky. One critic, Zinovy Zinik, even goes so far as to denounce the work as 'an act of literary terrorism' (for an overview, see Kannemeyer, 461).[1]

Elements of Coetzee's novel enter into dialogue with Dostoevsky's *Demons* and elements refer to historical events that concern Sergei Nechaev and his circle. Other elements, however, clearly diverge from both Dostoevsky's novel and actual events. Coetzee's story imagines Dostoevsky returning in secret from financial exile in Dresden, where he was living with his young wife Anaya Snitkina, in order to bury his only son Pavel (who was in fact a stepson, adopted by Dostoevsky when he married his first wife Marya Isayeva in 1857). In Coetzee's novel Pavel has been living under the name of his biological father Isaev, and Dostoevsky at first travels using Isaev's papers to hide from his creditors who might have him detained should they become aware of his presence in the city. Pavel, in Coetzee's story, has died mysteriously after a fall from a shot tower. He may have committed suicide, as the police maintain; he may have been murdered by the authorities because of his connections to Sergei Nechaev's circle, as Sergei Nechaev maintains when he meets Dostoevsky, or he might well have been, as comes to seem increasingly likely, and as Dostoevsky comes to contend, murdered by Sergei Nechaev to further his revolutionary plans which involve setting a trap for Dostoevsky and using his name on a pamphlet in order to foment unrest. Dostoevsky, in mourning Pavel, comes to occupy his rooms, wear his clothes, and form a perverse family with Pavel's landlady Anna and her daughter Matryosha. He mourns Pavel excessively before becoming caught up in a police case involving Nechaev who is wanted generally for

---

[1] For a reading of how Coetzee deconstructs an idea of Dostoevsky, see Reichmann.

his subversive views, but particularly for the recent murder of a vagabond working as a police spy, called Ivanov.

Crucial elements of this story differ markedly from the known facts. Dostoevsky did indeed have a stepson named Pavel, and elements of their real relationship match those described by Coetzee; yet, Pavel did not die until 1900 and there is no record of Dostoevsky attempting to enter St Petersburg in 1869. J. M. Coetzee also had a son, however, named Nicolas, who, aged 23, died mysteriously from a fall from a high balcony in 1989. Kannemeyer, Hayes, and Attwell discuss the relationship between these tragic events and the composition of *The Master of Petersburg* and demonstrate convincingly how the novel might be read, in part, as a meditation on loss, meaning, and the relationship between the father and the son (Kannemeyer, 422–470).

The book, then, is surrounded by controversy and fraught relationships. Therefore, it is important to step back and consider what is essential to the relations that are drawn between *The Master of Petersburg* and Dostoevsky's *Demons*. The major point of connection between Dostoevsky's novel *Demons* and Coetzee's *The Master of Petersburg*, which is only touched upon briefly by Kannemeyer who then turns to other questions (Kannemeyer, 460), relates to the daughter of the landlady with whom Dostoevsky stays while occupying Pavel's old room. Adelman, Kossew ('Anxiety'), Scanlan, Lawlan, and Attridge (*Ethics of Reading*) also discuss the nature of these relations but focus on different elements to those I will consider here, and do not link these to the ideas Coetzee develops in *Giving Offense*. Her name is Matryosha and she appears in a chapter that was suppressed from the published editions of *Demons* until it was rediscovered among Dostoevsky's papers in 1921. This excised chapter known as 'At Tikhon's' or 'Stavrogin's Confession' is now published as an appendix to most editions of *Demons*. It was felt to be crucial to the novel by Dostoevsky as it sets out important information that in part helps to explain the perverse psychological disposition of the character Stavrogin, who, for Dostoevsky, offers an example of the dissolute Byronic hero. Stavrogin is one of two characters in *Demons* (the other being Stepan Trofimovich Verkhovensky) who is based upon the real-life figure Sergei Nechaev, although Stavrogin also differs in important ways from Sergei Nechaev.

In Dostoevsky's censored chapter Stavrogin travels to a monastery to confess to a monk named Tikhon. During the course of this interview, where the priest and the dissolute atheist spar over their philosophical understanding of the world, Stavrogin presents Tikhon with a pamphlet (of which he has made 300 copies for distribution at a later date) confessing to his seduction of a young girl Matryosha, which results in her subsequent suicide, who is first spoken of as being 14 (*Demons*, 762) and then described as being 10 years old (*Demons*, 776). The theme of the rape of innocence by depraved heterosexual male sexuality pervades *The Master of Petersburg* where it is foreshadowed on a number of occasions before being explicitly tied to an idea of Matryosha developed by Coetzee's character Dostoevsky. Coetzee's Dostoevsky begins to write a text that is related to the character of Stavrogin who is conflated with Pavel and Nechaev in Coetzee's novel. While the idea of the seduction and perversion of the very young Matryosha connects with *Demons,* the text Coetzee attributes to his Dostoevsky in the chapter called 'Stavrogin' in *The Master of Petersburg* is Coetzee's own and does not relate to any specific text in the surviving draft of Dostoevsky's suppressed chapter 'At Tikhon's'.

Foe and the method of distortion

A similar deliberate distortion of intertextual relations is apparent in *Foe*, which Coetzee published in 1986, several years before *The Master of Petersburg. Foe*, indeed, draws attention to how distortion and appropriation lie at the heart of literary thinking. Yet paradoxically it also shows how such crooked or crab-wise thinking has the potential to address problems which might not otherwise be addressed. Such distortion can be related both to the method of A against B and the resonances achieved through these asymmetrical relations – resonances that build into refrains that connect territories. In *Foe* these problems relate to relations of difference: differences of race and gender.

As we relate Coetzee's novel *Foe* both to the novel *Robinson Crusoe* and to the life of its author, Daniel Defoe, we become aware of points of connection, but we also notice points of rupture, confusion, or discontinuity. Coetzee's 'Foe' is like the Daniel Foe of history who changes his name, through vanity perhaps, to Daniel Defoe (Novak, 116), but does not resemble him in other ways: there is a confusion, for example, of chronology. Coetzee's character Foe is working for an extended time on Susan Barton's story and seems already to have imagined or published other works such as *Memoirs of a Cavalier* (1720), *Captain Singleton* (1720), even *An Essay on the History and Reality of Apparitions* (1727), works which we know were written after, even, in the latter case, long after *Robinson Crusoe* appeared in 1719.

Unlike Defoe, whose wife stoically suffered his absence for many years while raising their children alone (Novak, 313), Foe's wife, we are told, is dead (though Susan Barton may simply have been misled on this point). There are many other points of nonrelation between Defoe's work and Susan Barton's story, in particular with regard to the story of the island and Crusoe and Friday.

Foe, then, encourages us to draw incomplete, unsustainable, conclusions. For Coetzee's Susan Barton the true and real are linked through the material body and the images which impress themselves on the body (Coetzee, *Foe*, 18). Yet we are reminded that 'realism', at its very core, is based on deception. *Foe* demonstrates how the territories that come to comprise the real are both generated through and undermined by stories.

The method of deception in *Foe* and Defoe

Daniel Defoe was himself a master of deception, a 'master of fictions' as his biographer Maximilliam Novak has it. Critics, such as Novak and Richetti, have argued that the role playing he undertook in life (the shifting of positions and adoption of personas) would have helped him, perversely, to develop into a successful writer of fiction. He was already able to imagine himself in someone else's shoes. He worked as a spy for the English government against the Scottish, and in performing his duties he wrote political pamphlets making use of personas, such as a 'Quaker gentleman'. He would disguise his handwriting because handwriting could be used as evidence to establish authorship. He would argue different sides of an argument under different pseudonyms in pamphlets he was asked to write by his patrons the chief ministers of the English Parliament, Harley and Godolphin, and even to promote that side of the argument which he himself believed in least in order to foster a given set of political interests (see Novak, 338–359, 464–482).

In his own defence Defoe argued that the times he lived in required these kinds of strategies. Justified deceit was the best means of both surviving and making a useful difference, and indeed it was the best way of governing, as people by their nature are unruly and irrational. 'An age of Mysteries and Paradoxes' he called his times on one occasion; on another in a private letter, he stated: 'This, Sir, is an Age of Plot and Deceit, of Contradiction and Paradox. It is very hard, under all these Masks, to see the true Countenance of any Man' (Novak, 356).

The most interesting defence Defoe makes of himself and by extension, the disposition of the writer of fiction, comes in a document offering advice to the Secretary of State Robert Harley, written in 1704 called 'Maxims and Instructions for Ministers of State'. Here he offers advice on the use of spies abroad to promote the national interest. As for how to rule at home, he suggests that this should be accomplished through justifiable deceit (Novak, 234). He writes:

Tho' this Part of conduct is Call'd Dissumulation, I am Content it shall be Call'd what They will, But as Lye Does Not Consist in the Indirect Positioning of words, but in the Design by False Speaking, to Deciev and Injure my Neighbour, So dissembling does Not Consist in putting a Different Face Upon Our Actions, but in the further Applying That Concealment to the Prejudice of the Person; for Example, I Come into a persons Chamber, who on a Surprise is Apt to Fall into Dangerous Convulsions. I Come in Smileing, and Pleasant, and ask the person to Rise and Go abroad, or any Other Such question, and Press him to it Till I Prevail, whereas the Truth is I have Discovred the house to be On Fire, and I Act thus for fear of frighting him. Will any man Tax me with Hypocrisye and Dissimulation. (cited in Novak, 235, variant spellings in original)

This argument, based on the truth of the intention rather than the statement, is justified along the lines that the ends justify the means. Yet does the analogy hold for literature? What possible good could we be led towards in being faced with deception in art, with the deceptions indeed that comprise art? In Coetzee's short introduction to *Robinson Crusoe* he asks how we are supposed to read the patent lie made in several prefaces by Defoe that Crusoe is a real person and the author of the tales. Coetzee concludes that what we see at certain moments is the character of the castaway merging with author who fashions that character: we get a true glimpse of a real man, then, a particular man, through the false image of his double (Coetzee, *Stranger Shores*, 21).

In *Despair* Vladimir Nabokov explains how the reflected mirror image corrects the original mirror image. The first mirror image shows us the world back to front: my reflection is left handed while I am right handed. Through the reflection of the reflection, however, it is possible to see the true image of the self (where I am returned to right handedness). In just this way we are able to understand the true nature of a self-deceptive character (such as Hermann's in *Despair*) through the various deceptions he attempts.

Techniques of refraction and perversion

The Master of Petersburg, among other things, is a meditation on the nature of the writing process.[2] The dialogue with Dostoevsky underlines how, for Coetzee, this necessarily involves processes of refraction, as primary materials (borrowed from real life or other fictions) are deliberately distorted and composed to generate new meaning. That is, refraction involves creating new meanings that exceed or go beyond those meanings apparent in the intertexts one refracts.

Coetzee forcefully ties refraction to the idea of perversion, while for Dostoevsky perversion through possession, or leading astray, is a major theme of his novel. Part of what *The Master of Petersburg* offers is an excoriation of the writing process, an excoriation of what it means to write, to be a writer: in this novel the writer is understood to be the one who perverts. Perversion too involves a kind of excess, a going beyond what is expected or allowed in order to open new spaces for interpretation. It might be distinguished

---

[2]For further consideration of this idea, see Watson, Reichmann.

from simple refraction, however, as the kind of excess it involves is confronting and likely to offend received opinion. The same is true of the other targets of excoriation in this novel: the figure of the father and his relation to the son, the daughter, and the mother; and the figure of male heterosexual desire (echoed in desire more generally).

Refraction is a kind of doubling that involves the distortions that occur when something passes from one medium (an event 'A' or a representation 'A') to another (representation 'B'). The simple idea I wish to establish here with regard to the method of composition adopted by both Coetzee and Dostoevsky in these works is that both take historical events and refract them in representing them as fictions. Speaking in an interview in which he defends his own methods in *The Master of Petersburg*, Coetzee underlines how Dostoevsky also distorts historical facts in order to present a sharper truth:

> In *The Possessed* the names of the personages are not historical names and the identities are not historical identities. Yet no one is going to say that *The Possessed* is not about the Russia of 1870. (Joanna Scott interview with Coetzee, cited in Kannemeyer, 463)

This idea of refraction is linked to perversion by both Coetzee and Dostoevsky, though in different ways. Etymologically the word 'perverse' is drawn from the Latin pervertire: 'through' (per) 'turning' (vertire). The word 'perversion', of course, does not have neutral connotations: it has a bad taste that carries the idea of corruption. This idea of corruption further brings with it an understanding of how influence or perverting the other (especially the very young or innocent) involves training or 'creating a taste' (as it is described in *The Master of Petersburg*, 244) or even possession. How ideologies or stories can infect and corrupt people and in particular the young is a key theme of Dostoevsky's novel, which uses the image of demon possession to express these ideas and is in turn addressed by Coetzee (though Coetzee widens the critique to include the writer within the potentially corrupting field).

Dostoevsky draws upon events related to the Nechaev affair in 1869 in which the young revolutionary was implicated in the murder of a student Ivanov, for no other reason than to display the seriousness of his own revolutionary project. Nechaev is thought to be the author of a deeply cynical handbook *Catechism of a Revolution*, which considers other people as objects that might be legitimately manipulated, used, and disposed of to serve the revolution. The revolution itself, for Nechaev, has no end other than the destruction of the current system. Dostoevsky takes these incidents as a background in *Demons,* which he develops as a novel of three parts involving a number of characters based on people associated with this affair either directly or, in Dostoevsky's view, indirectly. For example, Nechaev and Ivanov form the basis of characters, but so too do radicals of the previous generation with whom Dostoevsky had associated in the 1840s in the Petrashevsky circle: in particular the novelist Turgenev and the Hegelian Professor of History Timofey Granovsky. Dostoevsky does not follow the Nechaev affair to the letter, however; rather, he weaves together his understanding of the strands of Russian life that, in his view, have brought Nechaev into existence (see Frank, *Dostoevsky*; Frank, 'Nihilism'; Belknap).

Dostoevsky's *Notes from Underground* famously begins with an Author's note:

> The author of these notes and the *Notes* themselves are, of course, fictitious. Nevertheless, such people as the writer of these notes not only can but even must exist in our society – taking into consideration those circumstances in which our society was formed. (*Notes from Underground*, 3)

So too, in unsuccessfully pleading with Mikhail Katkov, the editor of the *Russian Herald* (in which the novel first appeared in serial form), to include the chapter 'At Tikhon's' despite the obscenity involved in Stavrogin's seduction of the innocent Matryosha, Dostoevsky asserts:

> I swear to you that I could not omit the essence of the matter; this is a whole social type ... a Russian, a person ... who has lost everything native and most importantly faith; a degenerate *out of ennui* ... Along with the nihilists this is a serious phenomenon. (*Demons*, 749)

Dostoevsky, then, dramatizes at once elements of the forces that possess his characters and bring them into being, and the consequences of this mode of being on their conduct. Here it is simply necessary to note the outlines of the method, which refracts real events through the medium of Dostoevsky's dramatic framework (which draws its power in part through overstatement and melodrama) and his understanding of Russian society, the psychology of nihilist revolutionaries, and human psychology generally (see Belknap; Frank *Dostoevsky*). This in turn generates a perversion from an ideal. For Stavrogin, the Europeanized Russian who has descended into Byronic decadence and ennui, that ideal is of the world portrayed in a painting by Claude Lorrain, which he has seen in the Dresden Gallery, called 'Acis and Galatea' but which he has thought of as being called 'The Golden Age' (*Demons*, 775–776). He dreams of this painting, the Greek archipelago and the earthly paradise filled with beautiful innocent children. In the myth, this idyll is about to be destroyed by the Cyclops Polyphemus who murders Acis after which Galatea expresses her love for Acis by turning his blood into a river. Yet in Stavrogin's description the painting is an image of lost innocence (*Demons*, 775–776). As we see it features an ideal nuclear family. Stavrogin's dream of innocence is followed by a real vision of the outraged innocent Matryosha prior to her committing suicide 'standing right in the doorway, with her tiny fist raised' (*Demons*, 776).

Coetzee, in turn, develops a compositional method that works through refraction of source material in *The Master of Petersburg*: he distorts events related to the Nechaev affair (adding Pavel to the mix and altering the role of Ivanov among many other inventions) and Dostoevsky's involvement in it. He also draws upon Dostoevsky's dramatic method (staging melodramatic scenes that give something of the flavour of Dostoevsky's compositions); he further draws in and distorts the tragedy of his own son Nicholas's death from a fall, which is echoed by Pavel's fall from the shot tower. Finally, in the last chapter 'Stavrogin', Coetzee distorts Dostoevsky's process of composition in reimagining his relations to the young girl Matryosha.

While Dostoevsky refracts events in order to reflect them back in more comprehensible form for his original Russian audience, Coetzee outrages and perverts the materials he takes from Dostoevsky, transforming him into a particular disposition, a figure of the writer, of the father, of male heterosexuality, that is subject to ferocious critique. Yet rather than a character or characters being that which gives offence (as is the case with Dostoevsky's work, which caused Mikhail Katkov to censor the chapter 'At Tikhon's'), in Coetzee's novel it is the writer who outrages and the work that draws offensive material to the surface.

Techniques of offence

Much of what has been said so far has been possessed by the language of offence: 'perverting', 'outraging innocence'. It is important to step back and consider the insights Coetzee offers into these terms in his essays in *Giving Offense*, because these essays complicate these ideas in important ways and allow us to better understand the complex nature of Coetzee's novel and its critique of the fabrications among which we live, and its understanding of how forms of fictional excess might allow us to glimpse otherwise hidden truths.

With regard to the idea of innocence and children Coetzee states:

> Innocence is a state in which we try and maintain our children; dignity is a state we claim for ourselves. Affronts to the innocence of our children or to the dignity of our persons are attacks not upon our essential being but upon constructs – constructs by which we live, but constructs nevertheless. This is not to say that affronts to innocence or dignity are not real affronts, or that the outrage with which we respond to them is not real, in the sense of not being sincerely felt. The infringements are real; what is infringed, however, is not our essence but a foundational fiction to which we more or less wholeheartedly subscribe, a fiction that may well be indispensable for a just society, namely, that human beings have a dignity that sets them apart from animals and consequently protects them from being treated like animals. (It is even possible that we may look forward to a day when animals will have their own dignity ascribed to them, and the ban will be reformulated as a ban on treating a living creature like a thing.) (*Giving Offense*, 14)

In *Giving Offense* Coetzee defines 'offence' being taken by the powerless who are named by those in power: the offence is taken at the powerlessness that is implied by the powerful figure describing you in terms that disparage you (1–3). Yet he is also interested in the offence that is taken by those in power. He notes that 'the power of the powerful to defend themselves against representations of themselves is surprisingly limited' (6); they are particularly susceptible to representations which imitate them with mockery.

The focus shifts from questions of what offence is and how we might avoid giving it, or how we might positively respond to it to those questions the taking of offence asks us about ourselves and the truth of our lives. That is, Coetzee suggests that how we take offence may be false in fundamental ways – that it is based on fictions of ourselves and our social norms. While these sustain us, he suggests that they are nevertheless acted out. Coetzee does not ask us to abandon these stories, which would be impossible, and he suggests that incautious shifts in the stories we tell about ourselves and our societies can be dangerous. Rather, he shifts the question, which now becomes: how are we to protect ourselves from falsity? Or more precisely, how are we to speak the truth about ourselves, which will, very likely, cause offence?

In short, fictions are important but we need to recognize their nature and hold to the stories on which they are based with a flexible grip. Following on from the passage cited above, Coetzee states:

> The fiction of dignity helps to define humanity and the status of humanity helps to define human rights. There is thus a real sense in which an affront to our dignity strikes at our rights. Yet when, outraged at such affront, we stand on our rights and demand redress, we would do well to remember how insubstantial the dignity is on which those rights are based. Forgetting where our dignity comes from, we may fall into a posture as comical as that of the irate censor. (*Giving Offense*, 14)

The notion of the comic and of playing roles that Coetzee alludes to here is drawn from his reading of the sixteenth-century Dutch thinker Desiderius Erasmus' work on humour and madness in *The Praise of Folly*, which is at the heart of the understanding of both offence and the possibility of speaking the truth that Coetzee develops in *Giving Offense*. The idea of folly links the notion of what the writer is and does to the idea of writing as a way of avoiding a fixed position, and so speaking the truth from a non-position. Coetzee's essay on Erasmus in *Giving Offense*, 'Erasmus: Rivalry and Folly', draws ideas from Foucault, Lacan, and René Girard into a reading of Erasmus' position. At the centre of Erasmus' book is the already well-established figure of the fool, 'who claims license to criticize all and sundry without reprisal, since his madness defines him as not fully a person and therefore not a political being with political desires and ambitions' (84). Because of this the fool is able to work between fixed or rival positions (political or otherwise) without choosing any side. That is, the fool exceeds the boundaries of these positions. The fool avoids censure because the madness of the discourse produced is ungrounded. The fool does not claim the ground of reason; yet, paradoxically, because of this the fool can, and often is the only one who can, speak the truth.

The arguments have important implications for Coetzee's understanding of fictional practice. In developing a reading of Foucault, he turns to Derrida's critique of Foucault's *The History of Madness* (Derrida, 36–76) underlining Derrida's suggestion that one cannot enter the discourse of madness through the discourse of reason as Foucault attempts to, or rather, that any such attempt must be 'fictional'. In Derrida's reading, to which Foucault responds in 1972 (550–574), thought is identified with reason and madness is conceived of as existing outside of 'thought'. The turn that interests Coetzee involves the move, which then places fiction alongside madness, outside of the thought of reason. Coetzee cites Shoshana Felman who has written at length about this debate:

> To state, as does Foucault, that the mad subject cannot situate himself within his fiction, that, *inside* literature, he knows no longer *where* he is, is to imply, indeed that fiction may not exactly be located '*inside of* thought,' that literature cannot be properly enclosed *within* philosophy, present, that is, to itself and at the same time present *to* philosophy: that the fiction is not always where we think, or where it thinks it is. (Felman, *Writing and Madness*, 50 cited in Coetzee, *Giving Offense*, 81)

From here Coetzee moves to the question of the kind of knowledge that is possible from a position that exceeds boundaries, a position that does not know itself (88). This is in contrast to the Apollonian instruction 'Know Thyself' that Coetzee points to elsewhere in his book as being of central importance to the figure of the sometimes overly serious liberal humanist intellectual (4). Coetzee further develops this idea in drawing upon Felman's reading of Lacan which understands the knowledge of writing as being a '*knowledge that escapes* the subject but through which the subject is precisely constituted as the one who *knows how to escape* – by means of signifiers – his own self presence' (Felman, 132, cited in Coetzee, 89).

Powers of fiction

Having developed a reading of Girard to consider the concept of rivalry as that which emerges through mimetic desire, Coetzee turns to a closer analysis of Erasmus on folly, who he sees as developing, in ways that remain important and original, a clear-sighted understanding of the manner in which there can be a truth spoken outside of reason, a truth spoken through fiction. Erasmus, he states, talks of two kinds of madness, the first, which is unreasonable, but which nevertheless emerges from within reason, is akin to fury or anger and 'manifests itself in bloodlust, greed, illicit passion' (93). A second kind, linked to the wisdom of the fool or simpleton who speaks the truth others cannot speak, is however very different and develops its own counter-authority. This authority comes from 'veracity'. What is different about this discourse is not its substance. The truth is the truth and can also be spoken (though with much greater danger to one's person) from within reason. It is not the substance of the truth that differs, then, but 'where it comes from': that is, it comes from 'the mouth of the subject assumed *not* to know and speak the truth' (94). That is, it is spoken by one who claims to be outside reason, who claims to be not serious.

For Coetzee, in his reading of Erasmus, Foucault, Derrida, and Girard, it is this aspect of fiction that gives it its power: a power to speak from no position or to exceed the boundaries of any given position. The one who speaks, then, becomes elusive and the fictional narrative voice cannot be simply identified with an author. In *The Master of Petersburg*, Coetzee pictures his figure of the writer, the non-Cartesian, Dostoevsky reflecting without clear purpose, stating, 'He cannot think, *therefore what*?' (Coetzee, *Petersburg*, 236). This voice from nowhere is precisely what gives fiction its critical power, and it is the potentials of this element of the writing process that Coetzee develops to an extremely high degree. Furthermore, it works without understanding itself. Erasmus' narrator and figure of the fool Moria claims to say just 'what pops into' her head.

In his essay on Erasmus, Coetzee states:

> Madness of the second type, then, is a kind of *ek-stasis*, a being outside oneself, a state in which truth is known (and spoken) from a position that does not know itself to be a position of truth [....] Such speech, in which the linear propulsive force of reason gives way to the unpredictable metamorphosis of figure into figure, yields a bliss [...] laughter, an anarchic convulsion of the body that marks the defeat of the defenses of the censor. (*Giving Offense*, 95)

Yet if fiction is related to truths that it is difficult to speak, there is a further paradoxical relation, which moves fiction away from a too pure, too destructive truth, to an understanding of the necessity of fictions within real life. That is, fiction affirms a level of playing along, of taking a part, or playing roles, and understands that this is necessary to society at a foundational level. Underlining these ideas, which he draws from Erasmus, Coetzee states: 'Without social fictions there is no society. It is madness of the first – not second – kind to *seriously* try to destroy these fictions' (98). Turning to Ernesto Grassi's reading of this passage from Erasmus, Coetzee affirms that to try and destroy the fictions on which the spectacle of the world is built, to try to destroy the spectacle itself, would be 'pure insanity' (99). That is, at a certain level it is necessary to be willing to be deceived. Coetzee cites Grassi:

> The wish not to be deceived any more destroys life [....] we can affirm folly as Erasmus did as *ratio vivendi* out of the recognition that otherwise life ... would have not meaning. (*Giving Offense*, 99)

Meaning, then, aligns itself with fiction, with the fictions necessary to supporting the spectacle that gives meaning, without which there would be no meaning. This is something that balances the idea we have already considered in detail, that there is truth in fiction. The fool, then, the writer, has a double role: on the one hand, she (Erasmus' fool Moria is a woman, and Erasmus sees women as having a privileged relation to the process of speaking from outside authorized discourse, 97) can speak the truth that is not able to be spoken from within reason, and, on the other hand, she affirms those fictions that are necessary to the generation of meaning.

The Master of Petersburg, which focuses on the writing process and the role of the writer (or at least a writer like Dostoevsky) in this process, offers a structure, which, using this clichéd figure for formal purposes, equates the Writer (as creator) with God. The Writer, here, is the one who creates the world, and this is part of what gives offence as we are tempted to hold the writer responsible for what happens. Yet for Coetzee there is no need to seriously believe in the existence of either the God or the Writer; rather, they become the figure (story element) of God and the figure (story element) of the Writer. As we have seen in the reading of his essay on Erasmus, it is fictions that underwrite our sense of meaning, but this sense of meaning is nevertheless real and important. That is, the question of the structure of the real in relation to its representation is doubled or reflected and refracted by Coetzee. So, the question becomes not, 'what is the real', but 'what is realism' (see Coetzee, 'What is Realism', which is reformulated as the first chapter of *Elizabeth Costello*). We have, then, an analogical structure in Coetzee that reflects this understanding of 'the real' of meaning: much of his art is built upon representations of representations. Yet this does not involve a process of reduction to simple imitation: the representations are that through which one creates, through which one lives and understands in what he considers a thinking outside rational thought.

The method of sacrifice

There is a second logic that links God to meaning in Coetzee's Dostoevsky. If God cannot be drawn out through a wager, through an outrage or dare, perhaps sacrifice can affirm meaning: the Son of God might stand in place of God as that which affirms the meaningful. Martyrdom or sacrifice might be understood as involving a process of foundation. Coetzee's Nechaev sacrifices Pavel (*Petersburg*, 181) to affirm the idea of his revolution, because 'if you do not kill you are not taken seriously' (*Petersburg*, 195). Christian martyrs sacrifice the self to affirm or legitimate an idea, which, in part, involves an imitation of Christ. Nechaev sees himself as a kind of Christ. So too, in sacrificing himself for his art, Coetzee's Dostoevsky might well see himself as a Christ. Yet for Coetzee it becomes apparent that a particular kind of sacrifice is required in order to be a writer: the sacrifice not of Christ, but of Judas, who betrays so that Christ (or the idea of the truth) might be revealed. The betrayal destroys the one who betrays because it gives offence and draws condemnation. Yet paradoxically, in drawing offence down on his head the writer is able to bring ideas into focus that might lead us to truths.

Giving offence: Provocation

In *Strong Opinions* Vladimir Nabokov often appears to be deliberately outrageous or controversial. His colourful and comically furious dismissal of Dostoevsky, among other canonical writers, offers examples of this outrageousness (*Strong Opinions*, 146). Nabokov, however, with *Lolita*, a novel about pedophilia, somehow failed to outrage or avoided outrage. While he had initial trouble finding a publisher for the work, once it was in print it became a best seller and remains in terms of simple sales figures one of the most successful works of literary art in the twentieth century (Boyd, 288–392). So too, rarely does one put down the book in horror, or recoil from its contents: Humbert Humbert is thought of with affection by many readers.

Dostoevsky caused offence, both in his life and through his works, and unlike Nabokov, his portrayal of pedophilia – 'At Tikhon's' or 'Stavrogin's confession' – was censored or self-censored. Coetzee's character 'JC' in the 'Strong Opinions' section of *Diary of a Bad Year* and other of Coetzee's characters and works throughout his career, like *Disgrace* and not least those events described in *The Master of Petersburg*, however, have seemed to provoke strong reactions which are best characterized as offence. The provocation of giving offence, indeed, seems a deliberate technique.

There are many possible examples of offensiveness in *The Master of Petersburg*, but the central idea, which both structures the novel in its relationship to Dostoevsky and opens the way to the main themes in the book, is the idea of the sexual abuse of the young girl Matryosha. In 'At Tikhon's', prompted by Stavrogin (whose own suicide was originally intended to echo that of Matryosha in *Demons,* but had to stand alone with the censorship of that episode; see Frank, *Dostoevsky,* 664–667; Belknap, xxii; *Demons,* 749), the priest Tikhon concedes that the crime Stavrogin has committed in seducing the child Matryosha is the most dreadful crime possible.

As part of the interrogation and accusation against the figure of the writer that Dostoevsky represents in *The Master of Petersburg*, a police officer asks Dostoevsky whether there is 'anything indecent' in what he writes:

Nothing indecent? He ponders. 'Nothing that could offend a child,' he responds at last.

'Good.'

'But the heart has its dark places,' he adds reluctantly. 'One does not always know.'

For the first time the man raises his eyes from his papers. 'What do you mean by that?' He is younger than Maximov. Maximov's assistant?

'Nothing. Nothing'. (*Petersburg,* 144–145)

At the end of the book Coetzee's Dostoevsky is overcome by the heat of inspiration; it is a heat that welds together the idea of Stavrogin with the idea of the nihilist Nechaev and the idea of his son Pavel, around the imagined perverse seduction of the child Matryosha. Possessed by this creative demon he remembers this moment again:

He remembers Maximov's assistant and the question he asked: 'What kind of book do you write?' He knows now the answer he should have given: 'I write perversions of the truth. I choose a crooked road and take children into dark places. I follow the dance of the pen'. (*Petersburg,* 236)

The seduction of Matryosha is prefigured a number of times, both in sexualized glances that pass between the girl and Dostoevsky and in events recounted that occur around Dostoevsky, such as the memory of having seen child prostitutes and that of a man he met while in prison in Siberia who had raped and murdered his own daughter, in *The Master of Petersburg* (13, 28, 76, 134, 149, 183, 232).

Nevertheless, the seduction or perversion of Matryosha is not something Coetzee's Dostoevsky witnesses within the novel; rather, he deduces that it must happen or must have happened as the character displayed by Nechaev and those around him attest to its necessity. In effect, then, the actual seduction of Matryosha in *The Master of Petersburg* that implicates the refracted or perverted image of Dostoevsky's own son (which is an image that in turn refracts or perverts the image of Coetzee's own son) is a matter of fiction. Coetzee's Dostoevsky writes of a figure, like that of his own son Pavel, making love to a woman his own age while knowingly allowing a child to watch as a deliberate strategy of perversion, in order to 'create a taste' in the child (Coetzee, *Petersburg*, 244). Yet why?

Coetzee's Dostoevsky, within the text Coetzee has him write, offers two answers on behalf of his character 'Stavrogin'. The first relates to Nechaev and the (anti)-logic of Nechaev (a kind of madness of the first type as described by Coetzee in his essay on Erasmus): 'History is coming to an end ... all things are permitted. He does not believe his answer particularly, does not disbelieve it. It serves' (*Petersburg*, 244). He has a second explanation, however: 'It is the fault of the Petersburg summer – these long, hot, stuffy afternoons with flies buzzing against the windowpanes' (*Petersburg*, 244). Yet these are only Stavrogin's explanations and are very similar to those offered by Dostoevsky's (as opposed to Coetzee's Dostoevsky's) Stavrogin (*Demons*, 749–787). Coetzee's Dostoevsky, however, offers another explanation, one that explains why all this might be written. That is, in order to reveal God and so create genuine meaning,

> it is an assault upon the innocence of a child. It is an act for which he can expect no forgiveness. With it he has crossed the threshold. Now God must speak, now God dare no longer remain silent. To corrupt a child is to force God. The device he has made arches and springs shut like a trap, a trap to catch God. (*Petersburg*, 249)

Writing and risk

Behind this reading of Dostoevsky's method, which echoes other readings Coetzee offers of Dostoevsky, is a further reading or critique of the nature of the writing process, which is not obviously found in Dostoevsky's notion of his own work but might, rather, be attributed to Coetzee's understanding of Dostoevsky. This underlines the point that Coetzee makes in an essay he wrote on Frank's biography of Dostoevsky, which I have touched upon above: that Dostoevsky is gambling his very soul in the game of his art (Coetzee, *Stranger Shores*, 123–124). The point is made on page 222 of *The Master of Petersburg*, where, rather than aligning himself with the figure of Christ (as the one who gives meaning through self-sacrifice), Dostoevsky comes to understand that he performs a role closer to that performed by the Devil's surrogate Judas: he is the one who betrays everything in order to allow for the possibility of sacrifice. This, indeed, is the role Nechaev, who in luring him to St Petersburg by murdering his son Pavel, has caused him to play. Judas, who lies, who betrays, is necessary to the one who reveals the truth because he helps to bring about the sacrifice that guarantees the meaning of the truth.

The idea is sufficiently important to the themes of the novel that it is restated at the very end. Having begun to write, perverting the story of his son in order to have something to write, he recognizes the betrayal and asks himself if betrayal (the demon that possesses him to write) tastes of vinegar or gall. Christ was given vinegar to drink, mixed with gall, when he asked for a drink while nailed to the cross.

> It seems to him a great price to pay. *They pay him lots of money for writing books,* said the child, repeating the dead child. What they failed to say was that he had to give up his soul in return.
> Now he begins to taste it. It tastes like gall. (*Petersburg*, 250)

Writing, reading, and possession

Yet there is still more to the critique of the writing process, one that points at the phantom of the author and the presence of the reader.

One of the figures of the demon or demon possession in *The Master of Petersburg* is the process of writing itself, and the process of reading that answers it. Both involve possession of sorts. We have just witnessed some elements of this idea related to the figure of the writer. Yet it is also suggested that this is true of reading. Coetzee's Dostoevsky asks his police interrogator Maximov about what he is afraid of when he reads the horrors that writers like Dostoevsky, or like Coetzee, describe:

> When you read about Karamzin or Karamzov or whatever his name is, when Karamzin's skull is cracked open like an egg, what is the truth: do you suffer with him, or do you secretly exult behind the arm that swings the axe? You don't answer? Let me tell you then: reading is being the arm and being the axe *and* being the skull; reading is giving yourself up, not holding yourself at a distance and jeering. (*Petersburg*, 47)

And Maximov replies: 'you speak of reading as though it were demon-possession' (*Petersburg*, 47).

We are implicated, as readers, in any reading process, then. We are part of all the elements described. What elements are being fused together in *The Master of Petersburg*? There are many strands one could follow but an important one conflates sexuality with the perversion of innocence, with the demonic, and the vain pursuit, through unimaginable grief, of something that has been lost. A key to this reading can be found in the relationship between Coetzee's Dostoevsky and Matryosha's mother Anna Sergeyevna. Their sexual encounters are always guilty, but they are also linked to the idea of both Christ and the Devil. Towards the end of the book Dostoevsky suggests to Anna that they have a child. After sex Anna says, 'So was that meant to bring about the birth of the saviour?' (*Petersburg*, 225). Later, while reaching orgasm she whispers, 'the devil' (*Petersburg*, 230). Yet throughout it is apparent that Dostoevsky is seeking neither Christ nor the Devil in these encounters. Anna knows very well that he is using her as a path back to Pavel. After making love to her, he feels, in his dreams, that somehow he can make contact with his dead son. He tells her this and she makes a huge effort on his behalf to help him. She explains this to him:

> Yes, because of Pavel, because of what you said. I was ready to try. But now it is costing me too much. It is wearing me down. I

would never have gone so far if I weren't afraid you would use Matryosha in the same way. (*Petersburg*, 232)

Dostoevsky rejects, in the strongest terms, the accusation that he desired the child in place of the mother. Yet the desire that remains, the perverse desire, which is linked to earlier sexually charged glances between Dostoevsky and Matryosha, is the desire for the son to still be alive: a perverse desire because everything, everything good, would be sacrificed to bring back to life one thing. All meaning would be reduced to the meaning that rests in the lover's love for the loved one who is lost.

Coetzee's relation to his lost son Nicholas no doubt casts a shadow over this desire: the perverse desire to run time backwards in the manner of Orpheus and find his lost love (a theme mentioned by many readers in response to this book; see Adelman, Kannemeyer, 466–467). Perhaps, in part, the hopelessness of this task gives some of the bitter flavour to *The Master of Petersburg* in its excoriation of supposed seats of meaning: the writer, the father. Both the writer and the father might be called master: one because he can so masterfully conjure worlds that create meaning, the other because he exercises power that determines what is meaningful without need of understanding: Pavel speaks of Coetzee's Dostoevsky in this way (*Petersburg*, 218). The bitter truth that is revealed is that the writer develops truths through sacrifice *and* betrayal – the sacrifice of one's soul through the betrayal of all trust, of everything one loves. The real must be distorted and perverted in order to offer a story that might speak the truth to somehow give meaning to what has happened. This truth, in turn, exceeds that real, going beyond it in order to give it some sense of meaning.

Ethology not only involves ideas of place and how these affect and implicate the writers and readers of works of fiction. It also involves questions of disposition. One might, with some effort, link Kant's concept of 'genius' to its Latin root *ingenium*. *Ingenium* involves the disposition of an individual. It is disposition, in effect, that determines what is good for you and what is bad for you in Spinoza's *Ethics*. Spinoza has often been misunderstood, even by some of his early libertine admirers, as moving to relative notions of ethical behaviour that give licence to all our lusts.[3] Yet

---

[3]On the early reception of Spinoza, see Israel.

this hopelessly misunderstands his system, which requires us to distinguish between addiction or compulsions, which enslave us to the passions, and our true desires, which involve increasing our power to realize our capacities. The latter involves joining with others in mutually beneficial ways, rather than seeking to enslave or objectify them. Giving oneself over to pure lust, then, would involve weakness not strength: it would involve being passively acted upon by our emotions rather than actively seeking true connections with others.

The Master of Petersburg offers an examination of disposition that brings to the surface the interplay between what writers and readers seem to desire and what is at stake in these desires. In doing so it allows us to glimpse the difference between passive desires that eat our soul and active desires that allow us to flourish. It is, however, a dark book, so the former, rather than the latter, kinds of desire are the main points of focus.

8

Truth in Fiction: *Elizabeth Costello* and *Disgrace*

If a good deal of attention has been paid in recent times to intersections between ethics and Coetzee's work, much of it has been focused upon *Elizabeth Costello: Eight Lessons*. A particular point of interest has been the lessons that appeared independently as *The Lives of Animals* because it enters into dialogue with questions of importance to philosophy, literature, and the sociopolitical world.[1]

The first part of this chapter develops a reading of *Elizabeth Costello* and the second part reads *Disgrace*. Both novels consider the problem of the limits of our understanding, although they do so in different ways. *Elizabeth Costello* is deeply concerned with the idea of the confusion caused by the cacophony of competing voices in the world to which, as an ethical imperative, we must attempt to listen. This concerns limits that occur within dialogue and through attempts to sympathetically engage with others through fictional understandings. That is, it involves a surfeit of meaning, or walking a tightrope between moments of understanding and moments of utter confusion. *Disgrace*, for its part, considers how dispositions and situations can impose limits on the imagination that in turn can cause the failure of understanding. Rather than a surfeit of meaning, then, *Disgrace* considers the struggle of moving towards meaning. In beginning to move, however, it accepts the kinds of contradictions and confusions considered in *Elizabeth Costello*.

---

[1] See, for example, Aaltola, Carruth, Dawn, Marais, Heister, Kompridis, Baker, Flynn, Sellbach, Geiger.

Elizabeth Costello, place and displacement

The question of the potentials of literary form to engage with 'real world' problems is at the heart of *Elizabeth Costello*. In turn each lesson considers how the form of literary fiction, which by definition is a form that is displaced, or distanced from the 'real world', nevertheless engages with questions of disposition in relation to situation and place (which are crucial to an ethological understanding of ethics). Here displacement becomes a site of confusion.[2] When you are removed from your habitual environment, you also necessarily find your capacity to understand coming under challenge from unfamiliar contexts.

Each of the lessons here struggles with displacement. 'Lesson 1 Realism' considers the nature of the realist mode and how this mode, despite its emphasis on action or the body, might be made to accommodate thought through interaction with the dialogue form that straddles the disciplines of literature and philosophy. The realist mode offers a form through which feelings of disposition, situation, and place might be established. The dialogue form offers the potential for a range of views to be held up for consideration in approaching problems or questions. This lesson introduces Elizabeth Costello and her situation, which involves her endeavour to make herself understood (as a writer of fictions) in an academic form (the lecture), which establishes itself by attempting to set the fictional aside. That is, she is displaced between the understandings she has developed through fiction and the academic form she is being required to use.[3]

'Lesson 2 The Novel in Africa' considers how ideas of place, politics, and disposition can be broken free of their moorings. A black African novelist finds himself on a cruise liner entertaining wealthy mostly white patrons, as well as engaging in dialogue with his former lover Elizabeth Costello, whose past intimate relations

---

[2]Wright considers the theme of displacement in detail in relation to Coetzee's works.
[3]Coetzee himself encountered the same problem: being asked to give public lectures as a writer of fiction. His response was to shift the form back to fiction by reading stories about a fictional writer (Elizabeth Costello) who had been asked to address the questions he (Coetzee) had been asked to address, such as animal rights, the humanities in Africa, and so on.

with him affect her judgements of his position. Emblematically, the situation brings to mind the situation of writers who might write from or about a particular place but find their audiences outside that place.

'Lesson 3 The Lives of Animals: ONE: The Philosophers and the Animals' and 'Lesson 4 The Lives of Animals: TWO: The Poets and the Animals' consider how literary form and philosophical form might each engage differently with the same sets of problems. They meditate on how the forms themselves might determine what can and cannot be said, what can and cannot be imagined about our relationship to the environment. Yet they further engage with the problem of misunderstanding that occurs when one form engages with another, with each form potentially challenging or seeking to displace the other.

'Lesson 5 The Humanities in Africa' considers the relation between theological and literary modes of making meaning and how each form might create and impose meaning on places and peoples. Again, the idea of a struggle over meaning is staged, and this struggle, in effect, calls into question the nature of meaning itself. Meaning is essential to how both theology and art see themselves and their purpose in the world, and yet each might erode the other, displacing the meaning the other claims for itself.

In 'Lesson 6 The Problem of Evil' the question of what literary form might do is confronted directly, with the charge being made (and laid at the feet of a real-life novelist, Paul West, for his work *The Very Rich Hours of Count von Stauffenberg*) that what writers choose to represent and the manner in which they represent can have profound effects upon the souls, not only of those who read but those who write. That is, if writing is not good *per se*, is not the very *raison d'être* of writing – to have a positive effect in some way on some things – undermined? Isn't the posited value of literary endeavour displaced?

'Lesson 7 Eros' turns to not just the question of sexual passion, but the relation between the gods and human kind, which Elizabeth Costello understands through the mythical representations of such encounters that have in turn been taken up and reimagined by poets. Questions of mortality and immortality, the difficulty of representing an experience or being that is foreign but nevertheless invites one to try and understand it through desire, emerge. Our idea of ourselves that was once linked to an idea of the divine is undermined or displaced.

'Lesson 8 At the Gate' takes Elizabeth to a threshold or gate, seemingly between life and death. She will only be allowed to pass beyond this threshold, it transpires, if she is able to adequately state what she believes. She hesitates and fails, because she recognizes that literary form, the form she has inhabited and that has in profound ways shaped her being, rests upon ambiguity and uncertainty rather than clear exact meanings. Yet what might be the value of such an endeavour? If it cannot give us something certain in which we might believe, what earthly or unearthly good might writing do? Again here, the illusion of ultimate purpose, which might have served as some kind of foundational reason for being a writer at all, is displaced.

If Lesson 8 deals with what might be considered a deficit of meaning, or uncertainty, the 'Postscript: Letter to Elizabeth, Lady Chandos', in contrast, considers how literary form is capable of generating a surfeit or excess of meaning. This surfeit in turn might not be a blessing; it might, in effect, prove a curse. That is, the proliferation of meaning that writing could supply might not stand in as a new foundation; rather, it might do nothing other than throw us into confusion, into displacement.

Dialogue (complexity and confusion)

In *The Good Story* Coetzee explains what he sees as Dostoevsky's 'fundamental moral position regarding true interchanges between human beings (human souls), namely that these have to be reciprocal. Only when there is reciprocity do we have true dialogue' (Coetzee, *Good Story*, 50). Coetzee goes on to set out his own position: 'I believe most exchanges between human beings to be exchanges between projected fictions ... [and so] my acquaintance with true dialogue is slight' (Coetzee, *Good Story*, 50).

While the novel explores the nature of the dialogue of projected fictions, something else is at stake. If it is not concerned with true dialogue between characters, the novel is deeply concerned with the nature of dialogue itself and how it might be extended both outwards and inwards from the disposition of a character to the world and vice versa.

Dialogue: Complexity and confusion

Elizabeth Costello: Eight Lessons, had a mixed, and at times, puzzled, initial reception. Oliver Herford, the reviewer at the *Times Literary Supplement* can barely contain his annoyance at the confusions that come to the surface in the work and does not attempt to come to terms with them, seeing them rather as flaws in the writing. Yet even two very positive reviews, by distinguished reviewers, James Wood in the *London Review of Books* and David Lodge in the *New York Review of Books*, also confess to feelings of confusion, to a failure to completely recognize what is being done.

Their first response is to try to compensate for the confusion by tying the work back to sturdy, recognizable, moorings: ideas they are comfortable with. Wood asserts that the book is important because Coetzee offers us what he really believes. That is, it is a confession, and this underwrites its claims and makes them worth attending to. Yet while, as Hayes and others have shown, the idea of confession is crucial to Coetzee's conception of the nature of fiction (see Hayes, 106–130), it is hard to see how Wood comes to this conclusion. Although we are tempted to read Elizabeth Costello as a proxy for Coetzee, it is often not clear what her ideas are exactly, or whether they are endorsed by the work itself. The book describes not so much the inner workings of a mind, but it's inner and outer workings, a mind in the world among people, a world which continues to undermine concepts of belief, and as many critics have noted, and as has just been touched upon, Elizabeth Costello herself is refused entry beyond the Gate in Lesson 8 because of a failure to believe.

In his review David Lodge suggests that the novel intimates Coetzee's weariness with the process of writing novels, which Lodge suggests Coetzee feels have now lost the power they once had to affect the world. Yet *Elizabeth Costello* seems to insist that works of art do matter, that they make us think in ways not possible using other methods.

Elizabeth Costello's form seems instantly recognizable, and it is immediately identified by Wood, Lodge, and Herford as making use of the dialogue form, a form that is at least as old as Plato. Yet, have we really understood this form? If *Elizabeth Costello* is confusing, it is in part because it questions the nature of the dialogue, not by holding it up to the light and examining the premises on which it is built, but by turning the form against itself, by questioning its implications.

In the first lesson, 'Realism', we confront dialogue at a tangent. The tangent involves how realism engages or fails to engage with ideas. The narrator states:

> Realism has never been comfortable with ideas. It could not be otherwise: realism is premised on the idea that ideas have no autonomous existence, can exist only in things. So when it needs to debate ideas, as here, realism is driven to invent situations – walks in the countryside, conversations – in which characters give voice to contending ideas and thereby in a certain sense embody them. The notion of embodying turns out to be pivotal. In such debates ideas do not and indeed cannot float free: they are tied to the speakers by whom they are enounced, and generated from the matrix of individual interests out of which their speakers act in the world. (*Elizabeth Costello*, 9)

Dialogue as ethology

Ideas, then, emerge through a dialogue between individuals, their situations, and the environments within which they thrive or wither. That is, dialogue is situated among dispositions, situations, and places and so is ethological in nature. There is an ethical dimension to the concept of dialogue, which is central to the novel.

We recognize 'dialogue'. We think we know what it is. How could it be made to disturb or confuse us? It is familiar because it is everywhere, both inside and outside the novel. Yet what if we were to take this seriously? If it is familiar, if it is recognized, is this not because it multiplies itself everywhere; that it can't be contained; that it is not just a dialogue between characters or positions, but a never-ending, deviously complex system of responses to responses? It might be claimed, further, that it is a process that does not just take place between ideas: you are not only in dialogue with others, but just as much with your own intuitions and feelings, your own memories, but also with the weather and the rest of the planet; with what you ate for breakfast and what that is doing to your digestion or, even, your soul; with the amount of sleep you had last night; with what you think of the person you are talking to;

with what you know about language and its traditions, ideas, and their history: in short, the whole of your world, more or less, past, present, and future.

This is no longer Plato nor Dostoevsky nor Bakhtin. In Bakhtin's books on Dostoevsky's method, *Problems of Dostoevsky's Poetics*, *The Dialogic Imagination*, and elsewhere, he claims that the novel is able to offer an overview of a whole range of ideas, a whole range of ideological positions, without choosing between them: it can show us how ideas engage with one another and refract and bounce off one another, making us think about the problems at stake, without telling us what to think.

Writing in *Stranger Shores* on Dostoevsky, Coetzee has offered a point of critique concerning the limits of Bakhtin's idea. It is not enough, Coetzee suggests, to simply recognize that Dostoevsky put ideas into play; that he, like the compulsive gambler he was, put them forward as stakes in a game. What we need to realize is that Dostoevsky was not just using anything as stakes; rather, among the things he put on the table were his own most cherished beliefs. The very idea of his soul, in effect, was bet and perhaps lost along with the other trinkets of the age. In reviewing Joseph Frank's biography of Dostoevsky, Coetzee states:

> Frank loses an opportunity to supply what is missing in Bakhtin, namely, a clear statement that dialogism as exemplified in the novels of Dostoevsky is a matter not of ideological position, still less of novelistic technique, but of the most radical intellectual and even spiritual courage. (*Stranger Shores,* 145)

Coetzee goes on to quote Frank, who underlines how Dostoevsky 'fearlessly submits his own most hallowed convictions to the same test that he had used for those of the Nihilists'. Yet, for Coetzee, if Bakhtin demonstrates how the concept might be developed within the work and act upon readers (thereby carrying with it a power to generalize ideas and free them somewhat from the moorings of their beginnings), he in turn understates the importance of those contexts: the disposition, place, and situations from which the work emerged.

Implicit in Frank's account is what Bakhtin leaves out: that to the degree that Dostoevskian dialogism grows out of Dostoevsky's own moral character, out of his ideals, and out of his being as a writer, it is only distantly imitable. (*Stranger Shores*, 145–146)

In effect, Coetzee points out that dialogue is not simply a cold intellectual matter. It is tied to specific dispositions, places, and situations from which the work emerges and with which it engages and as such it is deeply felt. In short, the inflection on Bakhtin's concept of dialogue in fiction Coetzee offers is that you *feel* dialogue, to the depths of your being, as much as you think through dialogue. We might read Plato, but do we stop to imagine how Socrates' hapless interlocutors might feel as the very fabric of their worlds is unravelled through what Mrs Curren in *Age of Iron*, calls 'ventriloquism' (*Age of Iron*, 98). How does the ebbing of a belief, or the collapse of a belief within the self, brought about by engagement with external forces that press upon that self in unrelenting dialogue, feel?

Belief and opinion

Clearly nowadays beliefs still exist and are at times held to passionately, even murderously. Yet all beliefs have been called into question: especially those stridently held, but even those justified by fact and evidence, such as climate change. In effect, both those beliefs for which one would kill and die, no matter how tenuous their grounds, along with those that are scientifically verifiable, have been reduced (by those who oppose them) to the status of opinion.

In *What Is Philosophy*, Deleuze and Guattari consider opinion as one of the enemies of philosophy, perverting the truth to align it with that opinion that has been given to and embraced by the majority:

> True opinion will be the one that coincides with that of the group to which one belongs by expressing it. [...] The essence of opinion is will to majority and already speaks in the name of a majority. [...] The philosophy of communication is exhausted in the search for a universal liberal opinion as consensus, in which we find again the cynical perceptions and affections of the capitalist himself. (*What is Philosophy*, 146)

A temptation arises then: to choose opinions through social convenience rather than examining issues rigorously and seeking genuine truths (which now seem forever just out of reach). *Elizabeth Costello* makes us feel the consequences of our condition, where, in the absence of certainty, we often feign it. Through the pretence of fiction, *Elizabeth Costello* makes us feel the anxiety at the heart of our real everyday pretence.

Elizabeth Costello traces a number of the many fault lines of our contemporary crisis, a crisis of belief or opinion that has been caused by vociferously held beliefs or lightly held opinions that often contradict fact, evidence, and intuitive understanding. The character Elizabeth Costello is aware at least of the limitations of her position. While Deleuze and Guattari claim that 'Art does not have opinions' (*What Is Philosophy*, 176), Elizabeth Costello underlines that, like everyone else, she does have opinions and beliefs. However, she does her best, by engaging with the potentials of the form of literary fiction, to keep these at bay:

> Of course, gentlemen, I do not claim to be bereft of all belief. I have what I think of as opinions and prejudices, no different in kind from what are commonly called beliefs. When I claim to be a secretary clean of belief I refer to my ideal self, a self capable of holding opinions and prejudices at bay while the word which it is her function to conduct passes through her. (*Elizabeth Costello*, 200)

The book, then, brackets off belief and instead goes in a different direction. The lessons, we are told by Elizabeth's daughter Helen, in a short story Coetzee published in the *New York Review of Books* (which was not included in the book), are about feeling. 'You teach people how to feel', she tells the novelist, her mother, Elizabeth. Elizabeth Costello, of course, responds with scepticism (Coetzee, 'As a Woman Grows Older'). Yet this is a challenge the book throws down. It claims a central, rather than a peripheral, importance for works of art, which try to make people *feel* thought. Feelings, in the gut, the heart, or some dark and difficult to illuminate corners of the head, can and do lead us. We might not know why, but they sometimes have a force that is not only emotional: it can be moral and intellectual in that it challenges us to think about what we do, about why and who we are. We see this in Lesson 6, 'The

Problem of Evil'. Elizabeth knows she has to challenge Paul West's artistic practice in his book *The Very Rich Hours of Count von Stuaffenberg*, but she isn't certain how to do this or even why she must do this. It is not a confused impression that urges her on; rather, it is a sharp, gut, intuition. What is confused is the means she has at hand (the forms of words and the techniques of linking and focusing the meanings of words, the systems of thought now available in the world) with which to describe her intuition. Yet, in describing her attempts, Coetzee teaches us something new about an old problem.

The method of making meaning and ethics

The epigraph at the beginning of the Postscript to *Elizabeth Costello* is taken from the 'Letter of Lord Chandos to Lord Bacon' written in 1902 by the German writer Hugo von Hofmannsthal. Here von Hofmannsthal takes on the persona of Lord Chandos, a fictional friend to the great English scientist and writer Francis Bacon, and the letter is supposedly written in 1603. In von Hofmannsthal's story Chandos replies to Bacon, who has asked why he has not seen any works published by Chandos in recent times, when he was at one time such a promising writer. Chandos writes to explain his strange affliction, which has stopped him from writing.

> At such moments even a negligible creature, a dog, a rat, a beetle, a stunted apple tree, a cart track winding over a hill, a mossy stone, counts more for me than a night of bliss with the most beautiful, most devoted mistress. [...] It is as if everything, everything that exists, everything I can recall, everything my confused thinking touches on, means something. (Hugo von Hofmanssthal, quoted in *Elizabeth Costello*, 226)

Coetzee then elaborates on the character of Chandos' wife, who is mentioned briefly in the original letter. The Elizabeth C or Elizabeth Chandos Coetzee invents here, then, answers or enters into dialogue with von Hofmannsthal's character Lord Chandos, and the ideas von Hofmannsthal develops:

All is allegory, says my Philip. Each creature is key to all other creatures. A dog sitting in a patch of sun licking itself, says he, is at one moment a dog and at the next a vessel of revelation. [...] But how I ask you can I live with rats and dogs and beetles crawling through me day and night, drowning and gasping, scratching at me, tugging me, urging me deeper and deeper into revelation – how? *We are not made for revelation*, I want to cry out, *nor I nor you, my Philip*, revelation that sears the eye like staring into the sun. (*Elizabeth Costello*, 229)

As we have seen the technique or form that is being used here involves A against B. One sign is paired with or brought into relation with another sign, and between the two there is a resonance, but there is also a gap which requires interpretation. Another way of thinking of this is a dialogue. A third way is (modern) allegory. It is at the heart of language. It is there in metaphor itself, but more or less also in every rhetorical figure of speech.

The play of the ideas that circulate in *Elizabeth Costello* is complicated by the dialogue of fictions Coetzee describes in *The Good Story*, whereby ideas are constantly referred to other, often contradictory, ideas. This aspect of the work tends to exasperate some readers: such as Peter Singer, who was asked to respond to *The Lives of Animals* (which would become Lessons 3 and 4 in *Elizabeth*) when the two chapters were first presented as the Princeton Tanner lectures of 1997–1998.

In his response, which unsuccessfully tries to mimic Coetzee's form, Singer sees Coetzee's approach as amounting to a kind of trick and states: 'Call me old-fashioned ... but I prefer to keep truth and fiction clearly separate' (*Lives*, 86). Yet this misses the subtle ways in which Coetzee demonstrates truth and fiction to be implicated. For those who like their truth and fiction clearly separated, then, Coetzee's form can be maddening, but Coetzee demonstrates in effect that truth and fiction *cannot* be clearly separated. They are in constant dialogue, challenging us to understand what is true and what is false. The form of dialogue itself is related to the species of madness described in the postscript to the novel.

The madness is not the madness of fiction *per se*, but of our relations to the world more generally. As we have seen, in the letter Elizabeth C(handos), whom we relate to Elizabeth C(ostello), refers to this madness, where one sign is always related to another sign, and everything, absolutely everything, seems meaningful. The novel shows us how we are harried by voices, each with their separate claims, which offer, not a plenitude, but a chaos. Who and what do we believe when, if we listen properly, the very stones of the earth and all its life forms, its winds, and waters, murmur to us, in what, if we cannot see it as holy and a gift, sounds like a lunatic cacophony?

'It will be over soon': Meaning and death

Other signs push forward, without obvious explanation: the letter from Elizabeth C is dated 'This 11 September … '. In 2003 it was impossible to refer to this date without readers thinking of 9/11/2001, when the twin towers were destroyed by Al Qaeda in New York. This is an idea underlined by David Attwell in an interview with Coetzee for the Swedish newspaper *Dagens Nyheter*, on 8 December 2003. Here Coetzee begins by underlining that he resists requests to read his own works, but nevertheless responds to the implied links to 9/11:

> As for September 11, let us not too easily grant the Americans possession of that date on the calendar. Like May 1 or July 14 or December 25, September 11 may seem full of significance to some people, while to other people it is just another day. (Coetzee, 'Interview')

Yet it nevertheless cannot be said that the date does not signify. Insofar as it does it signifies a time of uncertainly, when meaning itself becomes uncertain. This time of uncertainty, in turn, might be further generalized to that time when we are confronted by the reality of death: the imminence or unavoidability of death. This kind of confrontation necessarily makes us question what things mean.

In *The Good Story*, Coetzee claims, as a 'trader in fictions' to be more interested in using reality than in reflecting reality. Yet he claims:

> What ties one to the real world is, finally, death. One can make up stories about oneself to one's heart's content, but one is not

free to make up the ending. The ending has to be death: it is the only ending one can seriously believe in. What an irony then that to anchor oneself in a sea of fictions one should have to rely on death! (*Good Story*, 69)

Elizabeth Costello follows its eponymous character as she approaches death and becomes increasingly confused in the face of it. It is as if she is already putting her house in order. Lessons 1 and 2 consider the remainders of a career. Lessons 3 and 4 consider death as it relates to animals. Her son John comforts her at the end of Lesson 4, 'There, there. It will be over soon' (*Elizabeth Costello*, 115). In Lesson 5 the humanities themselves are thought to be on their deathbed, 'The *studia humanitatis* have taken a long time to die, but now, at the end of the second millennium of our era, they are truly on their deathbed' (*Elizabeth Costello*, 123). Lesson 6 concerns the representation of death and in particular its 'obscene' representation, which Elizabeth Costello argues has the power to infect us. Lesson 7 in part meditates on the relation between love and death (*Elizabeth Costello*, 189). Lesson 8 concerns the threshold to death. Death offers a ground from which meaning might emerge. Meaning, then, is strangely linked to death or our limits. Death itself, as Leibniz sets out in 'Monadology', involves a feeling of confusion or dizziness:

But when there are a great number of small perceptions with nothing to distinguish them, we are stupefied, just as it happens that if we go on turning round in the same direction several times running, we become giddy and go into a swoon, so that we can no longer distinguish anything at all. And death can throw animals into this state for a time. (Leibniz, *Philosophical Writings*, 182)

While the linking of signs to signs, with every relation generating more meaning, could be considered maddening or madness or even a kind of death, it could also be understood to be a kind of power. Precisely, the power of fiction, which leads to different kinds of understanding than those available through other, more narrowly conceived systems of thought. In Lesson 3, Elizabeth Costello underlines how some systems work through rigid constraint and arrive at their clear and unambiguous truths because of the nature of these systematic constraints themselves. They defeat the tendency to slip away into multiple levels of meaning through tautology: the systems answer themselves and can only answer themselves. Here the sign is related to itself alone and this is a foundation that allows a stable meaning:

> 'I don't know what I think,' says Elizabeth Costello. 'I often wonder what thinking is, what understanding is. Do we really understand the universe better than animals do? Understanding a thing often looks to me like playing with one of those Rubik cubes. Once you have made all the little bricks snap into place, hey presto, you understand. It makes sense if you live inside a Rubik cube, but if you don't ....' (*Elizabeth Costello*, 90)

Life: The idea of truth

In Lesson 3, Coetzee is engaging with a narrow conception of philosophy as it addresses a particular question: the understanding of the lives of animals and the value of those lives (to some entity other than the animals themselves). This involves a conception of ethics that cannot proceed via ethology because it does not consider how each living thing develops in accordance with its particular disposition and its own relationships to its situation and environment. Elizabeth Costello is using a different kind of thinking to shift the emphasis of the question from one of value to one of meaning: not what life is worth, but what it means to live. That is, rather than understanding the use value of a life and the ethical obligations, rules, and so on that attend particular definitions of the status of those lives, she attempts to consider a contemplation of how such lives might feel or be experienced, which returns us to ethology. That one can no longer believe in Dostoevsky's idea of true dialogue does not mean that one abandons the idea of truth. Rather, truth must be made to emerge from a dialogue of fictions, which, in order to achieve some feeling of truth, must push imagination to its limits, imagining not only the voices of other people but of the worlds with and without them.

If *Elizabeth Costello* attempts to walk this line between madness and insight, *Disgrace*, which was composed concurrently with parts of *Elizabeth Costello*, takes an almost opposite approach. Rather than considering the potentials of imagining the true nature of fictional dialogue, it considers the implications of the failure of the imagination. Rather than confronting confusion and attempting to ground it, it confronts misunderstandings of another kind, misunderstandings that occur through the failure to imagine the other.

Disgrace and the failure of imagination

Disgrace begins by positing, from David Lurie's point of view, the 'problem' of sex. The problem here is tied to ethology, to David Lurie's disposition, to his worldview and the understandings of the world he has aligned himself with and the situations and spaces he inhabits. This worldview involves an idea of the Romantic poets, with a dash of *Don Quixote*, in that he has been infected by fictions which distort his view of the relations he enters into.

So the problem is both a 'general' problem of the relations between the sexes, in terms of love in all its senses, and sex, and a particular problem. The point of crisis for this problem is the idea of rape. As numerous critics have pointed out there are two rapes in *Disgrace*: what can be interpreted as the rape of Melanie by David Lurie in the first half of the book, and the rape of Lucy by the intruders into her farm which dominates the second half of the book.[4]

In progressing to this crisis, however, or revisiting it twice, problems open in what, from David Lurie's point of view, are unexpected ways. That is, while the issue of rape affects him, it is no longer primarily his problem. The crises affect the women differently, more profoundly, and although they clearly also affect him, he struggles to comprehend each rape in turn. In the first instance he is unable to acknowledge that this is in fact what has taken place: the sexual contact with Melanie to him seems consensual. Yet in the face of her silence within the novel we are left to piece together

---

[4]A good deal has been written on the representation of rape in this novel. See, for example, Shattuck, Van Wyk Smith, Mardorossian, Cass, Geertsema, Graham, Cornwell, Bethlehem, Middleton, Barnard, Gane.

information, which allows us to understand that this does amount to rape. In the second instance he also fails to understand. This is something that Lucy explicitly makes plain to him:

> 'Stop it, David! I don't need to defend myself before you. *You don't know what happened*'. (*Disgrace*, 134)

This point is then made again by Bev Shaw, who affirms that David was not there (*Disgrace*, 140). David Lurie resents this, wondering if what they mean is that 'where rape is concerned, no man can be where the woman is' (*Disgrace*, 141), this thought leads to further outrage on David's part, outrage 'at being treated like an outsider' (*Disgrace*, 141). Yet this brings forth a fundamental problem: the failure of the imagination in relation to other people. This theme is developed in the novel in regard to relations both between men and women and between white and black Africans.

This is underlined in a scene where Lucy attempts to explain to David what happened to her. She speaks of being astonished by the hatred and wonders if this somehow concerns relations between men and women in general, in comments that bring back to mind David's liaison with Melanie, implicating them as relations of a kind he cannot admit to himself. Lucy explains:

> Hatred … When it comes to men and sex, David, nothing surprises me any more. Maybe, for men, hating the woman makes sex more exciting. You are a man, you ought to know. When you have sex with someone strange – when you trap her, hold her down, get her under you, put all your weight on her – isn't it a bit like killing? (*Disgrace*, 158)

There is a sense of what one can and cannot know, then, somehow linked to differences of subject position, disposition, and situation, in this case, gender or race. It is a provocative claim and one that David at last begins to confront. He thinks:

> Lucy's intuition is right after all: he does understand; he can, if he concentrates, if he loses himself, be there, be the men, inhabit them, fill them with the ghost of himself. The question is, does he have it in him to be the woman? (*Disgrace*, 160)

Complicating Elizabeth Costello's position in *The Lives of Animals*, in *The Good Story* Coetzee contends that 'by a strenuous effort of sympathetic projection one can reach a flickering intuition' of what it is like to be something other including an animal (*Good Story*, 136). While there are no necessary limits to sympathetic intuition, then, 'our sympathetic intuitions can be relied on only to yield fictional truths' (*Good Story*, 134). Further, he sees 'sympathy as an inborn faculty in human beings which may or may not grow [... or] atrophy' (*Good Story*, 134). There are limits, then, to each particular imagination and therefore limits of understanding. He states:

> Sympathetic identifications allow us to enter other lives and to live them from the inside. It goes without saying that the other lives we live at such times are not necessarily the true lives of the others to whom they belong. [...] [When reading novels] it is not necessarily the true life of the [fictional] other we are living – witness the very different understandings different readers have of characters in novels. (*Good Story*, 134)

The point is subtle but it is important to try and follow. Echoing the well-known passage from *Elizabeth Costello*, in *The Good Story* Coetzee disagrees with Thomas Nagle when Nagle claims that we cannot understand what it is like to be a bat. It is worth finishing a quotation cited in part above:

> I disagree with Nagle. I think that by a strenuous effort of sympathetic projection one can reach a flickering intuition of what it is like for a bat to be a bat. But this does not amount to the claim that one can have intuitions of what it is *really* like for a bat to be a bat. (*Good Story*, 136)

Our capacity to feel the experience of a bat, then, depends on our capacity to imagine. It requires effort. Yet the alternative to it is to be completely cut off from this experience:

> In Nagel's terms, the only true, real knowledge one can have of what it is like to be anyone or anything in the world is a form of knowledge of what it is like to be oneself. (*Good Story*, 136)

What is at stake, then, is a failure to create or imagine a truth. If, in a passage in Plato emphasized by Nietzsche, Socrates is urged to 'make music', it is in order to seek another kind of truth, one not available through pure reason: a truth of feeling or intuition (Nietzsche, *Tragedy*, 70–71). Coetzee concludes by reiterating: 'Other such knowledge may be true, but its truth is the truth of fictions' (*Good Story*, 136). In part, the story of David Lurie involves a movement towards an effort to make music, as he attempts to compose his opera based on the life of Lord Byron; an effort to imagine.

A common criticism of *Disgrace* is that the book offers an unsympathetic relation of African people.[5] For example, we are never given access to the point of view of Petrus, or the boy Pollux, or any other black African character. There are two possible explanations for this. Firstly, it might reflect the kind of difficulty Coetzee expressed with regard to the writing of *Life & Times of Michael K*: an incapacity to fully identify with subject positions because of the nature of his own subject position in relation to theirs (see Coetzee Archives Container 33.5, Notebook MK, pp. 6–7, 16 June 1980, passage cited in Chapter 6). To put this another way, he can only criticize or write with honesty from those positions within which he himself is implicated.

Secondly, the novel itself is concerned with the limits of the imagination and as such concentrates on the point of view of its main protagonist David Lurie, representing the conditions of his experience. The novel shows us in part how these conditions (which amount to a lack of self-knowledge and a lack of knowledge of others) make it extremely difficult for him to understand the experience of another being or to use his imagination to access sympathetic intuition. Yet it also shows how Lurie begins to make steps, begins to make the kind of effort necessary to achieving some glimpses of understanding, and such glimpses occur towards the end through his engagement with the animals he helps to die.

The book in effect is open to, or revealing of, these kinds of limits, and revealing the empathetic and imaginative incapacities of a certain subject position is an ethical process. The problem,

---

[5]Peter D. McDonald offers a useful overview of the reception of the novel around the question of Race in 'Disgrace Effects'.

however, is how to make something that addresses the ethical implications of otherness and conflicts (here of race and gender), while constrained to think from within a particular disposition and situation. *Disgrace* attempts this, in part, by creating a distance between the character and the reader, making us uneasy about our reading habits, requiring us to watch ourselves reading, to catch ourselves in habitual responses.

One example comes at the scene with Pollux, the boy who was one of Lucy's rapists when he appears at Petrus's party. We are given in a short space an astonishing set of contradictory responses: that of Lucy, who is appalled and needs to leave; that of David Lurie who is enraged and wishes to go to the police; that of Lucy in response to David who refuses to call the police, in part because she does not wish to ruin Petrus's party; that of Petrus and the guests who are stony in response to the prospect of having the police called by whites against black Africans after all that has happened in their long history (*Disgrace*, 130–131). The book urges us to read with care, but offers us nothing simple, nothing easy, no neat reading, no certain truth.

The (deliberate) failure to supply a preconceived interpretation is equally apparent with regard to Melanie. David Lurie never comes close to understanding her experience of what has gone on, and since we see largely from his perspective this lack is also present in the novel. We never hear her statement. Her response is mediated by others, and these are other men: her boyfriend, who seems abusive; her father, who seems not to see her experience, but rather to channel it through his own Christian faith. Her mother and sister are silent; she is silent. She would 'spit in his face' the boyfriend says, but we only have his word for it. David Lurie's relationship to her is purely physical and functional. The interaction with the dogs that he helps to put down is emblematic of this: the only possibility of understanding comes through the idea that they themselves might understand. Bev Shaw tells him to 'think comforting thoughts, think strong thoughts. They can smell what you are thinking' (*Disgrace*, 81).

This idea is initially disparaged by David Lurie, but later he returns to it as the only way (*Disgrace*, 142): an immediate, intuitive understanding of the way things are. Lurie indeed, when trying to comfort Bev as she is putting a goat to sleep, comes up with a slightly different version of this idea of immediate knowledge or foreknowledge, one that returns to classical forms and Plato:

'Perhaps he understands more than you guess,' he says. To his own surprise he is trying to comfort her. 'Perhaps he has already been through it. Born with foreknowledge, so to speak. This is Africa, after all. There have been goats here since the beginning of time. They don't have to be told what steel is for, and fire. They know how death comes to a goat. They are born prepared'. (*Disgrace*, 83–84)

It is not clear that there is comfort in the book itself, however. Although a strange idea of the path or the way emerges as a motif, it is not easy to draw this motif into a clear interpretation.

One potential reading, however, might focus on the title of the novel. The opposite of disgrace is grace: a word with religious connotations related to the possibility of our not being without hope. The word 'grace' only occurs three times in the book, first in the phrase '*coup de grâce*', a merciful blow that is *not* delivered to a dog that has been shot in the chest by the farm intruders (*Disgrace*, 95). It is mentioned at the end of the novel in relation to David's favourite dog, whose 'period of grace' is coming to an end and who will soon be put down (*Disgrace*, 215). It is mentioned by mistake by Lucy's mother and David's former wife Rosalind. She misremembers the name of Lucy's partner, who has left Lucy and the farm, as being 'Grace' when it was really 'Helen'.

Yet the idea of grace, as that which exceeds the limits placed on sympathetic identification and intuition, somehow remains before us in *Disgrace*. In the Christian tradition grace involves the salvation of those who do not deserve salvation: an aspect of God's infinite love (Erickson, 320–321). Given the prime example of grace in the Christian tradition is the sacrifice Christ makes to take on the sins of the world by dying on the cross, the theme of grace is linked to the theme of sacrifice. This in turn is linked to the biblical story of Isaac and Abraham in *Genesis*. Melanie's surname is Isaacs. Isaac, the son of Abraham, was to be sacrificed in the wilderness by Abraham himself at God's request, as a way of testing Abraham's loyalty. While Abraham loves his son he is about to go through with the demand, only for God to rescind it at the last moment, offering instead a lamb to be sacrificed in Isaac's place. This idea of sacrifice, as that which will allow grace, is echoed at the end with the sacrifice

David makes of his favourite dog, which he carries like a lamb to be put down (*Disgrace*, 219).

> Bearing him in his arms like a lamb, he re-enters the surgery. 'I thought you would save him for another week,' says Bev Shaw. 'Are you giving him up?'
>
> 'Yes, I am giving him up'. (*Disgrace*, 220)

There are a number of other mentions of the idea of sacrifice. Towards the end of the novel David Lurie says, 'I am prepared to do anything, make any sacrifice, for the sake of peace' (*Disgrace*, 208). The story of sacrifice is also there in the idea of the scapegoat, which David is unsure he would apply to his own story (*Disgrace*, 91). The sacrifice story is linked to others that involve being led by the gods. In his relations with Melanie, David Lurie claims to have been led by Eros (89). Mr Isaacs tells him he needs to be led by God's path (*Disgrace*, 174).

The whole story of Isaac and sacrifice involves giving oneself over to what will happen, to having faith in the ruling powers. It is connected to the idea of a 'way' or 'path': a method. This in turn is connected to an idea of becoming, or process, which is not fully understood and cannot be fully foreseen. While *Disgrace* does not embrace this worldview, it nevertheless points towards something structurally similar to it. That is, it is felt in the novel that there are processes in train that can only be inadequately resisted, that can only, in truth, be followed (the process that sees David leave in disgrace from the university due to his sexual misconduct; the processes that lead to the intruders' attack on the farm and the rape of Lucy). Yet these processes might somehow offer painful lessons from which some meaning might emerge. Such meanings begin with the provocative premise that meaning can be extracted from the world through understanding and that in order to open such possible understanding for oneself one needs to glimpse or feel that others, even those that you have wronged, even those that have wronged you, in turn might have some access to understanding.

Disgrace does not allow us to indulge ourselves in easy interpretations; rather, it forces us to think about things that are not easy to think about, which are not easy to understand. In giving us a feeling of the difficulties involved, however, in refusing to avoid these difficulties, the novel does give us something important: a sense that there *are* meanings here, even as we struggle to hold them in our heads, meanings that inhabit different dispositions, different territories or domains, meanings that co-exist without necessarily being shared. It allows us to glimpse or feel an intuition of this complexity, to feel its meaning, and thereby to attempt to take it into account as we try to live well, as we try to invent dignity for ourselves.

9

Creative Intuition:
The Childhood of Jesus

This chapter has two parts. The first returns to the concept of intuition and how it might relate to the truth in *The Childhood of Jesus*. The second offers a reading of the novel in relation to Gerald Murnane's work, work that Coetzee critiques, further reflecting on the question of how truth might be conveyed in fiction. In *The Childhood of Jesus* and *The Schooldays of Jesus* Coetzee engages most clearly with ideas of intuition, examining the idea and its aporias.

The truth of the forms

A number of critics have now commented on the importance of Plato to J. M. Coetzee's *The Childhood of Jesus* (see Rabaté; Pippin; Mosca; Wilmots, 151–174). The structure of the world in which the story takes place seems to relate to the Platonic notion of the recollection of ideas, ideals, or forms from the world above, which are forgotten once one returns to this world, but are recognized as eternal truths once re-encountered. This Platonic myth of the forgotten world above, which is the world of the forms or ideals, is discussed in a number of dialogues: *Phaedo, Meno, Ion, Philebus*, but the myth itself is most clearly set out in *Phaedrus*.

In *The Childhood of Jesus* the main protagonists, Simón and David, and perhaps all those who exist in the Spanish-speaking world that includes Novilla, Belstar, Estrellita del Norte, and the reform school of Punto Arenas have crossed the sea to reach a new world in which their old lives are forgotten and they are able to begin again, with new names, and little memory of what has gone before. It is suggested on a number of occasions that this process of entering into the new life relates to death, as one passes from one life to the next, forgetting one's former state and starting again (*Childhood*, 28–29, 31, 70, 76, 168). Simón tells David: 'After death there is always another life. You have seen that' (*Childhood*, 156), and 'Marciano has found peace. He is probably crossing the seas at this very moment, looking forward to the next life. It will be a great adventure for him, to start anew, washed clean' (*Childhood*, 185–186).[1]

This in turn is linked, by Simón's interlocutor Eugenio, to the concept of 'bad infinity': the *mise en abyme* of endless repetitions (*Childhood*, 292). The main protagonist, Simón, differs from others he meets in that he carries with him the shadows of the former life. He states, 'I am beginning to think there is something in my speech that marks me as a man stuck in the old ways, a man who has not forgotten' (*Childhood*, 168).

On the one hand then, an idea of understanding in *The Childhood of Jesus* brings with it the structure that underpins Plato's concept of recognition, which, as we have seen above, offers one explanation for the feeling of intuitive understanding. In *Phaedo*, Socrates states:

And unless we invariably forget it after obtaining it we must always be born *knowing* and continue to *know* all through our lives, because to 'know' means simply to retain the knowledge which one has acquired, and not to lose it. Is not what we call 'forgetting' simply the loss of knowledge … ? (Plato, *Phaedo*, 58, section 75d).

As we have seen, inspiration, which gives access to the memory of this knowledge, carries with it many of the same characteristics of intuition: an immediate recognition of the truth.

---

[1] There are other possible interpretations of the 'new life', relating it to migration, or the status of refugees, particularly in the context of Australian laws related to the control of immigration. See Ng and Sheehan; Rutherford. See also Coetzee, *Good Story* on Australian migration policy, 88.

The idea of the truth is further underlined in the novel through references to stars and their implied link to the heavens or the Platonic world above. Simón says they are on a star (*Childhood*, 208), and the names of places in the novel refer to stars: Belstar, Estrelitta. So too there is a link to *Pheadrus* and the myth of truth Plato develops. This is underlined through a vision Simón experiences, which directly refers to the chariots of the gods described in *Pheadrus*, which ascend the heavens to look upon the truths or forms of the intellect. For the Gods, the ascent to this region of the truth is easy, as their horses lead them truly, while for humans the ascent is difficult, as we are led by one true horse (perhaps symbolizing the mind or spirit) and one unreliable horse (perhaps symbolizing the desires of the body) (Plato, *Pheadrus*, 494–495, sections 247–248). In *The Childhood of Jesus* David seems more of the Gods than men in the dream-like vision Simón has of him late in the novel:

> With uncommon clarity he sees a two-wheeled chariot hovering in the air at the foot of his bed. The chariot is made of ivory or some metal inlaid with ivory, and is drawn by two white horses, neither of whom is El Rey. Grasping the reins in one hand, holding the other aloft in a regal gesture, is the boy, naked save for a cotton loincloth. (*Childhood*, 277)

This is far from all that is at stake because as well as forgetting what was known (including a form of truth) from the previous life, the protagonists in the new world have also lost some of the desires that are associated with 'normal' life in our world. They no longer feel intense particular desires such as love or lust, and this is something that preoccupies Simón (*Childhood*, 70–81).

Intuition: The feeling of understanding

They seem to have moved to a realm in which universal desires or universal goods have taken the place of particular desires. Rather than this being something he can easily understand this is a matter of concern for Simón. He does not wish to let go of his former desires; he does not wish to forget everything that has passed in the previous life and he actively seeks to resist this process of generalizing and the stripping away of desire.

The main way in which his resistance to this process of divestment of feeling manifests is through the counter-process of understanding itself. He seeks to claim a ground of understanding by 'finding' the former mother of the boy who has been given the new name 'David.' Simón seems to clearly remember details of their voyage together: David had at one time a letter fastened by a string around his neck which carried with it the answer to the question of the identity of David's mother and father. This string had broken, and the letter was lost. Simón claims, however, that the boy will recognize his mother the instant he sees her, and so he remains confident that the mother will be found.

In practice, however, the boy fails to instantly recognize his mother. In practice, Simón claims, through pure intuition, to himself recognize David's mother moments after he first sees her. He discusses this with David:

'Didn't you feel a strange movement in your breast when she spoke to us, when she said hello – a kind of tug at the heartstrings, as if you might have seen her before, in some other place?'

Doubtfully the boy shakes his head.

I ask because the lady may be the very person we are looking for. That, at least, is the feeling I have.

'Is she going to be my mother?'

'I don't know for sure. We will have to ask her'. (*Childhood*, 88)

As we can see, it is Simón and not David who claims this intuition or feeling, although it is not clear whether Simón had ever seen David's mother in the previous life. The validity of the intuition is questioned by Elena:

[Simón] 'Elena, she *is* his mother. I arrived in this land bare of everything save one rock-solid conviction: that I would know the boy's mother when I saw her. And the moment I beheld Inés I knew it was she'.

'You followed an intuition?'

'More than that. A conviction'.

'A conviction, an intuition, a delusion – what is the difference when it cannot be questioned?' (*Childhood*, 102)

Intuition and creating the truth

Here then, the idea of intuitive recognition, or its status as a foundation of truth, is called into question. Yet because intuition as a method for finding the truth is held in suspension, a second aspect of the power of intuition is underlined: it is suggested that while intuition might not, after Plato, recognize the truth, it nevertheless has the power to create or manufacture the truth.

That is, while it remains uncertain and unprovable through the evidence offered by the book as to whether Inés is in fact David's true mother, in practice Inés *becomes* David's mother, just as Simón becomes David's father. Rather than intuition, in Platonic fashion, pointing to an 'eternal' realm situated temporally before the present, a former life in which one had access to particular truths, intuition, in a manner that corresponds more closely to Henri Bergson, realizes the present that is coming into existence and allows it to be understood. To repeat a quote from Chapter 1, in Bergson's terms:

> Intuition [...] signifies first of all consciousness, but immediate consciousness, a vision which is scarcely distinguishable from the object seen, a knowledge which is contact and even coincidence. (Bergson, *Creative Mind*, 34–35)

Perhaps alluding to James Joyce, Coetzee's Simón has emphasized how the idea of 'the father' is a concept that must be inhabited, that has no physical existence.[2] What happens in the book is that 'the mother', which must have a non-conceptual physical existence, in turn becomes an idea that needs to be inhabited, a state that needs to come into being or needs to be created.

There are other links between knowledge and intuition: David seems to learn to read on his own; that is, he teaches himself how to read. So too, he understands mathematics in a mysterious way, as Baylee Brits demonstrates in her essay on the novel (see Brits). The moment he needs to add up five and three to get eight demonstrates how he thinks through visualizing and grasping an answer in a magical rather than a logical process that in turn carries with

---

[2]This is something James Joyce explores in *Ulysses* and I discuss this at some length in the chapter on Joyce in *Thinking in Literature*. See Joyce, *Ulysses*, 9.837–845.

it elements of intuition (Coetzee, *Childhood*, 263). Here, rather than a Platonic understanding of inspiration, which links it with a recognition of what he already knew, we are closer to the idea of intuition set out by Descartes, which sees it as an immediate grasping of a self-evident truth (see Gaukroger and Hughes). It also links to a reading of Bergson, which sees the intuition as coinciding with what is becoming true. David recognizes his 'brother' Juan, whom they pick up hitchhiking late in the book through a similar intuitive recognition; yet, the concept of 'recognition' is again held in suspension; or rather it is created: Juan becomes David's brother because of David's assertion (or intuition) that he *is* his brother.

Innate knowledge

This in turn reminds us of the innate knowledge David seems to possess, in learning to read and so on, in *The Childhood of Jesus*. At first this might be understood to involve intuition as recognition: how could David 'learn' to read in this way without innate knowledge, since, in effect, he claims to already be able to read from the very beginning. But if we look more closely this knowledge is not simply innate; rather, it is suggested or provoked and the provocations in turn transform the kinds of knowledge that become possible. That is, David is pushed to reveal this knowledge or demonstrate it, at first by Simón, who challenges his claims to understanding and rejects them. At this point, however, David merely asserts his understanding in passages I will return to below. The 'true' reading of the book (i.e. the one that corresponds with the expectations that his teacher señor León and Simón and others have for such knowledge) only emerges as knowledge of this kind once he is forced to formulate it in those terms. Something else is at stake here: the possibility that the kind of knowledge David claims is not a knowledge of forms at all, but something other, even opposite: it is a knowledge of things, a kind of nominalism rather than a kind of idealism. That is, rather than things being related to forms or types, as in idealism, each thing is particular and unique, as in nominalism. Simón sets this out:

> While I was in hospital with nothing else to do, I tried, as a mental exercise, to see the world through David's eyes. Put an apple before him and what does he see? An apple, just *an* apple.

Put two apples before him. What does he see? An apple and an apple. Now along comes señor León (señor León is his class teacher) and demands: *How many apples, child?* What is the answer? What are *apples*? What is the singular of which *apples* is the plural? (*Childhood*, 290)

Yet the clear contradictions here somehow remain viable in the novel, since while David might actually be a nominalist, he is provoked, tempted, or seduced into revealing his understandings as if they were kinds of idealism.

Provocation

The idea of provocation and its function in the 'creation' of knowledge is most forcefully demonstrated through the interventions of señor Daga. Daga enters the story as a peculiar exception: he does not follow the rules of the world of Novilla, which, as we have seen, urge people away from particular desires towards general ones, and he seems to be a kind of impossible throwback, a violent figure ruled by desire. After the scene on the docks where he steals from and assaults his work colleagues, Daga returns later in the novel as an influence on David. Here again he is a source of bad example for David, and Simón is deeply concerned about this (the pen with the naked woman, giving David alcohol, potentially exposing him to sexual examples). All this does not seem to worry his 'mother' Inés, and Simón reasons that this is because she is also in Daga's thrall, herself having been tempted by particular desires to abandon the general idea of the good. Daga, then, tempts and suggests and provokes. Yet the moment of major suggestion occurs late in the book when David makes use of the gift given to him, irresponsibly, by Daga, setting alight the magic powder. The sparkling dust Daga encourages David to ignite is magnesium and initially blinds the boy (*Childhood*, 312). The doctor in the town of Nueva Esperanza determines that David is not really blind, concluding rather that David is highly suggestible and that he has entered into a process of becoming in which he is taking on the properties of the magician or miracle worker Daga has suggested he might be (*Childhood*, 322).

There are of course a number of ways of interpreting this. Yet I contend that he is forging the truth out of an asserted intuition. This process is extremely complex, as it involves apparently conflicting understandings of intuition: on the one hand, it seems to be linked with a Platonic understanding of the truth as recognition, and on the other to a more Bergsonian understanding of intuition as the experience of the emergence of what is in the process of coming into being, an experience that involves understanding as that which bears witness to creation.

There are contradictory elements in play then: creation and discovery seem to be mutually exclusive, but this is not the only apparent contradiction at the heart of the idea of intuition as it appears in the novel. Against the seventeenth-century philosopher Leibniz who famously argued in his *Theodicy* that there is an infinity of possible worlds but that this world is the 'best of all possible worlds' underwritten by the judgement of God (a conclusion ridiculed by Voltaire in *Candide*), the stevedore Álvaro makes the provocative claim that there are no possible worlds, only this one (*Childhood*, 54). Álvaro's view is seemingly undermined by the worldview of the book as a whole. As we have seen above and as Simón argues, the world of the novel might be understood to involve some kind of revisiting and revising that builds upon former selves.

It is important to underline what is at stake, that is, that these two ideas are, in logical terms, mutually exclusive. There is either one world, or many. If we were attempting to resolve this contradiction, the obvious place to start would be another dialogue by Plato, *Parmenides*, where the question of the relation of the one and the many and the paradoxes put in play through this relation is set out in detail. With regard to intuition, however, the implications are as follows: (a) if there are many worlds, recognition comes into play as a means of understanding; (b) if there is only one world, there could be no recognition, only immediate understanding, a coincidence of ideas and things as they emerge. Again, as we have seen, the contradiction involves, on the one hand, the understanding of intuition as recognition of an ideal and immutable truth, and, on the other hand, the understanding of intuition as that which in some sense 'creates' or brings truths into being.

The Schooldays of Jesus

While *The Childhood of Jesus* examines and questions the idea of intuition from a number of angles, in *The Schooldays of Jesus* the word 'intuition' only occurs towards the end of the novel. In the second novel the focus shifts from the interpretation of the nature of intuition to the struggle between reason and intuition. That is, something like Kant's prevarication between our inability to grasp the thing in itself and our capacity to nevertheless sense or feel it might be seen to be in play in *The Schooldays of Jesus*. As set out above, for Kant there are limits to reason. Intuitive judgement allows us to sense the meaning of something without adequately grasping that meaning. So too, the ideas expressed in this novel might be seen to oscillate between Kant's insistence that we cannot get to the 'thing in itself' on the one hand, and Spinoza's and Bergson's claims that we both can know this (in relation to ourselves and our own consciousness), and that this knowledge can lead us to higher knowledge, including spiritual knowledge, on the other.

Reason versus intuition

The Schooldays of Jesus places reason in conflict with spiritual understanding or intuition. Here a clear demarcation is set up between the character of Simón, the father figure who, in *The Schooldays of Jesus*, is the voice of pure reason and who claims not to understand the idea of intuition, and a group of others which includes Simón's surrogate son David and those associated with David such as his dance teacher Ana Magdalena, her husband Juan Sebastian Arroyo, and her lover and murderer Dmitri who all affirm the importance of intuition.

Intuition is first mentioned by Simón in a letter he writes to a teacher of creative writing, where he confesses his own sense of inadequacy as a man of pure reason, a man who cannot understand through intuition. He explains how Dimitri claims that all children came into the world with intuition 'of what is good and true', but they have 'lost that power as they become socialized', except for David who has retained that power (*Schooldays*, 179).

Yet towards the end of the novel Simón does encounter intuition.

> Unable to see his soul, he has not questioned what people tell him about it: that it is a dry soul, deficient in passion. His own, obscure intuition – that, far from lacking in passion, his soul aches with longing for it knows not what – he treats skeptically as just the kind of story that someone with a dry, rational, deficient soul will tell himself to maintain his self-respect. (*Schooldays*, 194)

So Simón encounters and then refuses intuition. Again, speaking with Juan Sebastian Arroyo (whose Christian names remind us of Coetzee's favourite musician Johann Sebastian Bach, and whose surname means 'a watercourse in an arid region'), whose philosophy of art Simón disparages, Simón denies that he has access to intuition. Juan Sebastian alludes to the first meeting with David, which is described in both *The Childhood of Jesus* and *The Schooldays of Jesus* in terms that, as we have seen, *do* imply intuition. Yet Simón replies:

> You misjudge me. I may have memories but I have no intuitions. Intuitions are not part of my stock-in-trade.
> [Juan Sebastian] 'Intuitions are like shooting stars. They flash across the skies, here one moment, gone the next. If you don't see them, perhaps it is because your eyes are closed'. (*Schooldays*, 199)

Simón, then, comes to doubt his own disposition, which is predisposed to logical reasoning and is simply unable to apprehend the kinds of 'truths' or 'visions' seemingly afforded to David, Ana Magdelana, and Juan Sebastian with their artistic sensibilities. Yet at the very end of the book, having witnessed the power of David dancing, Simón moves from disparaging the alleged insights of these dances and the numerological philosophy of Juan Sebastian to attempting to embrace them. It is as if he is playing out the imperative that has come to Socrates throughout his life 'in different forms at different times' to 'practice and cultivate the arts' (Plato, *Collected Dialogues*, *Phaedo*, 43, section 61e), something which in the past Socrates understood to mean that he should continue to practise philosophy, but which, since his life has become threatened by his being put on trial for 'corrupting the youth' of Athens, he now believes relates to music and poetry. This imperative presupposes that there has been something lacking in the logical methods Socrates has come to embody and, as touched upon above, Nietzsche makes much of this supposed deficiency in *The Birth of Tragedy* (Nietzsche, *Tragedy*, 70–71). So too, Simón, comically, without elegance, takes up dance in an effort to simply *see* the truth, to understand through intuition.

The ideal and the real: Coetzee in dialogue with Murnane

We have considered the way in which the truth is understood through intuition (as recognition) and alternately how intuition (as consciousness of being) creates the true. Here, in relation to *The Childhood of Jesus*, Coetzee provocatively suggests that the temporal process of the life above, which for Plato precedes and underwrites the truths that emerge in this world below, is capable of being inverted, with ungrounded intuitions founding truths which then transform the world. In order to come to terms with some of what is at stake in these paradoxical understandings of intuition, it is useful to take another tack, moving away from Coetzee's interest in ideas drawn from philosophy to his interest in how understanding might emerge in fiction.

Fictional understanding

In December 2012, Coetzee published an article on the contemporary Australian novelist Gerald Murnane in the *New York Review of Books*. Coetzee has long written for the *NYRB* and many of these essays have been collected and republished in *Stranger Shores: Literary Essays, 1986–1999*, *Inner Workings: Literary Essays, 2000–2005*, and *Late Essays: 2006–2017*. This republication in itself demonstrates that the essays are not only occasional pieces, but contain insights of sufficient importance to Coetzee to justify their preservation. Their relevance to Coetzee's fiction is apparent: his review of Joseph Frank's biography of Fyodor Dostoevsky, for example, appeared soon after he published a novel concerned with Dostoevsky, *The Master of Petersburg*.

Yet a second engagement with Plato emerges in *The Childhood of Jesus* – one that questions the relation between the ideals (or forms) which carry the truth for Plato and the real to which these truths are applied. Here it is useful to engage with the intertextual methods Coetzee makes use of in many of his works, entering into dialogue with other writers who have addressed similar concerns to his.

The critical reading Coetzee offers of Gerald Murnane in *The New York Review of Books* is interesting in a number of ways: it not only tells us things that Coetzee sees in Murnane, it tells us that Coetzee considers Murnane's work to be important and worthy of wider attention. It also tells us that Coetzee sees things in Murnane that concern him, in every sense of the word concern. It is possible to go further, but not without risk. It is possible to claim that Coetzee's essay offers a kind of preface to a dialogue that is played out as one debate among others, but one of the most important, in *The Childhood of Jesus*.

Gerald Murnane is a well-known figure in the academic discipline of Australian literature and is considered by a small but committed group of readers, both nationally and internationally, to be among the most important novelists currently writing in English. But wider recognition, even in Australia, has proved elusive. In 2006, he was in contention for the Nobel Prize, with the international betting house Ladbrokes quoting him at 33–1, and he has recently re-entered the running as has been commented upon by *The New York Times* (see Binelli). Yet it is telling that the highest awards he has received in Australia are special awards – the Patrick White Literary Award and the NSW Premier's Special Prize – that are intended as recompense for authors who have been unfairly overlooked (see Genoni).[3]

In his review of Murnane, Coetzee examines passages from Murnane's *Barley Patch* in which the narrative voice contemplates the nature of fiction and the nature of the self. The self, Murnane's narrator states, is made up of a 'network of images'. It is worth citing at length from Coetzee, who concludes:

---

[3] As I write Murnane finally won a major award the Prime Minister's Award for Fiction (awarded in 2019 for his 2017 work *Border Districts*).

The activity of writing, then, is not to be distinguished from the activity of self-exploration. It consists in contemplating the sea of internal images, discerning connections, and setting these out in grammatical sentences ('I could never conceive of a network of meaning too complex to be expressed in a series of grammatical sentences', says Murnane, whose views on grammar are firm, even pedantic). Whether the connections between images lie implicit in the images themselves or are created by an active, shaping intelligence; where the energy ('feelings') comes from that discerns such connections; whether that energy is always to be trusted – these are questions that do not interest him, or at least are not addressed in a body of writing that is rarely averse to reflecting on itself.

In other words, while there is a Murnanian topography of the mind, there is no Murnanian theory of the mind worth speaking of. If there is some central, originary, shaping force behind the fictions of the mind, it can barely be called a force: its essence seems to be a watchful passivity.

As a writer, Murnane is thus a radical idealist. (Coetzee, 'Girl from Bendigo Street')

This passage underlines a feeling of unease, which seems to be paired with a feeling of admiration and further indicates an interesting point of difference: a philosophical difference about the nature of the writer and the nature of the reader; a philosophical difference about the kinds of meaning that might be generated through works of fiction. The problem of idealism is at the heart of these differences. 'Idealism' is a problem that also concerned Coetzee in a talk he delivered at the second *China Australia Literary Forum* in Beijing, where he shared the stage with the Chinese Nobel laureate Mo Yan. Here Coetzee discussed the history of the Nobel Prize for literature itself, which stipulates, following the will of Alfred Nobel, that the award should be given, not to the best writer *per se*, but to the writer who produces 'the most outstanding work in an ideal direction' (Writing and Society). The question of the ideal, and what this term means, and how, on the one hand, the ideal can adequately face what might be called the real, and how, on the other hand, the real as we understand or experience it might exist at all without ideas or the ideal, are interrelated questions that seem to be pressing, for Coetzee.

The nature of the interrelation between the ideal and the real provides one of the most important themes of *The Childhood of Jesus*. As we have seen we find ourselves in the midst of a world that is, in some sense, in the manner of Plato, washed clean of the memory of a former life – though in the case of the central character, Simón, not all of the images of our own imperfect and passion-filled world. It is, or offers, in an often-repeated phrase, a 'new life', but there is something here that Simón finds empty.

While it is not entirely clear, the emptiness might stem from the feeling of promise itself, a promise that could only be an idea. This idea might be that the ideal, which is universal, should inhabit the material of the personal and fill it with meaning:

> And why is he continually asking himself questions instead of just living, like everyone else? Is it all part of a far too tardy transition from the old and comfortable (the personal) to the new and unsettling (the universal)? Is the round of self-interrogation nothing but a phase in the growth of each new arrival ... If so, how much longer before he will emerge as a new, perfected man? (*Childhood*, 72)

But does the ideal give meaning to life, or is it the other way around: do things give meaning to ideas? Simón informs us that 'ideas cannot be washed out of us, not even by time. Ideas are everywhere. The universe is instinct without them' (*Childhood*, 136). Simón is also certain – at least, when he is forced to explain the world to David, the boy he is compelled to look after – that we are more than just earth, more than simple matter: 'What are we like if we are not like poo? We are like ideas. Ideas never die' (*Childhood*, 156). His own urges are physical in nature, but as the philosopher stevedore Eugenio explains to him, such urges are not directed towards a particular woman but 'the womanly ideal' (*Childhood*, 166). Who, then, is obsessed with the ideal, the spiritual philosopher or the earthy one who lusts? At first, we might think that the world Simón and David find themselves in is a world of universal ideals. But Elena, who belongs in this new world, chides Simón for failing to live in the present, for failing to correspond with the real.

The emptiness Simón feels stems not so much from either the real or the ideal, but from the fact that they correspond too neatly in this new world. For Simón, the sense that things have meaning is generated, paradoxically, by the *failure* of the ideal and the real to correspond. What seems lacking to him, both in Elena's views and this new life more generally, is a sense of doubleness:

> Elena is an intelligent woman but she does not see any doubleness in the world, any difference between the way things seem and the way they are. (*Childhood*, 80)

Meaning: Between the ideal and the real

The relation between the ideal and the real is complex, then, but what seems clear is that meaning, or the feeling that we have when we do not feel that things are empty, is generated by this fraught and unstable exchange of differences between what seems to be and what is. Here Coetzee has reimagined a theme that is classical, a favourite theme of Shakespeare. There is something essential in this tension, something essential to literature, because literature is formed through the act of drawing unstable signs into relation: A against B.

What, then, of the dialogue with Murnane? My argument is based around two broad premises. Firstly, a sense of meaning does not necessarily pre-inhabit every work of fiction; rather, it has to be created or constructed. Secondly, there are two main ways in which writers construct or create a sense of the meaningful in their works, both of which involve repetition and resonance, echoing, mirroring one sign with another. The first method involves correspondences between the book and something outside the book, which might be 'the real' (recognizable worlds that have been fictionalized), or might be other books or other imagined worlds. The second method involves the book building internal networks and references – to ideas, images, words, characters, and so on – that occur once in the work and are then varied through repetition. Through this repetition themes or images emerge that invite interpretation.

While all writers necessarily make use of both methods in generating a sense of the meaningful in their works, there are different degrees of emphasis, so that readers might notice one kind first and skate over the importance of the other in particular writers. In terms of emphasis Coetzee seems to be a writer who values the external: his works enter into a dialogue with what is outside, although what is outside his works are not only real-world problems, but other works, other books. As we have seen and has often been noted, intertextual relations dominate *Foe* and *The Master of Petersburg* but also occur in many other works. In terms of emphasis Murnane seems to be a writer obsessed with the internal: the networks of images he creates – his marbles, his plains, his horse races with their silks and patterns of movement – recur not only within individual works, but throughout all of his works, creating a field of meaning that seems somehow self-contained. Yet, in fact, Coetzee depends as much on internal resonance, just as Murnane depends as much on external resonance, to create meaning.

Coetzee can enter into a dialogue with Murnane in a way that Murnane, who claims he no longer reads new fiction, cannot with Coetzee. Even with what he has read Murnane claims it is his reading of them and not those works themselves that are important to his own work. Yet there is a similarity here because when Coetzee refers to other writers in his books, he never really refers to them, even when he names them. Rather, he offers deliberately distorted images of them – so that his character Foe is not Daniel Defoe but an idea of 'the writer', and his Dostoevsky is not the historical author but an idea of 'the writer'. Yet as we have seen this deliberate distortion is a kind of dialogue: a doubleness that enables meaning to emerge.

Coetzee's dialogue with Murnane is signalled ambiguously in *The Childhood of Jesus*. The boy at the centre of the novel, whom we necessarily relate to Jesus, is called David. Other clear links to the idea of Jesus have been pointed out by critics, in particular, Rabaté and Pippin, who underline the links to the apocryphal childhood gospels of Jesus. In addition, Jesus claimed to be a descendant of King David, and 'David' is undoubtedly also a reference to Coetzee's brother, David Keith Coetzee, who died in 2010, and indeed the novel is dedicated to 'DKC'. The idea of the brother is something that recurs throughout the novel: David wishes he had two brothers and that he was the youngest. In the *New Testament*, Jesus is said to have four older brothers, one of whom is called Simon (Mark 6:3; Mathew 13:55), although the Catholic Church, dedicated to the idea of Mary as a virgin, rejects this and asserts that these 'brothers' were either cousins or the sons of Joseph from a previous marriage. In the novel, David's mother (if she is in fact his mother) is called

Inés – the Spanish version of Agnes, one of the Catholic Church's more prominent virgin saints – and in learning this Simón, or the narrator, reflects: 'Inés! So that is the name! And in the name is the essence!' (*Childhood*, 99).

The confusion – if it can be called that, because it is clearly deliberate – allows these references to point in several directions at once. It is an example of Coetzee's method of deliberate dissonance or distortion. Furthermore, in Coetzee's novel we are told that David is not the boy's real name. Elena discusses this with Simón:

> She pauses. 'You keep referring to David as "the boy." Why don't you use his name?'
> 'David is the name they gave him at the camp. He doesn't like it, he says it is not his true name'. (*Childhood*, 71)

Yet there is also a story by Murnane, appended to *A History of Books*, called 'The Boy's Name was David'. Here Murnane writes:

> *The boy's name was David.* The man, whatever his name was, had known, as soon as he had read that sentence, that the boy's name had not been David. At the same time, the man had not been fool enough to suppose that the name of the boy had been the same as the name of the author of the fiction, whatever his name had been. The man had understood that the man who had written the sentence understood that to write such a sentence was to lay claim to a level of truth that no historian and no biographer could ever lay claim to. There was never a boy named David, the writer of the fiction might as well have written, but if you, the Reader; and I, the Writer, can agree that there might have been such a boy so named, then I undertake to tell you what you could never otherwise have learned about any boy of any name. (Murnane, *History of Books*, 182)

This is not the only clue that some reference to Murnane's work might be being made. In *Inland*, Murnane tells us that his book *Invisible Yet Enduring Lilacs* takes its title from the last paragraph of André Maurois' biography of Marcel Proust (Murnane, *Inland*, 190). Murnane's narrator underlines that his own interest in external references only involves passages or images from texts that have made a forceful impression on him, leaving behind a residue in words or images. *Invisible Yet Enduring Lilacs* includes the essay 'Some Books Are To Be Dropped into Wells, Others Into Fish Ponds', an essay that begins with an extended reflection on his memory of reading *Don Quixote*. Considering a theme he develops at greater length in *A History of Books*, Murnane reflects on what, exactly, he retains from his reading of this book and is surprised that he can remember almost nothing. He can only remember a passage read out by a university lecturer that involves the image of someone being struck in the face by wind-borne vomit. Murnane then cautions readers of the essay who might have a fuller knowledge of the book and might wish to correct him on this point by, for example, refuting the existence of any such passage in *Don Quixote*. To this potential objection Murnane replies: 'I am not writing about *Don Quixote* but about my memory of the books on my shelves' (Murnane, *Invisible*, 33).

Don Quixote is the book David both does not read and uses to learn to read in *The Childhood of Jesus*.[4] The version of *Don Quixote* that Simón reads to him is written not by Cervantes, but by a 'man named Benengeli': the fictional Moorish author to whom Cervantes attributed the work. The small boy David quickly claims that he can read the book himself, but Simón is scandalized by this claim, which involves asserting one's own images and imaginings (which might in no way in fact be related to the book itself) over what appears in the book:

No, you can't. You can look at the page and move your lips and make up stories in your head, but that is not reading. For real reading you have to submit to what is written on the page. You have to give up your own fantasies. (*Childhood*, 195)

The boy replies that he *can* read and 'quotes' a passage, which is not from *Don Quixote*, but begins, 'There was a man of double deed ... ' spookily citing an anonymous nonsense poem[5], and crying that 'It's not your book, it's my book!' Simón lectures him in response:

'On the contrary, it's señor Benengeli's book that he gave to the world, therefore it belongs to all of us – to all of us in one sense,

[4]On Coetzee's interest in Cervantes, see López.
[5]Coetzee cites this poem in full in his notebook to *Life & Times of Michael K*, Coetzee Archives Container 33.5, p. 67.

and to the library in another sense, but not to you alone in any sense. And stop tearing at the pages. Why are you handling the book so roughly?'

'Because. Because if I don't hurry a hole will open'.

'Open up where?'

'Between the pages'.

'That's nonsense. There is no such thing as a hole between the pages'.

'There is a hole. It's inside the page. You don't see it because you don't see anything'. (*Childhood*, 195)

In a passage from *Inland* that Coetzee cites in his review, Murnane's narrator reflects on a quote from Paul Éluard, a poet he claims to know nothing about and to have never read: 'There is another world but it is in this one' (Murnane, *Inland*, 148). Murnane's narrator tells us the quotation appears at the front of a book by Patrick White, which Coetzee identifies as *The Solid Mandala*. The narrator conjectures, purely by the light of his affirmed ignorance, about where the quote might have originally appeared, showing how the contexts that surround it might change it, but equally claiming the authority of his own ignorance to allow understandings to emerge that will open up this other world inside the pages:

The other world ... is a place that can only be seen or dreamed of by those people known to us as narrators of books or characters within books ... until Paul Éluard comes into my room I have only a copy of his written words. He wrote his words and at the instant of his writing them the words entered the world of narrators and characters and landscapes. (Murnane, *Inland*, 150–151)

It is apparent, then, how holes can open up within pages, at least the kinds of pages that Murnane and Coetzee, for all their many differences, write. What also becomes apparent is how these pages are concerned with the ideal, which is understood to involve the relation between seemingly 'identical' but actually incommensurable elements: the imagined world and the real world of the one who both *imagines* and *is*, but who, in imagining, is no longer what he was. He is no longer forced to exist, but becomes something that persists. That is, these pages are concerned with how the ideal is capable of creating meaning. This differs again, then, from the complex plays between the real and the ideal, nominalism and idealism, we have touched upon above. It is not just the real that can enter into and alter the ideal, but also the other way around.

The ideal is that which might be, in truth, ungrounded, but is nevertheless capable of generating the truth once it has been created in what Murnane calls a viable work of fiction. Or is the ideal in turn suggested by the real, as Coetzee also seems to suggest? That is, the real is *capable* of being idealized, and once this has been done, once a sensation of meaningfulness has been created, the newly minted ideal truth is intuitively recognized as being the truth. Or rather, intuition is the process through which the real is transformed into an ideal that serves as the truth. Making meaning is not easy: a viable fiction of the truth has to be created.

'Meaning' here refers to the *feeling* that things have meaning. 'Meaning' must always remain undefined in other than tautological terms, since it only exists as a relation that someone feels or senses. Via Kant, beauty might be linked to truth because something in the world resonates with something in me: a feeling of meaning. The artist conveys the resonance, not the thing in the world or the thing in me.[6]

Placing Coetzee's *The Childhood of Jesus* in dialogue with the work of Gerald Murnane shows how they, while very different, also seem, with their echoing relations of the ideal and the real, to offer distorted reflections of each other. Both writers' books are meaningful because they create signs that double each other by not exactly matching. Their works hold out signs for the soul towards readers, which are necessary because if a soul were to emerge it could only emerge between signs: there is no sign that is the soul.

Yet there is a difference of emphasis and tone. As Coetzee notes in his review, Murnane is supremely confident in the value of the truths generated through the power of the ideal, even as this power undermines and sets to one side the real. Coetzee, for his part, is troubled by the open question as to whether the sense of truth (which is provoked by an assertion that claims the status of intuition) can by any means be trusted, even as it consistently demonstrates its power to create such truths, which consistently carve themselves into the flesh of the real.

---

[6]See Paul Cézanne, 'What if I could create this impression by means of another, corresponding one' cited in Kendall, 296.

10

Experience, Insight:
Boyhood, Youth

Boyhood

While the intertextual elements of the *The Childhood of Jesus*, relating to other works of fiction, such as those of Gerald Murnane, are important, it is interesting that there are also very strong links to Coetzee's own work. In particular, there are strong points of connection between the *The Childhood of Jesus* and *Boyhood*. What is of interest in this regard is an understanding of knowledge based not on intuition *per se*, but experience (although as we will see experience too becomes inter-involved with intuition).

In *Truth and Method* Hans-Georg Gadamer develops a historical reading of the concept of *Erlebnis* or 'experience' through eighteenth- and nineteenth-century German thought. He shows how *Erlebnis* is understood as a unity of meaning that is tied to the concept of life which is, in the aesthetic realm, what underlies or guarantees meaning.[1] Yet for Gadamer there are also limits to experience as the source of meaning in literature, limits which are engaged with through symbolism and allegory (Gadamer, 61–70).

---

[1]Gadamer, 53–61. While a fuller reading of Coetzee in relation to Gadamer would be an important contribution to the field, I will not attempt this here.

Experience in *Boyhood*, *Youth*, and *The Childhood of Jesus*

While the child 'John', based on Coetzee's self as a child, is 10 at the beginning of *Boyhood* and 13 at its end, there are strong resonances between his behaviour and that set out in *The Childhood of Jesus*, where David is significantly younger. While it is important to list these and draw points of comparison, it is equally important to consider what these relations tell us about the status of knowledge and the kind of layering of knowledge, from one state of being or disposition to another, that occurs within a given life, something which, as we have seen, is outlined in important ways in *The Childhood of Jesus*. This involves a knowledge drawn from experience.[2]

Here the truth is equated with the particular experience of an immature being, a child, who builds the world through the understandings their experience opens to them. This process of understanding is not allowed to rest unquestioned, however. One might argue that a key capacity of thinking in literature involves the ability to represent many sides of a situation, even when that situation is focalized through a particular character. The mere fact that these perceptions are represented and portrayed changes them from purely subjective experience to experience that is being observed, at the very least by the narrator and the reader, although that process of observation is often (as it is in Coetzee) further amplified by the events or situations that affect the principal character. Added to this are the observations or reflections of that character upon their own self and situation as well as by

---

[2]In developing this reading of *Boyhood* and *Youth*, I am leaving to one side a set of questions related to the status of autobiography, autobiographical fiction, or what Coetzee calls 'autrebiography', and its relation to the truth, something which Coetzee himself has a strong interest in (see *The Good Story*, *Doubling the Point*). For works that attend to these questions closely, see Attwell, *Life of Writing*, 25–34, who ties all of Coetzee's writing to the idea of the self; Kannemeyer, who draws on the fiction in developing his biography; Boehmer, who contrasts the methods of Attwell and Kannemeyer; Attridge 'J. M. Coetzee's *Boyhood*' and *Ethics of Reading*, considers the implications of working between fictional and autobiographical modes. See also Cardoen; Shechan, 'Coetzee & Co.'; Cichoń; Collingwood-Whittick 'Fictionalisation'; Sévry; Lenta, 'Autrebiography'; Kossew, 'Scenes'.

interactions with and observations from other characters who offer different points of view or dispositions to the principal character. To an extent this relation, in which the self is an observer of the self in fiction and art more generally, merely amplifies a pre-existing situation within consciousness itself. Deleuze underlines this interaction between the subjective view and the objective view in representation in his work on film, drawing on the work of Descartes and Bergson:

> It is the *Cogito*: an empirical subject cannot be born into the world without simultaneously being reflected in a transcendental subject which thinks it and in which it thinks itself. And the *Cogito* of art: there is no subject which acts without another which watches it act, and which grasps it as acted, itself assuming the freedom of which it deprives the former. (Deleuze, *Cinema 1*, 73)

Deleuze then goes on to cite Bergson:

> 'Thus two different egos [moi] one of which, conscious of its freedom, sets itself up as an independent spectator of a scene which the other would play in a mechanical fashion. But this dividing-in-two never goes to the limit. It is rather an oscillation of the person between two points of view of himself, a hither-and-thither of the spirit ... ', a being-with. (Deleuze, *Cinema 1*, 73, citing Henri Bergson from *L'Énergie spirituelle*, 920)

Along these lines all experience might be understood to already involve this kind of doubling of the self, all observation involving the observation of the observation of the one who observes, in a *mise en abyme* that would have been familiar to Coetzee through his close study of Samuel Beckett, and French structuralist and poststructuralist theory. The nature of the kind of truths that might emerge through experience, then, is one of the central concerns of *Boyhood, Youth,* and *Summertime.* The truth is approached not through an obsessive concentration on the problem of observation itself, however; rather, it is focused through other elements that situate or determine the nature of the self being observed.

Family and disposition

One element is that of the family situation out of which the boy emerges and its interaction with his own disposition. Like *The Childhood of Jesus*, *Boyhood* begins with the position of the child within the family, situations that are linked to the disposition of the boy at the heart of each story (with the disposition both affecting and being affected by the situations it inhabits). Just as Inés is seen to coddle David, John is coddled by his mother in *Boyhood* (*Boyhood*, 11). Like David, John is the 'prince' of the household:

> As long as he can remember he has had a sense of himself as prince of the house, and of his mother as his dubious promoter and anxious protector – anxious, dubious because, he knows, a child is not meant to rule the roost. (*Boyhood*, 12)

In *The Childhood of Jesus*, the 'family' that emerges as the family of David has the child at the top with Inés beside him and the 'father', who is always a father in suspension, to one side. A near identical structure exists in *Boyhood* (*Boyhood*, 12).

Just as Inés, in *The Childhood of Jesus*, has two brothers with whom she spends time playing tennis, and who are distant from and even antagonistic to her surrogate 'partner' Simón, in *Boyhood* Vera has two brothers with whom she also plays tennis, who are barely on speaking terms with her husband Jack (*Boyhood*, 21–22, 42). Just as David leads Inés once she accepts him as her own, John leads Vera (*Boyhood*, 113). Like David, John has a creative relationship with the truth: 'His difference from other boys may be bound up with his mother and his unnatural family, but is bound up with his lying too' (*Boyhood*, 35). Like David, John makes friends with a Juan (John's best friend and first cousin in *Boyhood*), and another of his cousins is called Agnes (Inés in Spanish) (*Boyhood*, 93). Like David, John is 'special' but it is not always certain in what way he is special, that is, it is not certain whether he is gifted or handicapped.

In *The Childhood of Jesus* Inés has an Alsatian dog, Bolivar, of whom, like David, she is overly protective, worried that he might come to harm, although Simón is wary of the dog. In *Boyhood* there are a series of dogs. Vera had a pet Alsatian, Kim, before she was married:

his mother, together with other women in long white dresses, standing with tennis racquets in what looks like the middle of the veld, his mother with her arm over the neck of a dog, an Alsatian. (*Boyhood*, 48)

This dog is poisoned by eating meat that farmers had left out for jackels (*Boyhood*, 48). John too is given a pet Alsatian whom he names Cossack: 'Cossack is not quite full grown when he eats the ground glass someone has put out for him' (*Boyhood*, 50). Later John and his friends are disciplined by an Afrikaans farmer, accompanied by his Alsatian dog, for trespassing (*Boyhood*, 71). The only time John is beaten by his father is when his mother, exasperated by his behaviour, allows it and lets 'his father loose on him, like a dog from a chain' (*Boyhood*, 79).

So too, outside the frame of the family, there are more general similarities of situation with 'Scenes from a Provincial Life' and *The Childhood of Jesus*, situations that involve problems of interpretation, both of the self and the environment in which the self finds itself. Just as *The Childhood of Jesus* reflects on the idea of a second life, this idea also occurs in *Boyhood, Youth,* and *Summertime*, with each stage in the development of the character John, from childhood, young adulthood, and the prime of life being seen as somehow distinct, as if what had gone before both haunts the new present, but is also erased from it. After being rescued from drowning in *Boyhood*, in free indirect discourse the boy reflects: 'From that day onward he knows there is something special about him. He should have died but he did not. Despite his unworthiness, he has been given a second life. He was dead but is alive' (*Boyhood*, 17). Later this idea returns in slightly different form: 'He can imagine himself dying but he cannot imagine himself disappearing. Try as he will, he cannot annihilate the last residue of himself' (*Boyhood*, 112).

So too, the frames of meaning allowed to David and John, with which they might interpret their situations, are similar. Just as David is impressed by the story of the 'third brother' that his mother tells to him and in turn becomes obsessed with the idea of himself becoming the third brother (*Childhood*, 146–148), John too is obsessed with these stories (*Boyhood*, 65). In sections of *Boyhood* that deal with the fraught race relations John experiences in apartheid South Africa, John connects these stories with the nature of the whites, 'the Coloured people, and the Natives'. In these stories,

> the third brother is kind and honest and courageous while the first and second brothers are boastful, arrogant, uncharitable. At the end of the story the third brother is crowned prince, while the first and second brothers are disgraced and sent packing.
>
> There are white people and Coloured people and Natives, of whom the Natives are the lowest and most derided. The parallel is inescapable: the Natives are the third brother. (*Boyhood*, 65)

Just as David has issues with his school which causes his parents, led by Inés, to remove him from school and eventually head north as fugitives, John is concerned that he might be forced to take only Afrikaans classes, due to political moves afoot at the time. Should he be forced into this, John feels his only option is to refuse, 'as a last, desperate step to throw himself upon his mother's protection, refusing to go back to school, pleading with her to save him' (*Boyhood*, 111).

The power of stories: Jesus

Stories, myth, or fiction derive their power not merely from an understanding of the relation of the particular to the general (as one sees truth in the represented experience of fiction or the fable that can be applied by readers to their own experiences); rather, they also derive power by acting as models or exemplars of behaviour. The *New Testament* presents Jesus as one who should be imitated, one whose life should be taken as a model for our own. The application of this model does not necessarily involve wisdom, however: the identification might just as well stem from *hubris* or some other ill-understood emotion, as from a genuine desire to act upon the understandings one might see as being demonstrated by the model.

There are connections to the figure of Jesus in *Boyhood* and *Youth*. In *Boyhood*, despite at first suggesting he does not like Jesus but is prepared to put up with him because Jesus 'did not pretend to be God, and died before he could become a father' (*Boyhood*, 142),

John indicates that he blocks his ears when at school they reach the part in Luke's gospel where Jesus rises from the dead:

> If he were to unblock his ears and let the words come through to him, he knows, he would have to stand on his seat and shout in triumph. He would have to make a fool of himself forever. (*Boyhood*, 142)

The sentiment is echoed in *Youth*, where, towards the end of the book, the protagonist John goes to see a screening of Pasolini's *Gospel According to St Matthew*, 'when his tomb is revealed to be empty and the angel announces to the mourning women, "Look not here, for he is risen," [...] his own heart wants to burst; tears of an exultation he does not understand stream down his cheeks' (*Youth*, 154). On both occasions, the passionate response to representations of Jesus relates to his rising from the dead or overcoming death. Yet Pippin and Rabaté have demonstrated in their readings of *The Childhood of Jesus*, how David's manner imitates in many ways that of the boy Jesus from the apocryphal gospels related to Jesus as a child (see Rabaté, Pippin).

In his notebook to *Boyhood* (which involves movement between three works: *The Lives of Animals*, *Disgrace*, and *Boyhood*) on 8 May 1995, Coetzee writes: '"His" relation to Jesus. The powerlessness of teachers and preachers to spoil Jesus' (Coetzee Archives, Container 35.2, Casebound Notebook). Just as David reveals a sudden capacity to read, John understands, all of sudden, that he is capable of speaking Afrikaans:

> Then suddenly one day he opened his mouth and found he could speak, speak easily and fluently and without stopping to think. He still remembers how he burst in on his mother, shouting, 'Listen! I can speak Afrikaans!' (*Boyhood*, 125)

An idea of capacity emerges here, suddenly, inexplicably, intuitively, and this kind of capacity (David's capacity to read; John's to speak another language) in turn determines the kinds of interpretation that become possible. Both reading and speaking another language open doors to different points of view. Experience does not only relate to situations, disposition, models, but how they are interpreted, and specifically how they are interpreted with regard to the truth of the self.

Experience, insight, and the truth of the self

Throughout his notebook Coetzee considers how he should end *Boyhood*. On 1 January 1995 he writes:

> How to end? When despite himself he catches himself in a moment of pity or sympathy for his father – even of envy. Or when he stands back for a moment from himself and sees himself as a prim, judgmental little prig. (Coetzee Archives, Container 35.2, Casebound Notebook)

Further insight is offered into Coetzee's thoughts later in the notebook where he writes:

> As a memoir the thing may be OK, but as fiction it is too myopic, self-absorbed, closed. It leads nowhere. There must be a moment – refused, if necessary – when he sees that he is blind to the reality of his father and mother, that they have lives of their own, and that the childishness of childhood consists in this willful, self-indulgent ignoring of them. (13 June 1995, Coetzee Archives, Container 35.2, Casebound Notebook)

In order to become meaningful, then, experience needs to move beyond the self. This does not seem possible through experience alone. In the passage above Coetzee seems to suggest that the kind of understanding that is needed can only come as a flash of insight, an intuition. When he develops this idea towards the end of *Boyhood*, the passage brings with it an allusion to Plato and the realm above described in *Phaedrus*:

> The sky, that usually sits tight and closed over his head [...] opens a slit, and for an interval he can see the world as it really is. He sees himself [...] not a child, not what a passer-by would call a child, too big for that now, too big to use that excuse, yet still as stupid and self-enclosed as a child: childish; dumb; ignorant; retarded. In a moment like this he can see his father and his mother too, from above, without anger: not as two grey and formless weights seating themselves on his shoulders, plotting his

misery day and night, but as a man and a woman living dull and trouble-filled lives of their own. The sky opens, he sees the world as it is, then the sky closes and he is himself again, living the only story he will admit, the story of himself. (*Boyhood*, 160–161)

Indeed, *Boyhood* might be read as a critique of purely subjective understanding, which might be aligned with a limited form of reasoning through experience. That is, subjective experience alone is shown to be inadequate as a guide to understanding. The potential limitation of experience is that it can become self-absorbed and solipsistic. Yet it is made apparent that the young John himself is becoming increasingly conscious of his own selfishness and self-absorption, and is beginning to realize that this is what is childish in him, that this is what he is being forced to confront and refuse. A slightly modified version of this method is developed in *Summertime* where those who judge or describe John are now fictionalized familiars, bearing witness, with the narrative frame organized around a biographer drawing the strands together, again based on the evidence of observational experience.

In a passage immediately following that just quoted, something of the truth of John's nature is again revealed to his mother, who has always understood something of the truth of his selfishness 'when she is not wrapped up in illusion' (*Boyhood,* 161). The truth about the self, then, presupposes another observer, perhaps observing another self. In *Boyhood*, momentarily, the mother takes on this role:

> This is what he fears from her, from the person in all the world who knows him best, who has the huge advantage over him of knowing all about his first, most helpless, most intimate years, years of which, despite every effort, he himself can remember nothing; who probably knows as well, since she is inquisitive and has sources of her own, the paltry secrets of his school life. He fears her judgment. (*Boyhood*, 161)

The structure of one who observes, who oversees the one who experiences, is ultimately that which is in play in *Boyhood* and *Youth,* where the narrative voice, who writes 'he' rather than 'I', distances the observing eye of the writer from the self observed, since, as Carrol Clarkson sets out in detail in her reading of the stylistic implications of this division, the observer of the self is in some ways no longer the same self (Clarkson, *Coetzee: Countervoices*, 19–46). This difference, which emerges in the writing process, whereby the writing self is distanced from the selves described in the writing, is underlined by Coetzee in prefatory remarks he makes to his Nobel Prize acceptance speech, 'He and His Man'. Here in words that appear on the video but not in the written transcript, Coetzee states:

> I want to say a word about certain events that must have taken place in 1948 or 1949 when I, that is to say the one I call 'I' not the one I call 'he', was a boy of eight or nine reading for the first time the book called *Robinson Crusoe*.[3]

Here Coetzee alludes to a difference between his own self, which involves a relation to himself as a boy ('the one I call "I"'), and his writings about that self in *Boyhood* ('the one I call "he"'). The former involves the oscillation of points of view within the *Cogito* set out by Deleuze, while the second involves a further distancing, that divorces the self described from the self that writes more fully.

This kind of insight is there also in the fraught questions of race relations encountered by John as he grows up within apartheid era South Africa, something that is explored at length in the story of Eddie, the boy servant his age who is beaten for offering the slightest of refusals to obey the will of the white adults he serves.[4] This sits in stark contrast to the ongoing outrageous refusals John makes time and again throughout *Boyhood*. The contrast between his position in the world and that of Eddie haunts him and occurs to him again as a kind of intuitive flash, understood by the look he imagines seeing in Eddie's eyes, a look of hatred and lack of forgiveness.

> At this moment, in the leaky house in Ida's Valley, curled under a smelly blanket, still wearing his blazer, he knows that Eddie is thinking of him. In the dark Eddie's eyes are two yellow slits. One thing he knows for sure: Eddie will have no pity on him. (*Boyhood*, 77)

---

[3](http://www.nobelprize.org/mediaplayer/index.php?id=555).
[4]For more on the South African context to *Boyhood* and *Youth*, see Collingwood-Whittick 'Autopsy'; Vermeulen; Lenta, 'Group, Nation, State'; Medalie.

The idea of the eyes of others again allows John a flash of insight into experience beyond his own. This time it is into the lives of sheep on the family farm Voelfontain in the Karoo, animals that are killed with impunity and that, one is told, are blissfully ignorant of their fate. Looking into their eyes John recognizes that they do understand everything and that they carry with them a deep resignation or foreknowledge (*Boyhood*, 102).

Many lives in one: Fictions of the self

This otherness is further available through the idea of the layering of lives within a single life, which recurs through *Boyhood*, *Youth*, *Summertime*, and *The Childhood of Jesus*. The idea of a stumbling through a life filled with errors, which are passed over as one moves to a new life, carried over into the new life as one somehow fails to completely forget the previous sets of errors, the previous sites of misunderstanding. Yet each new life also offers a new beginning, and new potentials of understanding as residues from the former lives (like the forms of Plato's life above) allow insight into and potential understanding of a self.

The lives, then, are structured upon misunderstanding but occasionally open to insight or intuition that allows a glimpse of the truth behind those lives. It is not necessarily a matter of progress through the various lives; rather, different kinds of misapprehension replace one another successively. These kinds of misapprehension in turn are considered from a formal point of view by Coetzee.

In the notebook to *Boyhood* Coetzee writes:

The question of narration. Even novels that believe they are past 'realism' adhere to an elementary realism of narration, in the sense that the narrative position at any given moment must be either inside or outside. Thus the narrative source can be conceived realistically as the position of the narrator, inside or outside the action. What I have to do is to invent a position between the two that thus does not belong to realism, that is in effect a fictional construct. Neither a ten-year-old incapable of reflection on himself nor the same boy grown up, looking back seeing implications. (Coetzee Archives, 5 December 1994, Container 35.2, Casebound Notebook)

The 'between' position of *Boyhood* is perhaps what allows it to develop some of its startling tone, with the darkness of the narrative and the horror of the quasi-sociopathic characteristics of the boy 'he', who crushes his brother's finger while experimenting with the force of a grinding machine (*Boyhood*, 119), who imagines the suicide of his father with complete lack of concern (*Boyhood*, 159):

> What he would write if he could [...] would be something darker, something that, once it began to flow from his pen, would spread across the page out of control, like spilt ink. Like spilt ink, like shadows racing across the face of still water, like lightening crackling across the sky. (*Boyhood*, 140)

Youth, the examination or test

The idea of the examination or test as something John relished and excelled at is developed in *Boyhood* (130–131). Yet in *Boyhood*, the word 'examination' or 'test' is already filled with irony, since they do not involve any self-examination or real testing of the nature of the self. Here the examinations he takes as a child allow him to excel. He feels more at home in the exams and the competition it opens with others than in life itself, and rather than teaching him about life, they open something sociopathic in him, as he feels relief, for example, at the death of his academic rival Oliver, which is then overcome by disappointment, since he now no longer has a worthy competitor (*Boyhood*, 143).

In *Youth* the motif of the test recurs, but the nature of the exam has changed considerably from the childhood experience of it. Firstly, on entering university he no longer can effortlessly make his way to the top of the class and exams are now something he has to work towards with tremendous effort, rather than looking forward to as inevitably giving way to his will. The idea of the test, then, slowly begins to develop from the limited role played by study to the question of life itself.

The nature of study also begins to subtly turn from a desire to succeed for its own sake to a growth into one's own disposition. This is seen in his attraction to mathematics, with its deductive methods built on the interplay of ideal forms somehow unsullied by the impure experience which he struggles to understand:

> What draws him to mathematics, besides the arcane symbols it uses, is its purity. If there were a department of Pure Thought at the university he would probably enroll in pure thought too; but pure mathematics appears to be the closest approach the academy affords to the realm of the forms. (*Youth*, 22)

Yet John's disposition still very much lacks self-knowledge, which is ironically indicated by the narrator who notes that while he is attracted to the Greek alphabet used in mathematics, 'he knows no Greek works beyond *hubris* and *arete* and *eleutheria*' (23). While *arete* refers to 'moral virtue', and *eleutheria* to 'freedom', *hubris*, of course, refers to pride or foolish over-confidence and ignorance of self.

In moving to London he is, for the most part, seeking to test himself. This is apparent in the earliest notes to *Youth*:

> ('Youth') He hates London but can think of no alternative to it. There is nothing for him in Cape Town. Going back to Cape Town would be like admitting oneself to a ward where one learns basket-weaving and sleeps a lot [...]. Cape Town is no test. London is at least a test; but what it is a test for he does not know. He knows that there must be a test, testing; but he does not know how to find that test. Unless one has been tested one cannot be saved. He throws himself into whatever looks like a test. Women are a test; he throws himself at women, grits his teeth, does what has to be done. (6 August 1996, Coetzee, Folder 35.2, HRC)

There is, in turn, a reimagining of the idea of a test; rather than it being something which is easily overcome, the test now involves endurance, and failing or being found wanting is itself part of the test. It becomes a test of character or resilience.

Questions that emerge involve the manner in which good and bad and the nature of the artist are brought together. Does the artist have to be good? Can the artist be good and interesting at the same time? Being not interesting is seen to be a major failing for the young John: this is his major criticism of Ford Maddox Ford, for example, that he is not interesting (*Youth*, 56; 112).

The purpose of the truth

At the heart of *Youth* is a crisis around the understanding of the truth and the function of the truth. Near the beginning of the book is a scene in which an early girlfriend, Jacqueline, reads from John's diary and finds passages in which he complains of the burden she is placing on his life as a writer (*Youth*, 8–10). The breakup is comical and causes John to reflect on the truth of what he writes in his diary:

> Who is to say that the feelings he writes in his diary are his true feelings? Who is to say that at each moment while the pen moves he is truly himself? At one moment he might truly be himself, at another he might simply be making things up. How can he know for sure? Why should he even want to know for sure? (*Youth*, 10)

While this might be taken to stand for a statement of the truth and its variable nature in the context of the novel, and the pointed irony directed towards John at this moment, its status as insight is drawn into question. The same idea is stated again later in the book and here again it relates to a failure in a relationship with a woman.

> He does not like bad news. Particularly he does not like bad news about himself. I am hard enough on myself, he tells himself; I do not need the help of others. It is a sophistry he falls back on time and again to block his ears to criticism [....] He abominates scenes, angry outbursts, home truths ('Do you want to know the truth about yourself?'), and does all in his power to evade them. What is truth anyway? If he is a mystery to himself, how can he be anything but a mystery to others? There is a pact he is ready to offer the women in his life: if they will treat him as a mystery, he will treat them as a closed book. (*Youth*, 132–133)

Here it becomes clear that rather than affirming the banal idea that 'the truth is relative', this very claim is called into question as it is paired to a deeper insight that John, at this time, is unable to deal with criticism.

Rather than not knowing the truth, then, it becomes apparent that his problem is in acting upon it or accepting it once recognized. This is underlined towards the end of the book when John realizes he is directly assisting the Cold War effort of Great Britain through his work as a computer scientist developing the Atlas computer project, in part for the British military. He intuitively feels immediately that this is wrong or wrong for him. It endangers something about him: his sense of justice, his soul. Yet the question is deflected: should he suffer this test (of undermining one's soul) for the sake of experience, for the sake of leading an interesting life, one with deep lows as well as high highs that might later be transformed into art? The test needs to involve more than mere experience for its own sake. An exploration of the self needs to lead to some disposition that is ethically justifiable. This brings to mind Gadamer's reading of 'experience' and the literary tradition of formation, the *bildungsroman* contributed to by Rousseau, Goethe and added to by Tolstoy and James Joyce, among others.

> *Experience.* That is the word he would like to fall back on to justify himself to himself. The artist must taste all experience, from the noblest to the most degraded. Just as it is the artist's destiny to experience the most supreme creative joy, so he must be prepared to take upon himself all in life that is miserable, squalid, ignominious. It was in the name of experience that he underwent London – the dead days of IBM, the icy winter of 1962, one humiliating affair after another: stages in the poet's life, all of them, in the testing of the soul. (*Youth*, 164)

A methodical way to the truth

Following this passage he recognizes, more or less immediately, as if through intuition, what is right and wrong: the only question is how he should act upon that understanding. Such insights have been allowed to John from time to time: 'Now and again, for an instant, it is given to him to see himself from the outside' (116); yet, this has not led to much more than a disquiet at his own perceived inadequacies. Following the passage cited above however, John comes to understand an underlying truth about his life as a writer. Rather than undergoing tests in order to develop experience that in turn will make him sufficiently interesting to be a writer, he learns at last that writing itself involves something reasonably boring: being methodical.

That is, he retreats from the clichéd position that a writer cannot write unless visited by inspiration, 'he cannot begin writing until the moment is right' (*Youth*, 166). Then, led by the insight that his failings as a writer and a lover run parallel, he realizes that he is afraid both of women and of writing, and this fear causes him to do nothing. This fear is also a fear of failure, and he understands that it can only be faced by working doggedly, methodically at the tasks of living and writing: 'What more is required than a kind of stupid, insensitive doggedness, as lover, as writer, together with the readiness to fail and fail again?' (*Youth*, 167). The principal element of the method of being a writer, then, is writing, practising, labouring. This method in turn is connected to trusting an innate or intuitive understanding of what is true, of what is good or bad for you.

This is contrasted with a different idea of intuition that is set out earlier in the novel, which rings hollow through the manner in which it warms over Romantic and early Modernist ideas and tiredly echoes the epiphany James Joyce describes Stephan Dedalus experiencing in *A Portrait of the Artist as a Young Man*:

> The faraway cries of children, the birdsong, the whirr of insects gather force and come together in a paean of joy. His heart swells. At last! he thinks. At last it has come, the moment of ecstatic unity with the All! (*Youth*, 117)

In contrast to this, the recognition of the truth John experiences is mundane. So too is the way to being a writer. Elleke Boehmer and Carol Clarkson have warned us not to identify *Youth* too closely with the real John Coetzee. Yet in *Youth* J. M. Coetzee represents how one might move from not writing to beginning to write as 'he' begins, without at first knowing it, work on a novel. He is tasked with finding materials for Guy Howath and is drawn back through his study in the British Museum to South Africa and starts to trace elements of its colonial history (*Youth*, 135–139).

Here he understands that fiction allows a way of sharpening the truth or finding its aura: 'The difficult part will be to give to the whole the aura that will get it onto the shelves and thus into the history of the world: the aura of truth' (*Youth*, 138). The beginning of the project that might emerge as a novel is only one of the two projects that is mentioned, however. He also makes mention of a second. This begins from the intuition that people invented binary logic and that computing does not equal thinking. He wants to develop a different mode of thought, one that leads to 'and, or' not 'either, or'.

> He is reading in the history of logic, pursuing an intuition that logic is a human invention, not part of the fabric of being, and therefore (there are many intermediate steps, but he can fill them in later) that computers are simply toys invented by boys (led by Charles Babbage) for the amusement of other boys. There are many alternative logics, he is convinced (but how many?), each just as good as the logic of *either–or*. (*Youth*, 159–160)

It might be argued that this second project developed with the first. That is, that thinking in literature offers a way of working with an inclusive logic – a logic that allows paradoxical truths to emerge, truths that remain open.

Conclusion

In examining Coetzee's work in relation to three provocations – that there is truth in fiction; that meaning can be created through process and method; that fiction can be adequate to ethical concerns – it is apparent that the four central terms – truth, meaning, fiction, and ethics – are all connected to ideas of understanding and knowledge. As this book and my previous book attempt to demonstrate, literature is a mode of thinking; yet, it remains difficult to establish this convincingly in the terms usually applied to thought in the academy. Here research is defined as a contribution to knowledge; yet, in practice this needs to be counted; hence, the systems of accounting for knowledge prefer those things that can be related to metrics.

While it is not my purpose to align literary thinking with functional definitions, it becomes apparent where some of the difficulties arise. If knowledge is defined as data or the quantifiable, one might, in literary study, point to numbers of books, numbers of readers, and to numbers of citations. Yet this says nothing about the process of thinking or the nature of the contribution to thinking provided by works of literature. It is more useful to think in terms of understanding rather than quantifiable data. That is, rather than seeing knowledge as fixed, a 'thing', we need to see it in terms of process: thinking not thought; knowing or understanding rather than knowledge.

Spinoza's three kinds of knowledge point to processes rather than entities. The imagination is an abstract noun, but only has meaning in relation to its gerund, imagining (which for Spinoza includes all of our perceptions: seeing, hearing, touching, and so on), as well as to the processes of relation that we equate with knowledge (associating night-time with darkness, fire with heat, for example).

The memory provides a store of these kinds of associations, but even remembering, or the memory, in the human mind, can be understood as a process.[1] The second kind of knowledge, reason, is equally a process: reasoning. Here we do not possess a thing, but a way of thinking, moving say, through the geometrical method, from one certain premise to another in order to build upon what we know, or working with an algorithm by applying terms to the algorithm which then process that data. Spinoza's third kind of knowledge, intuition, too, is a process. We feel that we immediately know, we sense that something is meaningful, but this does not involve the *recognition* of a fixed form but an *understanding* of forms.[2] Knowing that existence exists, as an immediate foundational intuition, for example (Spinoza, *Ethics,* I, Definitions 1, 7, and 8, 408–409), means experiencing existence; it means, that is, existing, with existing here not being cut off from anything but rather being felt as part of what is greater. Knowing, following Descartes, that I think therefore I am, also implies a process: in experiencing existing and thinking at once, and associating them with understanding.

Implying that his system, involving the first, second, and third kinds of knowledge, is in some ways circular as well as hierarchical, for Spinoza understanding itself is already tied to intuition. That is, to understand is to already be in understanding:

To have a true idea means nothing other than knowing a thing perfectly, or in the best way. And of course no one can doubt this unless he thinks that an idea is something mute, like a picture on a tablet, and not a mode of thinking, viz. the very [act of] understanding. And I ask, who can know that he understands some thing unless he first understands it? I.e., who can know that he is certain about some thing unless he is first certain about it? (Spinoza, *Ethics,* II, P43, 479)

---

[1]Confusions arise of course, because we come to associate memory with collections of data, such as those we store on computers; yet in practice, whenever we access that data in order to use it for a purpose, we bring it into relation with whatever method of thinking we are using in order to develop our conclusions. Hutto argues that narrative capacities provide such a method in recreating autobiographical memory.

[2]This is no doubt 'anti-Platonic', but in Deleuze's sense, where anti-Platonism can be found, already, in Plato, and uses insights from Plato rather than simply rejecting them (Deleuze, *Logic of Sense,* 253–265).

An idea is not data inscribed on a hard disk: it is a mode of thinking, the process or act of understanding.

That there is truth in fiction means that fiction can provide ways of understanding truths, processes through which truths might emerge. Truth itself is a feeling of understanding, and such feelings are our experience of the meaningful. So when we say that fictions can help us to create meaning, we mean they provide a way in which we can access this meaningful feeling. Ethics too are not fixed as rules (in the manner of morals); rather, we experience the ethical (or balanced relations to other beings and things, that is, how to live well) as the process of living, which necessarily involves situating our disposition within our environment. Ethics is equally linked to truth and meaning: living well is endeavouring to experience the meaningful, and understanding truths, insofar as we are capable.

Literature is capable of helping us to understand by engaging us in processes of understanding, and Coetzee's literature offers an example of works of this kind. They provoke us to create meaning (which have to be true to be felt as understanding, with understanding always having an intuitive quality).

Art, then, can involve understanding. It is a process of seeking to know, of trying to understand or developing methods of understanding.

WORKS CITED

Ackerley, Chris, 'Style: Coetzee and Beckett', in *A Companion to the Works of J. M. Coetzee*, edited and introduction by Tim Mehigan, Rochester, NY: Camden House, 2011, pp. 23–38.

Adams, Carol, J., *The Sexual Politics of Meat: A Feminist-Vegetarian Critical Theory*, London: Continuum, 2010.

Adams, Kelly, 'Acts without Agents: The Language of Torture in J. M. Coetzee's *Waiting for the Barbarians*', *ARIEL: A Review of International English Literature*, vol. 46, no. 3, July 2015, pp. 165–177.

Adelman, Gary, 'Stalking Stavrogin: J. M. Coetzee's *The Master of Petersburg* and the Writing of *The Possessed*', *Journal of Modern Literature*, vol. 23, no. 2, 2000, pp. 351–359.

Appel, Jr., Alfred, '*Lolita*: The Springboard of Parody', *Wisconsin Studies in Contemporary Literature*, vol. 8, no. 2, Spring 1967, pp. 201–241.

Ardoin, Paul, S. E. Gontarski, and Laci Mattison (eds.), *Understanding Bergson, Understanding Modernism*, New York: Bloomsbury, 2013.

Argamon, Shlomo, Moshe Koppel, James W. Pennebaker, and Jonathan Schler, 'Automatically Profiling the Author of an Anonymous Text', *Communications of the ACM*, vol. 52, no. 2, 2009, pp. 119–123.

Aristotle, *Posterior Analytics*, translated by G. R. G. Mure, Oxford: Clarendon Press, 1928.

Armbruster, Frank E., Raymond D. Gastil, and Herman Kahn, *Can We Win in Vietnam?: The American Dilemma*, with the assistance of Thomas F. Bartman and Carolyn Kelley, New York: Frederick A. Praeger, 1968.

Attridge, Derek, *J. M. Coetzee and the Ethics of Reading: Literature in the Event*, Chicago: University of Chicago Press, 2005.

Attridge, Derek, 'Sex, Comedy, and Influence: Coetzee's Beckett', in *J. M Coetzee in Context and Theory*, edited and introduction by Elleke Boehmer, Katy Iddiols, and Robert Eaglestone, London, England: Continuum, 2009, pp. 71–90.

Attwell, David, 'The Problem of History in the Fiction of J. M. Coetzee', *Poetics Today*, vol. 11, no. 3, Autumn 1990, pp. 579–615.

Attwell, David, *J. M. Coetzee: South Africa and the Politics of Writing*, Berkeley: University of California Press, 1993.

Attwell, David, *J. M. Coetzee and the Life of Writing: Face to Face with Time*, Melbourne: Text Publishing, 2015.

Auster, Paul and J. M. Coetzee, *Here and Now, Letters: 2008–2011*, New York: Viking, 2013.

Aydede, Murat, 'Aristotle on *Episteme and Nous: The Posterior Analytics*', *Southern Journal of Philosophy*, vol. 36, no. 1, 1998, pp. 15–46.

Baker, Geoffrey, 'The Limits of Sympathy: J. M. Coetzee's Evolving Ethics of Engagement', *ARIEL: A Review of International English Literature*, vol. 36, no. 1–2, January–April 2005, pp. 27–49.

Bakhtin, Mikhail, *Problems of Dostoevsky's Poetics*, edited and translated by Caryl Emerson, introduction by Wayne C. Booth, Minneapolis: University of Minnesota Press, 1984.

Bakhtin, M. M., *The Dialogic Imagination: Four Essays*, edited by Michael Holquist, translated by Caryl Emerson and Michael Holquist, Austin: University of Texas Press, 1981.

BBC News, 'Democrat Hack: Who Is Guccifer 2.0?' 28 July 2016, available at: http://www.bbc.co.uk/news/technology-36913000, accessed 28 July 2016.

Beckett, Samuel, *Watt*, London: Picador, 1988 [1953].

Beckett, Samuel, *Molloy*, London: Faber, 2009.

Belknap, Robert, 'Introduction', in Fyodor Dostoevsky, *Demons*, edited by Ronald Meyer, translated by Robert A. Maguire, London: Penguin Classics, 2008, pp. xi–xxiv.

Bell, David, *Spinoza in Germany from 1670 to the Age of Goethe*, London: Institute of Germanic Studies, University of London, 1984.

Bell-Villada, Gene H., 'The Idea of Art for Art's Sake: Intellectual Origins, Social Conditions, and Poetic Source, *Science & Society*, vol. 50, no. 4, Winter 1986/1987, pp. 415–439.

Bergson, Henri, *The Creative Mind*, translated by Mabelle L. Andison, New York: Philosophical Library, 1946.

Bergson, Henri, *Matter and Memory*, translated by N. M. Paul and W. S. Palmer, New York: Zone Books, 1991.

Bergson, Henri, *Creative Evolution*, translated by Arthur Mitchell, Mineola: Dover, 1998.

Binelli, 'Is the Next Nobel Laureate in Literature Tending Bar in a Dusty Australian Town?' *The New York Times Magazine*, 27 March 2018, available at: https://www.nytimes.com/2018/03/27/magazine/gerald-murnane-next-nobel-laureate-literature-australia.html, accessed 2 April 2018.

Boehmer, Elleke, 'Reading between Life and Work: Reflections on J. M. Coetzee', *Textual Practice*, vol. 30, no. 3, 2016, pp. 435–450.

Boletsi, Maria, 'Barbaric Encounters: Rethinking Barbarism in C. P. Cavafy's and J. M. Coetzee's *Waiting for the Barbarians*', *Comparative Literature Studies*, vol. 44, no. 1–2, 2007, pp. 67–96.

Boyd, Brian, *Vladimir Nabokov: The American Years*, Princeton: Princeton University Press, 1991.

Bréhier, Émile, *Chrysippe et l'ancien stoïcisme*, Paris: Félix Alcan, 1910.

Bréhier, Émile, *La théorie des incorporels dans l'ancien stoïcisme*, Paris: Librairie philosophique J. Vrin, 1997.

Brits, Baylee, 'The Name of the Number: Transfinite Mathematics in *The Childhood of Jesus*', in *J.M. Coetzee's The Childhood of Jesus: The Ethics of Ideas & Things*, edited by Jennifer Rutherford and Anthony Uhlmann, New York: Bloomsbury, 2017, pp. 129–146.

Buning, Marius, 'Allegory's Double Bookkeeping: The Case of Samuel Beckett', in *Samuel Beckett 1970–1989*, series *Samuel Beckett Today/Aujourd'hui 1*, edited by Marius Buning, Sjef Houppermans, and Dinièle de Ruyter, Amsterdam: Rodopi, 1992, pp. 69–78.

Buzzati, Dino, *The Tartar Steppe*, introduction by Tim Parks, translated by Stuart Hood, Edinburgh: Canongate Books, 2007.

Canepari-Labib, Michela, *Old Myths – Modern Empires: Power, Language, and Identity in J.M. Coetzee's Work*, Berne: Peter Lang, 2005.

Cardoen, Sam, 'The Grounds of Cynical Self-Doubt: J. M. Coetzee's *Boyhood*, *Youth* and *Summertime*', *Journal of Literary Studies/Tydskrif vir Literatuurwetenskap*, vol. 30, no. 1, March 2014, pp. 94–112.

Carlson, N. R., *Physiology of Behavior* (8th ed.), New York: Pearson Education, 2004.

Cichoń, Anna, 'Boyhood Scenes from Provincial Life and Youth – J. M. Coetzee's Autobiographies', in *A Universe of (Hi)stories: Essays on J. M. Coetzee*, edited by Liliana Sikorska, Frankfurt, Germany: Peter Lang, 2006, pp. 59–66.

Clarkson, Carrol, *J. M. Coetzee: Countervoices*, London: Palgrave Macmillan, 2013.

Clément, Bruno. *Le récit de la méthode*, Paris: Seuil, 2005.

Coetsé, Jacobus Jansz, *Relaas … Door … Jacobus Coetsé Jansz. Noopens de Door Hem Gedaene Togt in en Door 't Land der Groote Amacquas [A Narrative … by … Jacobus Coetsé … Concerning the Journey Made by Him in and Through the Land of the Great Amacquas]*, translated by E. E. Mossop, no. 15, Cape Town: Publications of the Van Riebeeck Society, 18 November 1760.

Coetzee, J. M., *The English Fiction of Samuel Beckett: An Essay in Stylistic Analysis*, Dissertation, the University of Texas, Austin, 1969.

Coetzee, J. M., 'Nabokov's *Pale Fire* and the Primacy of Art', *UCT Studies in English*, vol. 5, no. 5, 1974, pp. 1–7.

Coetzee, J. M., *Foe*, London: Penguin, 1987.

Coetzee, J. M., *White Writing: On the Culture of Letters in South Africa*, New Haven: Yale University Press, 1988.

Coetzee, J. M., *Doubling the Point: Essays and Interviews*, edited by David Attwell, Cambridge, MA: Harvard University Press, 1992.

Coetzee, J. M., *Giving Offense: Essays on Censorship*, Chicago: Chicago University Press, 1996.

Coetzee, J. M., *What Is Realism?* Bennington, VT: Bennington College, 1997.

Coetzee, J. M., *Boyhood*, London: Vintage, 1998.

Coetzee, J. M., *Stranger Shores: Literary Essays, 1986–1999*, London: Secker & Warburg, 2001.

Coetzee, J. M., *Elizabeth Costello: Eight Lessons*, Sydney: Knopf, 2003.

Coetzee, J. M., *Youth*, London: Vintage, 2003.

Coetzee, J. M., 'As a Woman Grows Older', *The New York Review of Books*, vol. 51, no. 1, 15 January 2004, pp. 11–14.

Coetzee, J. M., *Dusklands*, London: Vintage, 2004.

Coetzee, J. M., *In the Heart of the Country*, London: Vintage, 2004.

Coetzee, J. M., *Life & Times of Michael K*, London: Vintage, 2004.

Coetzee, J. M., *The Master of Petersburg*, London: Vintage, 2004.

Coetzee, J. M., *Waiting for the Barbarians*, London: Vintage, 2004.

Coetzee, J. M., *Inner Workings: Literary Essays, 2000–2005*, London: Harvill Secker, 2007.

Coetzee, J. M., *Diary of a Bad Year*, London: Vintage, 2008.

Coetzee, J. M., 'Eight Ways of Looking at Samuel Beckett', *Samuel Beckett Today/Aujourd'hui*, vol. 19, 2008, pp. 19–31.

Coetzee, J. M., 'Is There Thought without Language?', in *Literature and Sensation*, edited by Anthony Uhlmann, Helen Groth, Paul Sheehan, and Stephen McLaren, Newcastle: Cambridge Scholars Publishing, 2009, pp. 74–77.

Coetzee, J. M., *Summertime: Scenes from a Provincial Life*, London: Vintage, 2010.

Coetzee, J. M., Archives, Harry Ransom Humanities Research Center, University of Texas, Austin, 140 Containers, Full list of holdings and Container descriptions, available at: http://norman.hrc.utexas.edu/fasearch/findingAid.cfm?eadid=00717. 1864–2012, 1 September 2015.

Coetzee, J. M., *The Childhood of Jesus*, Melbourne: Text Publishing, 2013.

Coetzee, J. M., 'J. M. Coetzee Gives the Opening Provocation at Worlds Literature Festival Salon', Writers Centre Norwich, UK, available at: https://www.youtube.com/watch?v=1EaxNqutqDk, published 5 July 2013, accessed 25 April 2015.

Coetzee, J. M., *Two Screenplays*, edited and introduction by Hermann Wittenberg, Cape Town: University of Cape Town Press, 2014.

Coetzee, J. M. and Arabella Kurtz, *The Good Story: Exchanges on Truth, Fiction and Psychotherapy*, New York: Viking, 2015.

Coetzee, J. M., 'He and His Man', Video of Nobel Acceptance speech, including prefatory comments not included in the transcript, available at: http://www.nobelprize.org/mediaplayer/index.php?id=555, accessed 12 December 2016.

Coetzee, J. M., 'The Quest for the Girl from Bendigo Street', review of Gerald Murnane *Barley Patch* and Gerald Murnane *Inland*, The *New York Review of Books*, 20 December 2012, available at: http://www. nybooks.com/articles/2012/12/20/quest-girl-bendigo-street/, accessed 1 May 2016.

Coetzee, J. M., *The Schooldays of Jesus*, Melbourne: Text Publishing, 2016.

Coetzee, J. M., 'An Exclusive Interview with J.M. Coetzee', with David Attwell, *Dagens Nyheter*, 8 December 2003, available at: http://www. dn.se/kultur-noje/an-exclusive-interview-with-j-m-coetzee/, accessed 26 February 2017.

Collingwood-Whittick, Sheila, 'Autobiography as Autrebiography: The Fictionalisation of the Self in J. M. Coetzee's *Boyhood: Scenes from Provincial Life*', *Commonwealth Essays and Studies*, vol. 24, no. 1, 2001, pp. 13–23.

Collingwood-Whittick, Sheila, 'Autopsy of an Afrikaner Childhood: J. M. Coetzee's Ethical and Psychological Stock-Taking in Post-Apartheid South Africa', in *Healing South African Wounds/Guérir les blessures de l'Afrique du Sud*, edited and introduction by Gilles Teulié and Mélanie Joseph-Vilain, Montpellier, France: PU de la Méditerranée, 2009, pp. 283–306, 456–457.

Costas, Procope S., 'Review of *History of Mehmed the Conqueror* by Kritovoulos', *Renaissance News*, vol. 8, no. 1, Spring 1955, pp. 30–32.

Damasio, Antonio, *The Feeling of What Happens*, London: Vintage, 2004.

Damasio, Antonio, *Looking for Spinoza*, London: Vintage, 2004.

Damasio, Antonio, *Descartes' Error*, London: Vintage, 2006.

Davidson, Donald, 'On the Very Idea of a Conceptual Scheme', *Inquiries into Truth and Interpretation*, Oxford: Oxford University Press, 2009, pp. 183–198.

Defoe, Daniel, *Robinson Crusoe*, edited by Michael Shinagel, New York: W. W. Norton, 1994.

Deleuze, Gilles, *Cinema 1: The Movement-Image*, translated by Hugh Tomlinson and Barbara Habberjam, Minneapolis: University of Minnesota Press, 1986.

Deleuze, Gilles, *Spinoza: Practical Philosophy*, translated by Robert Hurley, San Francisco: City Lights Books, 1988.

Deleuze, Gilles, *Proust and Signs*, translated by Richard Howard, Minneapolis: University of Minnesota Press, 2000.

Deleuze, Gilles, 'The Method of Dramatisation', in *Desert Islands and Other Texts: 1953–1974*, edited by David Lapoujade, translated by Michael Taormina, Los Angeles: Semiotext(e), 2004, pp. 94–116.

Deleuze, Gilles and Félix Guattari, *A Thousand Plateaus*, translated by Brian Massumi, Minneapolis: University of Minnesota Press, 1987.

Deleuze, Gilles and Félix Guattari, *What Is Philosophy?* translated by Hugh Tomlinson and Graham Burchell, New York: Columbia University Press, 1994.

Dienes, Z. and D. Berry, 'Implicit Learning: Below the Subjective Threshold', *Psychonomic Bulletin and Review*, vol. 4, 1997, pp. 3–23.

Doctorow, E. L., *Ragtime*, London: Penguin, 2006.

Dooley, Gillian, '"Hades This Place, and I a Fugitive Shade": Classical Cultures and Languages in J. M. Coetzee's *Age of Iron*', *English in Africa*, vol. 43, no. 1, May 2016, pp. 101–108.

Dostoevsky, Fyodor, *Demons*, edited by Ronald Meyer, translated by Robert A. Maguire, introduction by Robert Belknap, London: Penguin Classics, 2008.

Dostoevsky, Fyodor, *Notes from Underground and The Double*, translated by Ronald Wilks, introduction by Robert Louis Jackson, London: Penguin Classics, 2009.

Douglas, Paul, *Bergson, Eliot, and American Literature*, Lexington: University of Kentucky Press, 1986.

Downey, Glanville, 'Review of *History of Mehmed the Conqueror by Kritovoulos* by Charles T. Riggs', *Speculum*, vol. 30, no. 1, January 1955, pp. 122–124.

Durrant, Sam, 'J. M. Coetzee, Elizabeth Costello, and the Limits of the Sympathetic Imagination', in *J. M. Coetzee and the Idea of the Public Intellectual*, edited and introduction by Jane Poyner, Athens, OH: Ohio University Press, 2006, pp. 118–134.

Easton, Kai, 'Coetzee, the Cape and the Question of History', *Scrutiny2: Issues in English Studies in Southern Africa*, vol. 11, no. 1, 2006, pp. 5–21.

Falkenstein, Lorne, 'Kant's Account of Intuition', *Canadian Journal of Philosophy*, vol. 21, no. 2, 1991, pp. 165–193.

Ferguson, Robert, *The Short Sharp Life of T. E. Hulme*, London: Penguin, 2002.

Fink, Hilary L., *Bergson and Russian Modernism 1900–1930*, Evanston, Illinois: Northwestern University Press, 1999.

Fletcher, Angus, *Allegory: The Theory of the Symbolic Mode*, New York: Cornell University Press, 1964.

Förster, Eckart and Yitzhak Y. Melamed (eds.), *Spinoza and German Idealism*, Cambridge: Cambridge University Press, 2012.

Foucault, Michel, 'The Order of Discourse', in *Untying the Text: A Poststructuralist Reader*, edited by Robert Young, London: Routledge & Kegan Paul, 1981, pp. 48–78.

Foucault, Michel, *The Archeology of Knowledge*, translated by A. M. Sheridan Smith, London: Routledge, 1991.

Frank, Joseph, 'Nihilism and "Notes from Underground"', *The Sewanee Review*, vol. 69, no. 1, Winter 1961, pp. 1–33.

Frank, Joseph, 'The Rebel', *The New Republic*, 16 October 1995, p. 53.

Frank, Joseph, *Dostoevsky: A Writer in His Time*, Princeton, NJ: Princeton University Press, 2009.

Gallagher, Susan, *A Story of South Africa: J. M. Coetzee's Fiction in Context*, Cambridge, MA: Harvard University Press, 1991.

Gallagher, Susan Van Zanten, 'Torture and the Novel: J. M. Coetzee's *Waiting for the Barbarians*', *Contemporary Literature*, vol. 29, no. 2, Summer 1988, pp. 277–285.

Gatens, Moira, *The Amsterdam Spinoza Lectures: Spinoza's Hard Path to Freedom*, Assen: Van Gorcum, 2011.

Gatens, Moira, 'Cloud-Borne Angels, Prophets, and the Old Woman's Flower-Pot: Reading George Eliot's Realism alongside Spinoza's "Beings of the Imagination"', *ALS*, vol. 28, no. 3, 2013, pp. 1–14.

Gatens, Moira, 'Spinoza on Goodness and Beauty and the Prophet and the Artist', *European Journal of Philosophy*, vol. 23, no. 1, 2015, pp. 1–16.

Gaukroger, Stephen. *Cartesian Logic: An Essay on Descartes's Conception of Inference*, Oxford: Clarendon Press, 1989.

Genoni, Paul, 'The Global Reception of Post-National Literary Fiction: The Case of Gerald Murnane', *JASAL*, vol. 9, 2009, pp. 1–13.

Gillies, Mary Ann, *Henri Bergson and British Modernism*, Montreal and Kingston: McGill-Queen's University Press, 1996.

Goldstein, Rebecca, *Incompleteness: The Proof and Paradox of Kurt Gödel*, New York: W. W. Norton, 2006.

Gordimer, Nadine, 'The Idea of Gardening', *The New York Review of Books*, 2 February 1984, available at: http://www.nybooks.com/articles/1984/02/02/the-idea-of-gardening/, accessed 15 February 2017.

Graef, Ortwin de, 'Suffering, Sympathy, Circulation: Smith, Wordsworth, Coetzee (But There's a Dog)', *European Journal of English Studies*, vol. 7, no. 3, December 2003, pp. 311–331.

Hayes, Patrick, *J. M. Coetzee and the Novel: Writing and Politics after Beckett*, Oxford, England: Oxford University Press, 2010.

Head, Dominic, *J. M. Coetzee*, Cambridge: Cambridge University Press, 1997.

Heister, Hilmar, 'Mirror Neurons and Literature: Empathy and the Sympathetic Imagination in the Fiction of J.M. Coetzee', *Mediatropes*, vol. 4, no. 2, 2014, pp. 98–113.

Hodgkinson, Gerard P., Janice Langan-Fox, and Eugene Sadler-Smith, 'Intuition: A Fundamental Bridging Construct in the Behavioural Sciences', *British Journal of Psychology*, vol. 99, no. 1, February 2008, pp. 1–27.

Hoegberg, David E., '"Where Is Hope?": Coetzee's Rewriting of Dante in *Age of Iron*', *English in Africa*, vol. 25, no. 1, May 1998, pp. 27–42.

Hogarth, Claire Milne, 'Epistolary Constructions of Identity in Derrida's *Envois* and Coetzee's *Age of Iron*', *Dissertation Abstracts International, Section A: The Humanities and Social Sciences*, vol. 64, no. 4, October 2003, p. 1250.

Hooton, William, 'Wordsworth, Coleridge and the Politics of Pantheism', *Coleridge Bulletin: The Journal of the Friends of Coleridge*, vol. 14, Autumn 1999, p. 14.

Hughes, Joe, 'The Cold Quietness of the Stars: Proof, Rhetoric, and the Authority of Reason in the *Ethics*', in *Spinoza's Authority: Resistance and Power in Ethics*, edited by A. Kiarina Kordela and Dimitris Vardoulakis, London: Bloomsbury, 2017, pp. 113–134.

Hume, David, *A Treatise of Human Nature*, edited by L. A. Selby-Bigge, Oxford: Clarendon Press, 1888 [1739–1740].

Hume, David, *An Enquiry Concerning Human Understanding*, Chicago: The Open Court Publishing Co, 1900.

Hutto, Daniel D., 'Memory and Narrativity', in *Routledge Handbook of Philosophy of Memory*, edited by Sven Bernecker, Kourken Michaelian, London: Routledge, 2017, pp. 192–203.

Israel, Jonathan, *Radical Enlightenment: Philosophy and the Making of Modernity*, Oxford: Oxford University Press, 2001.

Jameson, Fredric, *Postmodernism, or The Cultural Logic of Late Capitalism*, Durham, NC: Duke University Press, 1991.

Jung-Beeman, M., E. M. Bowden, J. Haberman, J. Frymiare, S. Arambel-Lui, R. Greenblatt et al., 'Neural Activity When People Solve Problems with Insight', *Public Library of Science (Biology)*, vol. 2, no. 4, 2004, pp. 500–510.

Kannemeyer, J. C. *J. M. Coetzee: A Life in Writing*, translated from the Afrikaans by Michiel Heyns, Johannesburg: Jonathan Ball, 2012.

Kant, Immanuel, *Critique of Judgement*, translated by Werner S. Pluhar, Indianapolis: Hackett, 1987.

Kant, Immanuel, *Critique of Pure Reason*, translated and edited by Paul Guyer and Allen W. Wood, Cambridge: Cambridge University Press, 1997.

Kendall, Richard (ed.), *Cézanne by Himself: Drawings, Paintings, Writings*, London: Macdonald Orbis, 1988.

Knaller, Susanne, '"There Has Been Something Staring Me in the Face, and Still I Do Not See It": Untersuchungen zu J. M. Coetzees *Waiting for the Barbarians* und Dino Buzzatis Il deserto dei tartari', *Germanisch-Romanische Monatsschrift*, vol. 51, no. 3, 2001, pp. 349–366.

Knox-Shaw, Peter, '*Dusklands*: A Metaphysics of Violence', *Commonwealth Novel in English*, vol. 2, 1983, pp. 65–81.

Kossew, Sue, 'The Anxiety of Authorship: J.M. Coetzee's *The Master of Petersburg*; and André Brink's *On the Contrary*, *English in Africa*', vol. 23, no. 1, May 1996, pp. 67–88.

Kossew, Sue, 'Scenes from Provincial Life (1997–2009)', in *A Companion to the Works of J. M. Coetzee*, edited and introduction by Tim Mehigan, Rochester, NY: Camden House, 2011, pp. 9–22.

Kritovoulos, *History of Mehmed the Conqueror*, translated by Charles T. Riggs, Princeton, NJ: Princeton University Press, 1954.

Lamey, Andy, 'Sympathy and Scapegoating in J. M. Coetzee', in *J. M. Coetzee and Ethics: Philosophical Perspectives on Literature*, edited and introduction by Anton Leist and Peter Singer, New York, NY: Columbia University Press, 2010, pp. 171–193.

Lawlan, Rachel, '*The Master of Petersburg*: Confession and Double Thoughts in Coetzee and Dostoevsky', *Ariel*, vol. 29, no. 2, 1988, pp. 131–155.

Leibniz, Gottfried Wilhelm, *Philosophical Writings*, edited by G. H. R. Parkinson, London: Dent, 1973.

Leibniz, Gottfried Wilhelm, *Theodicy: Essays on the Goodness of God the Freedom of Man and the Origin of Evil*, edited and introduction by Austin Farrer, translated by E. M. Huggard, Chicago: Open Court, 1990.

Leist, Anton and Peter Singer (eds. and introd), *J. M. Coetzee and Ethics: Philosophical Perspectives on Literature*, New York: Columbia University Press, 2010.

Lenta, Margaret, 'Autrebiography: J. M. Coetzee's *Boyhood* and *Youth*', *English in Africa*, vol. 30, no. 1, May 2003, pp. 157–169.

Lenta, Margaret, 'Group, Nation, State: J. M. Coetzee and Problems of Nationality in Postcolonial Countries', *Journal of Literary Studies/ Tydskrif vir Literatuurwetenskap*, vol. 27, no. 4, December 2011, pp. 1–16.

Lesher, James, 'The Meaning of NOYΣ in the Posterior Analytics', *Phronesis*, vol. 18, no. 1, 1973, pp. 44–68.

Levin, Yael, 'Metalepsis and the Author Figure in Modernist and Postmodernist Fiction', *Twentieth Century Literature*, vol. 62, no. 3, September 2016, pp. 289–308.

Levinson, Marjorie, 'A Motion and a Spirit: Romancing Spinoza', *Studies in Romanticism*, vol. 46, no. 4, 2007, pp. 367–408.

Lodge, David, 'Disturbing the Peace', *New York Review of Books*, 20 November 2003, available at: http://www.nybooks.com/ articles/2003/11/20/disturbing-the-peace/, accessed 9 February 2017.

López, Maria J., 'Miguel De Cervantes and J. M. Coetzee: An Unacknowledged Paternity', *Journal of Literary Studies/Tydskrif Vir Literatuurwetenskap*, vol. 29, no. 4, December 2013, pp. 80–97.

Marais, Michael, '"One of Those Islands without an Owner": The Aesthetics of Space in *Robinson Crusoe* and J. M. Coetzee's *Life & Times of Michael K*', *Current Writing: Text and Reception in Southern Africa*, vol. 8, no. 1, April 1996, pp. 19–32.

Marais, Michael, 'The Incurious Seeker: Waiting, and the Search for the Stranger in the Fiction of Samuel Beckett and J.M. Coetzee', *MediaTropes*, vol. 4, no. 2, 2014, pp. 6–30.

Masterson, John, '"I Speak with the Voice of Things to Come": Reading "The Vietnam Project" Today', *Journal of Literary Studies/Tydskrif vir Literatuurwetenskap*, vol. 29, no. 2, July 2013, pp. 62–81.

Mayer, R. E., 'The Search for Insight: Grappling with Gestalt Psychology's Unanswered Questions', in R. J. Sternberg and J. E. Davidson (eds.), *The Nature of Insight*, Cambridge, MA: The MIT Press, 1996, pp. 3–32.

McDonald, Peter, D., 'Disgrace Effects', *Interventions*, vol. 4, no. 3, 2002, pp. 321–330.

McDonald, Peter D., 'The Writer, the Critic, and the Censor: J. M. Coetzee and the Question of Literature', in *J. M. Coetzee and the Idea of the Public Intellectual*, edited and introduction by Jane Poyner, Athens, OH: Ohio University Press, 2006, pp. 42–62.

Medalie, David, '"Such Wanton Innocence": Representing South African Boyhoods', *Current Writing: Text and Reception in Southern Africa*, vol. 12, no. 1, April 2000, pp. 41–61.

Meihuizen, N. C. T., 'Beckett and Coetzee: Alternative Identities', *Literator: Tydskrif vir Besondere en Vergelykende Taal- en Literatuurstudie/Journal of Literary Criticism, Comparative Linguistics and Literary Studies*, vol. 32, no. 1, April 2011, pp. 1–19.

Mensch, Jennifer, 'Intuition and Nature in Kant and Goethe', *European Journal of Philosophy*, vol. 19, no. 3, 2009, pp. 431–453.

Mosca, Valeria, 'Ideas and Embodied Souls: Platonic and Christian Intertexts in J. M. Coetzee's *Elizabeth Costello* and *The Childhood of Jesus*', *European Journal of English Studies*, vol. 20, no. 2, August 2016, pp. 127–138.

Moses, Michael Valdez, 'The Mark of Empire: Writing, History, and Torture in Coetzee's *Waiting for the Barbarians*', *The Kenyon Review*, vol. 15, no. 1, Winter 1993, pp. 115–127.

Mulhall, Stephen, *The Wounded Animal: J. M. Coetzee and the Difficulty of Reality in Literature and Philosophy*, Princeton, NJ: Princeton University Press, 2009.

Murnane, Gerald, *Invisible Yet Enduring Lilacs*, Sydney: Giramondo, 2005.

Murnane, Gerald, *Barley Patch*, Sydney: Giramondo, 2009.

Murnane, Gerald, *A History of Books*, Sydney: Giramondo, 2012.

Murnane, Gerald, *Inland*, Sydney: Giramondo, 2012.

Nabokov, Vladimir, *The Real Life of Sebastian Knight*, London: Penguin, 1982.

Nabokov, Vladimir, *Lolita*, New York: Vintage, 1989.

Nabokov, Vladimir, *Pale Fire*, New York: Vintage, 1989.

Nabokov, Vladimir, *Strong Opinions*, New York: Vintage, 1990.

Nabokov, Vladimir, *The Gift*, New York: Vintage, 1991.

Nabokov, Vladimir, *Despair*, London: Penguin, 2000.

Neruda, Pablo, *The Heights of Macchu Picchu: A Bilingual Edition*, translated by Nathaniel Tarn, New York: Farrar, Straus and Giroux, 1966.

Ng, Lynda, 'The Violence of Forgetting: Trauma and Transnationalism in Coetzee's *Dusklands*', *Textual Practice*, vol. 30, no. 3, May 2016, pp. 417–433.

Ng, Lynda and Paul Sheehan, 'Coetzee's Republic: Plato, Borges and Migrant Memory in *The Childhood of Jesus*', in *J. M. Coetzee's* The Childhood of Jesus: *The Ethics of Ideas and Things*, edited by Jennifer Rutherford and Anthony Uhlmann, London: Bloomsbury, 2017, pp. 83–103.

Nietzsche, *The Birth of Tragedy: Out of the Spirit of Music*, translated by Shaun Whiteside, edited by Michael Tanner, London: Penguin, 1993.

Nisbett, R. E. and T. D. Wilson, 'Telling More Than We Can Know: Verbal Reports on Mental Processes', *Psychological Review*, vol. 84, 1977, pp. 231–259.

Novak, Maximilian E., *Daniel Defoe: Master of Fictions: His Life and Works*, Oxford: Oxford University Press, 2003.

Panza, John R., 'Coetzee's Nabokov's *Pale Fire* and the Primacy of Art', *Explicator*, vol. 57, no. 4, Summer 1999, pp. 244–247.

Pappas, Nickolas, 'Plato's Aesthetics', *The Stanford Encyclopedia of Philosophy*, 27 July 2008, available at: https://plato.stanford.edu/entries/plato-aesthetics/, accessed 14 July 2014.

Pippin, Robert B., 'What Does J. M. Coetzee's Novel, *The Childhood of Jesus* Have to Do with the Childhood of Jesus', in *J.M. Coetzee's* The Childhood of Jesus: *The Ethics of Ideas & Things*, edited by Jennifer Rutherford and Anthony Uhlmann, New York: Bloomsbury, 2017, pp. 9–32.

Pirandello, Luigi, *Six Characters in Search of an Author*, translated by Jennifer Lorch, Cambridge: Cambridge University Press, 2004.

Plato, *The Collected Dialogues, Including the Letters*, edited by Edith Hamilton and Huntington Cairns, translated by Lane Cooper, Bollington Series LXXI, Princeton: Princeton University Press, 1989.

Pluhar, Werner S., 'Translator's Introduction to Immanuel Kant', in *Critique of Judgement*, Indianapolis: Hackett, 1987, pp. 23–109.

Popescu, Monica, 'Waiting for the Russians: Coetzee's *The Master of Petersburg* and the Logic of Late Postcolonialism', *Current Writing: Text and Reception in Southern Africa*, vol. 19, no. 1, 2007, pp. 1–20.

Pugliese, Cristiana, 'Waiting on the Border: A Comparative Study of Dino Buzzati's *Il deserto dei Tartari* and J. M. Coetzee's *Waiting for the Barbarians*', *Studi d'Italianistica nell'Africa Australe/Italian Studies in Southern Africa*, vol. 14, no. 2, 2001, pp. 57–79.

Quigley, Megan, *Modernist Fiction and Vagueness*, Cambridge: Cambridge University Press, 2015.

Rabaté, Jean-Michel, 'Pathos of the Future Writing and Hospitality in *The Childhood of Jesus*', in *J.M. Coetzee's* The Childhood of Jesus: *The Ethics of Ideas & Things*, edited by Jennifer Rutherford and Anthony Uhlmann, New York: Bloomsbury, 2017, pp. 33–56.

Reber, A. S., *Implicit Learning and Tacit Knowledge: An Essay on the Cognitive Unconscious*. New York: Oxford University Press, 1993.

Reichmann, Angelika, 'Possessed by the "Exhilarating Monster": J. M. Coetzee's Reading of Dostoevsky in *The Master of Petersburg*', *European Journal of English Studies*, vol. 20, no. 2, August 2016, pp. 139–151.

Roberts, Sheila, '"City of Man": The Appropriation of Dante's *inferno* in J M Coetzee's *Age of Iron*', *Current Writing: Text and Reception in Southern Africa*, vol. 8, no. 1, 1996, pp. 33–44.

Rutherford, Jennifer, 'Thinking through Shit in *The Childhood of Jesus*', in *J. M. Coetzee's* The Childhood of Jesus: *The Ethics of Ideas and Things*, edited by Jennifer Rutherford and Anthony Uhlmann, London: Bloomsbury, 2017, pp. 59–82.

Scanlan, Margaret, 'Incriminating Documents: Nechaev and Dostoevsky in JM Coetzee's *The Master of Petersburg*', *Philological Quarterly*, vol. 76, no. 4, 1997, pp. 463–477.

Sellbach, Undine, 'The Lives of Animals: Wittgenstein, Coetzee, and the Extent of the Sympathetic Imagination', in *Animals and the Human Imagination: A Companion to Animal Studies*, edited by Aaron Gross and Anne Vallely, New York: Columbia University Press, 2012, pp. 307–330.

Sévry, Jean, 'Coetzee the Writer and the Writer of an Autobiography', *Commonwealth Essays and Studies*, vol. 22, no. 2, Spring 2000, pp. 13–24.

Shapiro, G., 'Reading on the Edge of Oblivion: Virgil and Virgule in Coetzee's *Age of Iron*', in *Literary Studies and the Pursuits of Reading* [e-book], edited by Eric Downing, Jonathan M. Hess, and Richard V. Benson, Rochester, NY: Camden House, 2012, pp. 233–248.

Sheehan, Paul, 'Coetzee & Co: Failure, Lies and Autobiography', *Textual Practice*, vol. 30, no. 3, 2016, pp. 451–468.

Shklovsky, Viktor, 'Art as Technique', in *Twentieth-Century Literary Theory: A Reader*, edited by K. M. Newton, New York: St. Martin's, 1997, pp. 3–5.

Skow, John, 'Parallel World: A First-Rate Novelist Adapts Dostoyevsky's life Too Freely', *Time Magazine*, 28 November 1994.

Spencer, Robert, 'J. M. Coetzee and Colonial Violence', *Interventions: International Journal of Postcolonial Studies*, vol. 10, no. 2, 2008, pp. 173–187.

Spinoza, Benedictus de, *Ethics*, in *The Collected Works of Spinoza, Volume 1*, edited and translated by Edwin Curley, Princeton: Princeton University Press, 1985.

Sulk, Kay, '"Visiting Himself on Me" – The Angel, the Witness and the Modern Subject of Enunciation in J.M. Coetzee's *Age of Iron*', *Journal of Literary Studies*, vol. 18, no. 3–4, 2002, pp. 313–326.

Szczurek, Karina, 'Coetzee and Gordimer', in *J. M. Coetzee in Context and Theory*, edited and introduction by Elleke Boehmer, Katy Iddiols, and Robert Eaglestone, London, England: Continuum, 2009, pp. 36–46.

Tajiri, Yoshiki, 'Beckett's Legacy in the Work of J. M. Coetzee', *Samuel Beckett Today/Aujourd'hui: An Annual Bilingual Review/Revue Annuelle Bilingue*, vol. 19, 2008, pp. 361–370.

Tajiri, Yoshiki, 'Beckett, Coetzee and Animals', in *Beckett and Animals*, edited and introduction by Mary Bryden, Cambridge, England: Cambridge University Press, 2013, pp. 27–39.

Tolstoy, Leo, Childhood, Boyhood, *and* Youth, London: Penguin, 2011.

Tuckwell, Jason, *Creation and the Function of Art: Techné, Poiesis and the Problem of Aesthetics*, New York: Bloomsbury, 2017.

Uhlmann, Anthony, *Beckett and Poststructuralism*, Cambridge: Cambridge University Press, 1999.

Uhlmann, Anthony, *Samuel Beckett and the Philosophical Image*, Cambridge: Cambridge University Press, 2006.

Uhlmann, Anthony, *Thinking in Literature: Joyce, Woolf, Nabokov*, London: Continuum, 2011.

Uhlmann A., 'J. M. Coetzee and the Uses of Anachronism in *Summertime*', *Textual Practice*, vol. 26, no. 4, 2012, pp. 747–761.

Veres, Ottilia, 'Homo Solitarius: Intersubjectivity in Coetzee's *Life & Times of Michael K* and Beckett's *Molloy*', in *Intertextuality, Intersubjectivity, and Narrative Identity*, edited and introduction by Péter Gaál-Szabó, Newcastle upon Tyne, England: Cambridge Scholars, 2017, pp. 135–148.

Vermeulen, Pieter, 'Wordsworth's Disgrace: The Insistence of South Africa in J. M. Coetzee's *Boyhood* and *Youth*', *Journal of Literary Studies/Tydskrif vir Literatuurwetenskap*, vol. 23, no. 2, June 2007, pp. 179–199.

Voltaire, *Candide*, translated by John Butt, London: Penguin Classics, 2001.

Von Kleist, Heinrich, 'Michael Kohlhaas', in *The Marquise of O and other Stories*, edited and translated by David Luke and Nigel Reeves, London: Penguin, 1978, pp. 114–213.

Waters, Anne, 'Language Matters: Nondiscreet Nonbinary Dualism', in *American Indian Thought: Philosophical Essays*, edited by Anne Waters, London: Blackwell, 2004, pp. 97–116.

Watson, Stephen, '"The Writer and the Devil": J. M. Coetzee's *The Master of Petersburg*', *New Contrast*, vol. 22, no. 4, December 1994, pp. 47–61.

Weitz, Morris, *Philosophy of the Arts*, Cambridge, MA: Harvard University Press, 1950.

Wenzel, Jennifer, 'Keys to the Labyrinth: Writing, Torture, and Coetzee's Barbarian Girl', *Tulsa Studies in Women's Literature*, vol. 15, no. 1, Spring 1996, pp. 61–71.

West, Paul, *The Very Rich Hours of Count von Stauffenberg*, New York: Harper & Row, 1980.

White, Patrick, *The Solid Mandala*, London: Vintage, 1995.

Williams, T. C., 'Kant's Philosophy of Language: Chomskyan Linguistics and Its Kantian Roots', *Philpapers. org*, 1993, available at: http://philpapers.org/rec/WILKPO-2, accessed 1 December 2016.

Wilm, Jan, *The Slow Philosophy of J. M. Coetzee*, London: Bloomsbury Academic, 2016.

Wittenberg, Hermann, 'Towards an Archaeology of *Dusklands*', *English in Africa*, vol. 38, no. 3, October 2011, pp. 71–89.

Wood, James, 'A Frog's Life', in *London Review of Books*, vol. 25, no. 20, 23 October 2003, pp. 15–16, available at: https://www.lrb.co.uk/v25/n20/james-wood/a-frogs-life, accessed 11 October 2015.

Worton, Michael, '*Waiting for Godot* and *Endgame*: Theatre as Text', in *The Cambridge Companion to Samuel Beckett*, edited by John Pilling, Cambridge: Cambridge University Press, 1994, pp. 67–87.

Writing and Society Research Centre (with the China Writers' Association), *The China Australia Literary Forum 2*, available at: http://www.uws.edu.au/writing_and_society/research/current_research_projects/chna_australia_literary_forum_2013, accessed 1 May 2016.

Yeoh, Gilbert, 'J. M. Coetzee and Samuel Beckett: Ethics, Truth-Telling, and Self-Deception', *Critique: Studies in Contemporary Fiction*, vol. 44, no. 4, Summer 2003, pp. 331–348.

Zimbler, Jarad, *J. M. Coetzee and the Politics of Style*, Cambridge: Cambridge University Press, 2014.

Zinik, Zinovy, '"The Spirit of Stavrogin," Review of *The Master of Petersburg*. Novel by J. M. Coetzee', *Times Literary Supplement*, 4 March 1994, p. 19.

INDEX

idealism 183, 190
'the idea of gardening' 102, 106–7
ideas
  adequate 20–1
  rational 26
imagination 115–16
'Inaugural Dissertation' 23
inductive method 71–2
inference and intuition 18–19
Ingenium 147
Inland (Murnane) 187, 189
innate knowledge 176–7
inner time 115
*Inner Workings: Literary Essays,
  2000–2005* 181
Innocence 136
In Search of Lost Time 45
insight, experience and 198–201
instinct 11, 92–5, 97, 106–15,
  112–14, 121, 184
intellect 114–15
intellectual intuition 23–5
intelligence 93–7
intention and meaning 43–6
interpretations 48–51, 60–1, 64–5,
  71
intertextuality, techniques of
  110–12, 126–9
In the Heart of Country (Coetzee)
  83
intuition 64, 67–8, 80, 97, 172
  and Aristotle 14–15
  Bergsonian 27–31
  cognitive science and 31–2
  concept of 11–13, 22–3
  and creating the truth 175–6
  empirical 24
  and ethology 8–9
  false and true 69–71
  feeling of understanding
    173–4
  and foundation 16
  inference and 18–19

intellectual 23–5
Kantian 23–7
and knowledge 175
vs. reason 179–81
Spinoza's third kind of 20–1
sympathetic 165, 168
intuitive method 69
Invisible Yet Enduring Lilacs
  (Murnane) 187–8
Ion (Plato) 13–14
'Isaac Newton and the Ideal of
  a Transparent Scientific
  Language' 3, 31

*J. M. Coetzee and the Life of
  Writing: Face to Face with
  Time* (Attwell) 1, 75
James, William 30, 50
Jesus
  in *Boyhood* 196–7
  power of stories 196–7
  in *Youth* 196–7
Joyce, James 93, 205–6

Kafkaesque narrator 83
Kahn, Herman 41, 62
Kannemeyer, J. C. 52
Kant, Immanuel 12, 22–3, 179
  intuition 23–7
Kinbote, Charles 48
knowledge 12–13, 31, 94
  innate 176–7
  and intuition 175
  kinds of 76
  Spinoza's third kind of 20–1
  tacit 11
Know Thyself 138–9
Knox-Shaw, Peter 53
Kossew, Sue 1
Kritoboulos 78–9
  meaning of 80–2
Kritoboulos, Michael 78
Kurtz, Arabella 45